Also by William C. Davis

THE ORPHAN BRIGADE
BATTLE AT BULL RUN
DUEL BETWEEN THE FIRST IRONCLADS
BRECKINRIDGE: STATESMAN, SOLDIER,
SYMBOL

The Battle of New Market

William C. Davis, 1946-

Louisiana State University Press

Baton Rouge and London

Published by arrangement with Doubleday & Company, Inc.
Manufactured in the United States of America
Louisiana Paperback Edition, 1983
10 9 8 7 6 5 4 3 2

LIBRARY OF CONGRESS CATALOGING IN PUBLICATION DATA

Davis, William C., 1946–
  The battle of New Market.

  Bibliography: p.
  Includes index.
  1. New Market, Battle of, 1864.   I. Title.
E476.64.D37   1983   973.7'36   82-18705
ISBN 0-8071-1078-7 (pbk.)

ACKNOWLEDGMENTS

One of a writing historian's chief occupations is the accumulation of debts. Research is based on cooperation, and the greater the research, the more the indebtedness. My search for sources on New Market ranged from America's chilly Alaska to behind the Iron Curtain, leaving in its path many fond memories and a host of obligations for which only brief acknowledgment can be made. As always, libraries and archives have been indispensable, and I invariably received kindness and helpful attention from the following: Mrs. Georgia Bumgardner, American Antiquarian Society; Archie Motley, Chicago Historical Society; Winston Broadfoot of the George Washington Flowers Collection and Mrs. Sharon E. Knapp of the Perkins Library, Duke University; Jon M. Williams, Eleutherian Mills Historical Library; James R. Bentley, the Filson Club; Dr. Györö Ember, Magyar Orszagos Leveltar, Budapest; Harriet McLoone, Henry E. Huntington Library and Art Gallery; Mr. Dennis F. Walle, Illinois Historical Survey, Urbana; Mrs. Nancy Boles, Maryland Historical Society; Kurt Brandenburg, Museum of the Confederacy; Elmer O. Parker, Old Military Records Division, National Archives; James Heslin, New-York Historical Society; Patricia B. Gatherum, Ohio Historical Society; Caroline Wallace, Southern Historical Collection; Colonel George Pappas, Colonel James Agnew, and Richard J. Sommers, U. S. Army Military History Research Collection; Howson W. Cole, Virginia Historical Society; Louis H. Manarin, Virginia State Library; Mrs. M. B. Hansen and Betty Kondayan, McCormick Library, Washington and Lee University; Virginia R. Hawley, Western Reserve Historical Society; and Rodney A. Pyles, West Virginia University Library.

Particularly helpful in opening up to me privately held papers of their ancestors were descendants of some of the participants at New Market. George Hugh Banning, La Jolla, California, and Hancock Banning, San Marino, California, were very helpful for their grandfather Colonel George H. Smith. Mrs. Lawrence Coe,

Memphis, Tennessee, kindly searched papers of her grandfather George M. Edgar. B. A. Colonna of Waco, Texas, was a great deal of help on his Cadet father; I shall always cherish the week we spent together in the Shenandoah Valley, walking over the New Market battlefield, reminiscing at Virginia Military Institute, making and sharing memories. Mrs. Franklin Hanger, Staunton, Virginia, granddaughter of General John Echols, kindly looked through his papers for me. I owe a special debt to Brigadier General George S. Patton, Fort Knox, Kentucky, Ruth Ellen Patton Totten, South Hamilton, Massachusetts, George P. Waters, Baton Rouge, Louisiana, and Major John K. Waters, Jr., Montgomery, Alabama. They kindly granted me access to the papers of General George S. Patton, Jr., in the Library of Congress, which collection was closed to researchers at the time of my writing. Mrs. Totten also very kindly allowed me to use the Civil War letters of Colonel George S. Patton. Anne S. von Poederoyen, Van Nuys, California, and William R. Wharton, Jr., White Plains, New York, opened the papers of General Gabriel C. Wharton to me. And I am greatly indebted to old friends Mr. and Mrs. John M. Prewitt of Mount Sterling, Kentucky, for allowing me the use of the papers of Mrs. Prewitt's grandfather Major General John C. Breckinridge.

A number of fellow historians gave freely of their time and wisdom, among them E. B. Long, Laramie, Wyoming, and Ezra J. Warner, Solana Beach, California. James J. Geary, Director of the New Market Battlefield Park was a constant ally throughout. And to the entire staff of the Virginia Military Institute I am most grateful. Major Edwin L. Dooley, Jr., Betty Mohler, and Julia Martin of the Office of Public Information were most gracious in my research in the Alumni Files, as was Lieutenant Colonel George B. Davis of the Preston Library. Joseph D. Neikirk of the V.M.I. Foundation and Mr. and Mrs. Henry A. Wise of Lexington, Virginia, were also most cordial.

Many personal friends contributed measurably to this book. Darryl Bertolucci, Silver Spring, Maryland, many times put up an unexpected overnight guest on my research trips to Washington. Christine C. Ritter of New Oxford, Pennsylvania, spent many hours laboriously translating into English Franz Sigel's letters to his wife during the campaign, written in excruciatingly illegible German. Robert J. Younger, Dayton, Ohio, gave service above and beyond the call of friendship in supplying me with hard-to-find journals and rare books. James I. Robertson, Jr., Virginia Polytechnic Institute and State University, very kindly read and criticized the entire manuscript, and I have benefited immeasurably from his comments. And then, of course, there is Pamela Davis, without whose patience and forbearance I could not write a line.

Contents

Illustrations

Photographs

Maps

Preface

Just west of the Blue Ridge Mountains lies the great Valley of Virginia, the Shenandoah. Second only to the Mississippi River in its strategic importance to the Confederacy, this Valley was one of the most hotly contested areas in the Civil War. Four major campaigns and a host of other, smaller, actions took place here. One of the most significant of these campaigns which, in turn, led up to one of the most significant small battles of the war, occurred in May 1864, when a Federal army under Major General Franz Sigel advanced up the Valley toward the farm community of New Market.

Who could try to stop Sigel? Perhaps no one. Pressed on all sides, the Confederates in Virginia had no one to spare. Only a few hundred cavalry in the Valley stood between the Federals and the destruction of the Shenandoah's vital resources, the back door to Lee's beleaguered army facing Grant, and Richmond. Finally, only after a series of hairbreadth near misses, an undermanned scratch force was hastily assembled. The man who would lead it had once been Vice President of the United States and a candidate for the presidency. His mission would be to drive Sigel out of the Valley. On his success or failure would rest the fate of a Confederate Virginia.

1
"The Romance of the War"

"All the romance of the war is in this valley," wrote journalist Major Charles G. Halpine of the Union army in May 1864. And he was right. If there had been or could be left any romance in the catastrophic, bloody civil war that had ravaged the land for the past three years, then surely it was here in "this valley," the mighty Shenandoah. From the war's very beginning its land and its people knew the conflict as few other places in the beleaguered Confederacy. Great armies and phantom raiders tracked its abundant fields; spies, renegades, and bushwhackers passed through its shadows. Every conceivable act in the drama of warfare played this troubled stage until, by 1864, its unwilling audience, the people of the Shenandoah, could tell Halpine "stories that surpass in pure interest & excitement all the wildest creations of romance." Indeed, the major, like so many others now, fully believed that "there is no romance to compare with the varying fluctuations of war in this ravaged but still beautiful Paradise." And there was more to come.[1]

It was more than romance that made this paradise so fought over, so desirable, for the Shenandoah possessed more strategic importance than any other valley in the country. It was not hard to see why. Situated between Virginia's lovely Blue Ridge Mountains and the eastern reaches of the Alleghenies, it ran from its beginnings at Lexington, Virginia, deep in the Confederacy, 165 miles northeast to Harpers Ferry, West Virginia, the doorway to the North. Generally about thirty miles in width, it offered ample room for troop maneuver and movement. Because of the fact that the Valley began at a relatively high altitude at Lexington and gradually descended toward Harpers Ferry and the Potomac, men marching south through the Shenandoah were said to be going "up" the Valley; those moving to the north were heading "down" it.

This Valley provided a natural pathway for invasion for both of the contending armies. Since it could be reached from the east through only a select few gaps in the Blue Ridge, an army entering it from either end could move its entire length unseen by the enemy simply by closing off these openings. With such an avenue available, neither side could hope for a successful campaign in eastern Virginia unless its strategy included denying the Shenandoah to the enemy, for while the two main armies faced each other on the Richmond-Washington front a hostile force in the Valley could speed through one of the Blue Ridge gaps to deliver a fatal blow to an exposed flank barely sixty miles away.

Equally important as its geographical features, and more important to the Confederacy, was what the Shenandoah Valley contained. Across it ran the Virginia Central Railroad, the chief link between the east and west sides of the Blue Ridge. In Staunton, the Valley's chief depot on the line, the Confederacy maintained important hospitals, rail yards, and supply warehouses. And in the soil of the Shenandoah itself lay its richest asset. The crops from this abundantly fertile land were chiefly responsible for keeping the Confederate army in the East fed. Grain, fruit, livestock, all poured forth from this verdant cornucopia, and upon its produce rested much of the hope, and fate, of a struggling young nation.

The people of the Valley believed that its name "Shenandoah" had been left to them by a band of Indians now long disappeared from the land. It meant, they said, "Daughter of the Stars." If so, it was aptly named, for this Valley and its exploits beamed as bright as any star in the Confederate constellation, perhaps brighter. The reasons lay in a mountain and a man.

The mountain was the brooding Massanutten, itself an Indian name, but one that translated into a more prosaic "big mountain." Running down the center of the Valley from Harrisonburg north to Strasburg, it divided the Shenandoah in two for a distance of forty-five miles. Close to its center, near New Market, lay the only substantial gap that would allow the movement of large bodies of infantry or cavalry to pass from one side to the other. Denied New Market Gap, an army had to march south fourteen miles to Harrisonburg or north thirty-one miles to Strasburg to reach the opposite side. It was through this gap and in sight of the slopes of the Massanutten that, in a single campaign, enough military history was written to make it the most significant piece of geography of the Civil War.

The author of this history was the man. He sucked on lemons, avoided pepper because it made his left leg ache, often passed among his men giving out religious tracts, and seemed always to fight his battles on Sundays. Regarded by many as peculiar and by a few as insane, all came in time to recognize him as a genius. Thomas J. Jackson had lived in the Valley, at Lexington, and when he took command of its meager Confederate forces in November 1861 he brought with him not only the immortal sobriquet "Stonewall," earned at Bull Run, but also an intimate knowledge of the Shenandoah and the Massanutten. This knowledge served him well. Using the mountain as a screen for his movements and, by controlling New Market Gap, as a wedge to keep the Federal forces from uniting against him, he managed deftly to move back and forth across it, defeating one army on one side while another lay helpless on the other. In the end, this mountain and his genius drove back three Union armies whose combined forces numbered four times his own. Yet in almost every case Jackson actually managed to confront his antagonists on equal or better than equal terms, so well had he and the Massanutten divided

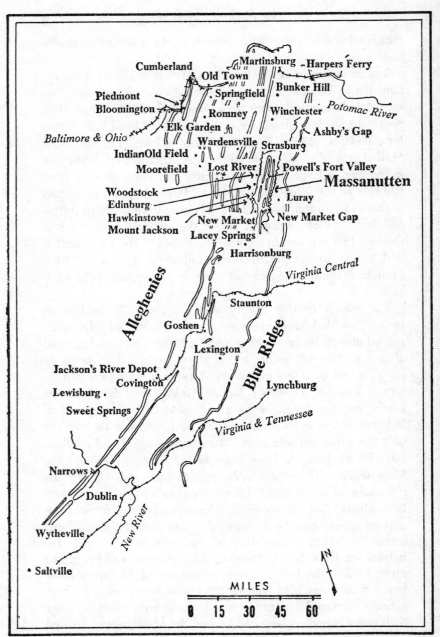

The Shenandoah Valley and southwest Virginia, including the
scene of McNeil's and Imboden's operations in West Virginia.

his enemies. His campaign in the Shenandoah electrified the South, almost paralyzed the Union high command, and added a new chapter to the annals of warfare.

Thereafter it was Stonewall's valley. He became to its people and its soldiers a saint; in time, a legend. And it seemed almost as if the legend itself was enough to protect his beloved Shenandoah, for fully a year passed before another serious threat to the Valley appeared. But by that time Jackson was no more. On November 25, 1862, he had ridden his awkward, ungainly warhorse, Little Sorrel, out of the Valley, never to see it again. There followed for him command of the Second Corps in R. E. Lee's mighty Army of Northern Virginia, smashing victory at Fredericksburg in December, and an even more brilliant performance at Chancellorsville the following May. But with his glory at Chancellorsville came accidental shots in the dark and, on May 10, 1863, the Lord who had blessed him with victory in so many battles claimed his mighty soldier. Five days later Jackson was returned to the Shenandoah to rest forever in his beloved Lexington.

Who would save Stonewall's valley now? For a time it would lie in the hands of two of Jackson's successors in the Second Corps, Lieutenant General Richard S. Ewell and Major General Jubal A. Early. Together they routed and nearly destroyed a Federal garrison at Winchester, seventeen miles north of Strasburg. In two days of fighting just one month after Stonewall's burial, they captured nearly 4,000 Yankees, in some cases taking whole regiments prisoner. From this victory the Confederates marched on down the Valley and into Maryland on their way to Pennsylvania, and Gettysburg. Just one month later they came back in defeat, their enemies in blue moving down the east side of the Blue Ridge in pursuit, trying to get through the gaps and into the Shenandoah. The Federals failed. Aside from minor skirmishes and brief unsuccessful forays, the Valley was preserved inviolate to the Confederacy for another year.

But then came May 1864 and a terrible new threat. The Valley was about to assume a greater role than ever before.

New men were coming to the Shenandoah. Major Halpine would be one of them, and as they came they would bring afresh the triumphs and horrors of this war. With them would come the fate of the Valley, this "still beautiful Paradise."

2
"The Hour for Action Has Arrived"

The Federals could use a new man. The Department of West Virginia, which bordered the Shenandoah on the north, had been the scene of almost total inactivity since its creation in the aftermath of Major General Robert H. Milroy's terrible defeat at Winchester in June 1863. Brigadier General Benjamin F. Kelley took the new command and did nothing with it. As the spring campaign of 1864 was about to open in the East, the Union hierarchy felt that more energy must be displayed on the Shenandoah front. Kelley would have to be replaced.

His relief would also solve two recurrent problems in Washington, one military, the other political. In a war where change in command was frequent, the Army had many officers of high rank out of active duty, "awaiting orders," among them several major generals. When a brigadier like Kelley was given a department, a responsibility commensurate with a higher rank, these dormant officers and the politicians who always seemed to attach themselves to shelved generals plagued the War Department and even the President over the supposed inequity. Replacing Kelley with one of these major generals would ease the burden.

At the same time it would stem a much greater outcry, one bound up with the complexion of the population. Of the five largest immigrant groups in the Union in 1860, only the

Germans came from a non-English speaking country. As the war broke out, Germans numbered over one and a quarter million. In several parts of the country, and particularly in cities, they made up the majority of the population and were being felt in national politics. With them had come some 4,000 officers and intellectuals, refugees from the European revolutions of the previous two decades. Spurred by these leaders, the Germans enlisted with the North in grand numbers and, as a result, they expected their favorites to be taken into high councils. Many were thus promoted beyond their talents, and they frequently turned up on the rolls of those "awaiting orders." Among them now, as the spring of 1864 approached, was perhaps the most popular German in America, Major General Franz Sigel.

Nowhere else in the Union Army could there be found such an example of the folly of letting politics govern promotion as Franz Sigel. Born in 1824 at Sinsheim, Baden, he took part as a young officer in the revolts of 1848. August Willich gave him command of one of four columns of his German Republican Army in April, and Sigel promptly went down in defeat at Freiburg, himself fleeing to Switzerland. The next year, in a new revolution, he led troops guarding Baden's frontier and was again beaten, this time running back to hide in shock in a hotel room. Though his men wanted a new commander, Sigel showed a remarkable staying power, and revolutionary leader Lorenz Brentano soon made him secretary of war and then adjutant to his new army commander. In command of a part of the army, Sigel was defeated yet again at Waghäusel and on the retreat, his superior having been beaten as well, he assumed to himself the now meaningless title of commander in chief.

Sigel fled at last to New York in 1852. Here he became administrator of a German language school. Moving on to St. Louis, Missouri, he assumed the position of director of the city schools in a community with a very heavy German immigrant population. At the same time, never forgetting past glories, he helped organize the Turnverein, a group devoted to preparing itself for the liberation of the homeland.

At the outbreak of hostilities Sigel was drilling a regiment in St. Louis and took part in the successful capture of militant Rebel sympathizers at Camp Jackson on May 10, 1861. He fought again in the skirmish at Carthage on July 5. Though relatively insignificant, these little victories made him a hero among his fellow Germans, and it was deemed politically expedient to appoint him a brigadier, a move calculated to bring thousands of his fellow Germans into the army. It worked, but at a high cost. Three days after his promotion, on August 10, 1861, his poor, almost negligent, performance in the Battle of Wilson's Creek, Missouri, contributed to a severe Union defeat. Blamed sharply for this reverse, he found his people still behind him. In November, when Major General Henry W. Halleck replaced Major General John C. Frémont in command of Union forces in Missouri, the Germans were outraged that Sigel had not received the command instead.

Sigel, too, was angry. He called Halleck a "slick lawyer" in a private letter that somehow found its way into print, and a feud began. Sigel tendered his resignation from the army while his friends made a martyr of him. He journeyed to Washington, speaking to influential Germans on the way, rallying Midwest Congressmen to his support, and finally won promotion to major general in March 1862. That same month, back at his command, he fought ably, for a change, at the Battle of Pea Ridge, Arkansas, and soon replaced Frémont in command of a corps in Virginia. In August, however, he turned in his usual poor performance at the Second Battle of Bull Run, only shortly after being beaten with the rest of the Union forces in Jackson's great Shenandoah campaign. Though he took no part in the Fredericksburg campaign that December, he did accede temporarily to command of one of the grand divisions that had fought at Fredericksburg, but a few days later was returned to his corps. This was too much. He would not be reduced in command; it was "exceedingly unpleasant." He asked to be relieved and in February 1863 went on extended leave for "medical" reasons.[1]

Despite his continual reverses, Sigel's standing among his fellow Germans was greater than ever, and a public outcry followed his relief. He did his best to foster it, making speeches in major cities in which he bitterly criticized the treatment he had received. German soldiers now, when asked what unit they served in, answered only with "I fights mit Sigel." His supporters began to claim, in response to a rumor that he had been called back to the field, that his presence "was equal to the addition of ten thousand men to the army." Indeed, some were now demanding that he be given command of all Union forces, saying that he would end the war in two months. A wag might have asked how he would have ended it—in victory or defeat.[2]

By the dawn of 1864 their campaign was working. Several members of the West Virginia legislature signed and submitted a petition that Sigel come to replace Kelley, and President Lincoln, perhaps with an eye on a potentially large German vote in his upcoming campaign for re-election, acquiesced. By mid-February the decision was made, in part because Sigel himself lobbied shamelessly for the position. He would have the West Virginia command. The Germans were elated. "It was a very judicious measure in every respect," wrote one of them, Major General Carl Schurz, to the President. But there were other people who found the news disturbing. Poor Milroy, vainly hoping for another command after his defeat at Winchester, saw in it the end of his chances. Worse yet, he felt, the move had been taken without any thought for "the wishes of the people of W. Va. or the good of the service." Perhaps most indignant of all was Colonel David H. Strother, whom Sigel now would shortly command. It was sad, he thought, "but the Dutch vote must be secured at all hazards for the Government and the sacrifice of West Virginia is a small matter."[3]

The War Department made the appointment official on February 29, 1864. Ten days later Sigel assumed the command, and the next day, March 11, he reached Kelley's headquarters at Cumberland, Maryland. An artillery salute announced his arrival as he took quarters in the Revere House, escorted by Kelley. The next morning the ousted brigadier lined up his staff in a parlor to meet the new commander and, when Sigel entered, they saw a man "small in stature and ungraceful."

Colonel Strother, seeing him for the first time, was disappointed. "His hair and beard are tawny, his jaws and cheek bones square and angular, his eyes light blue, forehead narrow, and too small for his face." Furthermore, as he stood before them incongruously dressed in the full uniform of a major general topped off by a shabby slouch hat, Sigel, after lobbying and planning for some time to get this position, now proceeded to say in hesitating, broken English, that he felt himself unequal to the task.[4]

Not everyone was disappointed. Many in the rank and file saw promise in the new appointment. "We are all much pleased with the change in the Department Commander," Captain Henry A. du Pont wrote his mother: "we shall have great changes here." There were those who feared that Sigel had made a mistake by accepting such a politically motivated appointment, but many more agreed with a private in the 123d Ohio Infantry: "I think he is the man that is needed here." Service in this department was odious, whoever the commander, and any change might be for the better. Besides, even if "I fights mit Sigel" had lost some of its meaning by 1864, still this new man had led whole wings of armies. When the post band serenaded him in his new headquarters a few days later, and as he spoke to them afterward, the men were confident. Surely, they felt, for all his faults, here was a man who would not be overwhelmed by a mere backwoods department.[5]

Sigel jumped into his new duties like a man of energy. Sensibly retaining Kelley's staff as his own for the time being, he began getting acquainted with his command, while Kelley himself would take over a reserve division. Perhaps taking the advice of a Wheeling editor that "Great military talent is of less consideration in this department . . . than is a practical knowledge of the country," he had his inspector general, Strother, prepare a lengthy and detailed description of the department, its boundaries, and the tenor of its people, as well as a listing of its forces and where they were posted.[6]

It was a large department, including all of Maryland west of the Monocacy River, part of Loudoun County, Virginia, at the West Virginia border, all of the Shenandoah Valley, and

West Virginia in its entirety. The populace was of every complexion, loyal to the Union in Maryland and most of West Virginia and intensely secessionist in the Valley. Its troops, though numerous, were widely scattered, thanks largely to the necessity of guarding the Baltimore & Ohio Railroad line which ran straight through the department from Harpers Ferry west. Long and difficult to hold, this major lifeline of Union supply was an easy target for Confederate guerrillas.

Wasting no time, Sigel set out on a tour of his garrisons on March 14. At Harpers Ferry, at Martinsburg, in Maryland, and elsewhere on his trip, he inspected the troops closely, passing slowly along the lines of men and looking sharply into their eyes, "apparently," thought one, "to see if there was fight there."[7]

If he did see fight in their eyes, it was not enough. The department had 23,397 men of all arms and 118 pieces of artillery, but the figures hardly told the full story. Inactivity had made them soft, and dispersion had seriously impaired their organization. To make matters worse, he could not pull his troops together enough to drill and refit them effectively without exposing the B&O line, three hundred miles of which from Cumberland west was almost totally unprotected. Sigel was not optimistic. "I will do the best I can under the circumstances."[8]

It was not encouraging that almost from the date of his arrival, Sigel received a stream of reports of anticipated Confederate raids. He had a small but efficient signal corps in operation with posts as far south as Winchester; and through the snows that fell in March and April, the rumors flowed into headquarters. Kelley, still in the department but in a subordinate command, was sure that "a movement, and a formidable one, will at an early day be made." Reports said that Confederates were threatening from the Valley, then that there were no Rebels in the Shenandoah, and again that a fearful raid was forming. Who and what to believe became frustratingly difficult.[9]

No matter who he believed, Sigel knew that the warming of spring would bring renewed hostilities in his department, as well as elsewhere. He must look to his defenses. On March 15, as part of his general reorganization, he placed Brigadier General William W. Averell in charge of the department's entire mounted arm. With his fascination for the trappings of soldiering, Sigel prepared meticulous—but quite superfluous—colored diagrams of his command, from division down to regiment, and then pored over them like a draftsman over his drawings. But the fact remained that he was doing good work in readying his command. As a result of his efforts, Sigel soon put the department on a better footing than it had enjoyed since its creation. He confidently expected to have 20,000 men ready for the field by the middle of April. Despite his continuing skepticism, Strother was forced to admit that "this looks toward activity."[10]

New appointments were made in his staff and command, but here Sigel showed one of his chief weaknesses—he was a terrible judge of men. Colonel Jacob M. Campbell of the 54th Pennsylvania Infantry told the general that "you were surrounded by many who would sacrifice the country's cause, for the purpose of bringing you into disrepute." Several of Sigel's enemies managed to get positions very close to headquarters, and he would suffer for it. Worst of all, though, was the favoritism Sigel showed for fellow Germans. This had been feared by the West Virginia press when he took the command. One of his first acts was to ask that his classmate at the Karlsruhe military school in Germany, Brigadier General Max Weber, be assigned to him. Soon, other countrymen were asking for positions with him, among them Schurz, while at least two of the units serving under him, the 28th Ohio Infantry and 1st New York (Lincoln) Cavalry, were almost entirely German. Many could hardly converse with fellow soldiers in other commands.[11]

One friend brought in by Sigel would have a heavy impact in days to come. Major General Julius Stahel-Szamvald, then thirty-eight years old, had been born at Szeged, Hungary. As a young man he kept a bookshop in Pest, later joined the Hungarian rebel army as a lieutenant in the revolts of the 1850s, won the War Cross of Bravery, and finally in 1856 had to take refuge from his troubled homeland in England. Coming to America, he worked as a journalist for the New York *Illustrated News* and, when war broke out, helped raise the 8th New York Infantry. Sigel formed a fondness for him early in the war, and Sigel's urgings for Stahel's promotion made the latter (who dropped the second half of his last name) a particular problem for President Lincoln. Nevertheless, when Lincoln went to Gettysburg in November 1863 to deliver his immortal address, Stahel commanded the guard of honor. By March 1864 when he was ordered to Sigel, Stahel was a major general serving on an obscure examination board. On arriving, he became chief of cavalry and then, a few days later, Sigel made him his chief of staff.

Stahel was "a little fellow, rather insignificant, looking for all the world like a traveling clerk," found Strother. "Stahel is a very good fancy cavalry officer," he continued, "who has never done anything in the field and never will do anything." With his arrival, all of the Federal actors in the coming drama were at hand.[12]

And there was no doubt that the curtain would rise soon. Growing bold now, Rebel guerrillas began raiding again, and some penetrated deep enough to capture one of West Virginia's state senators, an assemblyman, and the state's attorney. Meanwhile, the word came in with increasing frequency: The enemy would move on him in force, and soon. They were reported massing in numbers to move into West Virginia on April 1. Some thought they would advance from as far off as eastern Tennessee. Others said they would invade Kentucky through Sigel's department. Their numbers were reported at between 250 and 5,000 and more. Everything was confusion. All Sigel could do was pull in his troops, concentrating them for what might or might not come, asking West Virginia's militia to fill their places. Then came the word. No one could pass in or out of the Shenandoah. The Rebels had shut it off completely.[13]

What did it mean?

For one thing, it meant that Sigel was not the only new man in western Virginia. The Confederates had one too. Their Department of Western Virginia, whose rather nebulous borders included all of southwestern Virginia, portions of eastern Tennessee, and any parts of Kentucky and West Virginia that could be held, was as much a problem child for the Confederacy as Sigel's department was for the Union. The same political difficulties and divided loyalties plagued it; the same sort of lackluster generals had commanded in it. Since December 1862 it had been under the charge of Brigadier General Samuel Jones, a capable officer, but one unable to manage it to Richmond's satisfaction. By February 1864 Confederate authorities decided to replace him. They needed, said Secretary of War James A. Seddon, someone "better adapted to secure the confidence of the people"—their selection was "an officer of distinction in the Western army, who has political as well as military influences to aid his administration." He was John C. Breckinridge of Kentucky.

Where Jones was relatively obscure, there was not a household in the South or, for that matter, in the Union that did not know John C. Breckinridge. He came from a distinguished family, pioneers to Kentucky's Bluegrass. One grandfather had been Jefferson's attorney general. Another grandfather served as president of the College of New Jersey, and a great-grandfather, John Witherspoon, was the only clergyman to sign the Declaration of Independence.

But this Breckinridge's achievements outshone them all. Born in 1821 in Lexington, Kentucky, he studied the law, and rose rapidly in popularity and esteem in his community. When war came with Mexico, he received an appointment as major in the 3d Kentucky Infantry and was with it in a bloodless march to Mexico City in 1847. He saw no action in the war, but his service nevertheless gave extra impetus to his bid for a seat in the Kentucky legislature in 1849. He won the race, and two years later beat War of 1812 hero General Leslie Combs in a rough-and-tumble battle for Congress in the so-called "Ashland district," Henry Clay's old bailiwick. Indeed, from the friendship which the old Whig Clay displayed for Breckinridge, many thought that he intended to pass on his mantle of leadership to the young Democrat. Breckinridge won re-election in 1853, and then retired two years later when his district was gerrymandered out from under him. While in office the Kentuckian gained a national reputation. It came in part from his brilliant oratorical abilities. He could spellbind an audience. Tall, handsome, extremely personable, his friends and admirers were legion, even among his political opponents. Always moderate in politics and a sure vote-getter, he found himself nominated in 1856 to be James Buchanan's running mate in the coming presidential contest, despite the fact that, at thirty-five, he had only been eligible for the office for five months. "Buck and Breck" won handsomely, and John C. Breckinridge became the youngest Vice President in United States history.

As the sectional controversy grew during Buchanan's administration, Breckinridge became increasingly associated with the South in the public mind. In fact he did not favor secession and had once actually stated that slavery was such an evil that force, if necessary, should be used to eradicate it. When 1860 came, and the Democratic party split, the Southern "fire-eaters" nominated him for the presidency. He wanted to decline but finally accepted on the assurance that doing so would force the nominee of the Northern Democrats, his friend Stephen A. Douglas, to withdraw as well, opening the way for a moderate compromise candidate. It did not work and, once having accepted, he went down to defeat, polling second in the Electoral College to the husband of a distant cousin, Mary Todd Lincoln. He sat in the Senate until well after the war started, determined to voice his opposition to Lincoln's war policies to the last. Finally, in September 1861, when Union authorities in Kentucky decided that he was dangerously disloyal and ordered his arrest, he had no choice but to go to jail—or to Richmond. He chose the South.

Commissioned a brigadier general, Breckinridge fought well at Shiloh, Corinth, Vicksburg, Baton Rouge, Stones River, Jackson, and Chickamauga. By late 1863 he had risen to major general and temporary command of a corps in General Braxton Bragg's army besieging the Federals in Chattanooga. Like so many others, he incurred Bragg's wrath and a celebrated "feud" ensued, one in which he refused to take any part. Nevertheless, it ruined his effectiveness with the Army of Tennessee, and Richmond thought it best to transfer him. Western Virginia seemed the very spot, and he came to it with the confidence of all parties concerned. "I knew him as intimately as a boy from 17 to 20 could know a man," wrote his aide Lieutenant James B. Clay, Jr., grandson of Henry Clay, "and I can say with truth that he was the truest, greatest man I was ever thrown in contact with."[14]

Assigned officially to the new command on February 25, Breckinridge reached department headquarters at Dublin, Virginia, on March 4, assuming command the next day. Faced with warnings of an early Federal campaign, he set out almost at once on a four-hundred-mile tour of his department, all on horseback. He found some two brigades of infantry led by Brigadier General John Echols and Colonel John McCausland, totaling 2,985 effectives. His cavalry, one brigade and several scattered regiments, numbered 1,769, but scarcity of forage for their animals had forced them to send their horses away to far-off pastures, leaving the men dismounted. He had seven batteries of artillery but, in fact, only three of them had guns. In all, there were fourteen pieces. At the other end of the Shenandoah, Sigel's command numbered four times his own. The prospect was not heartening.[15]

What made a bad situation seem worse was that Breckinridge's five thousand-odd troops had grown soft on garrison duty. Indeed, few of them had ever seen a hard campaign. Their war had so far been largely one of boredom. Colonel George S. Patton of the 22d Virginia Infantry lamented this winter that "at night we can do nothing . . . but sit around the fire, fight our battles over again, and conjecture what we will do in the coming campaign."

The new general would change that. Even as he was making his tour, he instituted twice-daily drills, set up classes of instruction for the officers, and cracked down on the problem that desertions were giving his commanders in the field. He ordered the construction of defensive works on the key avenues of invasion and directed that all commands gather thirty days' rations and forage in anticipation of the coming campaign. Taking full advantage of every asset at hand, he personally addressed the troops all along the line. The men found this new general confident, if not inspiring, and they received him enthusiastically. In less than a month he managed to increase his forces by 10 per cent, and orders went out for the regiments to send their baggage to the rear. "This order looks as if Breck had something in his head," mused Colonel Patton. He was right. As Breckinridge told the men on his tour, "the time for speeches has passed . . . the hour for action has arrived."[16]

It seemed to be coming fast. Both Echols and McCausland expected an enemy move on the department soon, and Breckinridge could not argue. Breckinridge felt that reports of Federal build-ups in the Kanawha Valley of West Virginia and at Martinsburg seemed to confirm their fears, and the word from the Confederate actually commanding in the Shenandoah, Brigadier General John D. Imboden, was not heartening. "I have little or no doubt," he told General Robert E. Lee, "that we shall have a big raid here some time this month."[17]

Fortunately, March passed without the anticipated raid, but it remained a time of intense activity for the Confederates. While Breckinridge built up his department and drilled his men, Imboden worked feverishly to prepare some sort of defense against a move up the Shenandoah for, in case of an enemy advance, he would have to hold them back until Breckinridge's troops could move the 130 miles or more from Dublin to join him.

This Imboden was a rare man. Not blessed with extraordinary talents, he was one of the few in this or any other war who realistically viewed his own limitations. When his promotion to major general was broached to him by friends, he told them frankly that "I do not desire it. . . . I really feel that I have as high military rank as I am qualified for." He had been an ardent and early secessionist in 1861 and served for a time as captain of the Staunton Artillery before organizing his own unit, the 1st Virginia Partisan Rangers in April–May 1862. He performed well in Jackson's campaign in the Shenandoah Valley and at Gettysburg and was placed in command of the Valley District on July 28, 1863. Imboden found his headquarters in Staunton a lonely place. His secessionist views had made him many enemies in 1861 in this largely loyal community, and now only two or three families in all the city offered him any hospitality. "I have but few intimate personal friends," he told one of the few, "and the number is perhaps growing less as I grow older."[18]

He had just over 2,000 men to defend the Valley, and they were spread widely. His largest unit, the 18th Virginia Cavalry, moved its camp once and sometimes twice a week. There were too many avenues to guard and too few men.

One of the biggest jobs facing Imboden was the organization of the Valley reserves, but by April 30 he had four companies from Augusta County ready. In all, over 1,000 reserves stood in their companies. It was a great task preparing this department for more war, and Imboden found the "desk employment" it required most disagreeable.[19]

It would pay off when the time came, though. While Lee was and would remain for several weeks sanguine in the belief that the enemy would not move up the Shenandoah this spring, those in the Valley knew better. Imboden and Breckinridge knew something was coming. Echols and McCausland felt it would happen soon, and Patton quietly told his wife that "I look for quiet until about the middle of April, and then I look for activity." No one would argue with Imboden that, whenever the enemy came, "we shall be sorely put to meet him."[20]

3

"We Are in for Business Now"

On March 29, 1864, the Union plan began to unfold. Major General E. O. C. Ord arrived at Franz Sigel's headquarters in Cumberland with a letter from Lieutenant General Ulysses S. Grant. The General-in-Chief would move against Lee in early May. He wanted a two-pronged advance from West Virginia to coincide with his own movement. It would have the threefold effect of a diversion, to take troops away from Lee, as well as to regain loyal territory while destroying valuable enemy industry and supplies. Sigel was to assemble immediately 8,000 infantry, three batteries, and 1,500 cavalry at Beverly, West Virginia. Ord would command the column, his orders being to move via Covington, Virginia, to the easiest point of attack on the Virginia & Tennessee Railroad. He was to destroy as much of this lifeline between the Confederacy's east and west as possible, and then proceed to the supply depots at Lynchburg. Another column under Brigadier General George Crook would move on the railroad some hundred miles due south from Charleston and then turn northeast toward Staunton.

The benefits of such a raid could be far-reaching, especially from Crook's part in it. Besides destroying railroad mileage, he would be able to attempt the destruction of the invaluable salt works at Saltville, Virginia, chief source of the South's supply. Nearby lead mines at Wytheville provided bullets for

Rebel guns. Federal estimates predicted that, given just one full day unmolested, Crook could do enough damage to these Rebel facilities to put them out of the war for good. Then there was Staunton. It stood, thought many Federals, second only to Richmond in importance to the eastern Confederacy. If lost, "it would be fatal." The hub of the supply and communication systems for Virginia and its western connections, its fall would take the Old Dominion with it.[1]

If Grant knew this, then, it is strange that the nucleus of the main advance on Staunton appeared as an afterthought. Grant maintained a sufficiently low opinion of Sigel to want to keep him out of the way in this campaign. Consequently, he decided a few days after sending Ord to Cumberland that since Ord, Crook, and a small cavalry raid under Averell—leaving Logan Court House, West Virginia, to strike the Virginia & Tennessee—might be able to return north by way of the Valley, Sigel should be ready with a sufficient force to march south to Staunton to meet them. His chief purpose would be to bring them fresh supplies for the move on Lynchburg. Of course, there were other things Sigel could do as well. His move would cover the North from invasion down the Valley, Sigel might destroy some stores, and he could even help isolate Richmond by cutting communications lines. Underestimating the resistance Sigel could meet, Grant told him that his force for the campaign need not be "much more than an escort for the wagon train."

On the whole, Grant expected very little of all operations in West Virginia. "I do not calculate on very great results," he told his friend Major General William T. Sherman. It was the only way that Sigel's troops could be utilized in his grand strategy. Sherman would move against Atlanta, another army would advance into Louisiana, while a third force was to move up the James River against Petersburg. Grant, of course, would fight Lee, now stretched along the Rapidan River barely fifty miles east of Harrisonburg and New Market. While all this took place, something had to be done in West Virginia to prevent Lee being reinforced through the Blue Ridge gaps by troops from the Valley. Thus, Sigel, Crook, Ord, all of them, need accomplish nothing more than keeping Breckinridge and Imboden in their own front and away from Grant's. "In other words," Grant told Sherman, borrowing a phrase from President Lincoln, "if Sigel can't skin himself, he can hold a leg whilst some one else skins."[2]

The order to move would not be forthcoming yet, however. Sigel and Ord had quarreled. Indeed, they may never have been civil with each other. Ord, one of Grant's favorites from his western campaigns, was no master of tact. Here in Sigel's domain, perhaps a bit full of himself for being picked by the commanding general for the task ahead, Ord haunted Sigel's headquarters, highly put out that the troops being sent for him numbered only 6,500 when Grant had ordered 8,000. For his part, Sigel only added to the growing breach. He could scarcely hide his anger at the way this whole business was being conducted. "In fact," he would bitterly complain, "all dispositions *were made in such a manner as if I did not exist at all.*" As a result, he made little effort to accommodate Ord, and when asked to meet him at some point in the campaign with fresh supplies, Sigel, "in so many words," told him "I don't think I shall do it." Incensed, Ord immediately asked to be relieved of his command, and Grant acceded to his wishes on April 17.[3]

That same day another Grant man arrived at Sigel's headquarters, Lieutenant Colonel Orville E. Babcock. Ord's resignation required a new plan, and fast, for the opening of the spring campaign was set for barely two weeks off. Together Babcock and Sigel decided to postpone the raid planned for Ord, and to use Brigadier General Jeremiah C. Sullivan's division to strengthen Crook's column and Sigel's own. Crook, then, with 10,000 men would advance as scheduled earlier, while the German, with 7,000 or more, would move up the Valley to Cedar Creek, near Strasburg. From this point he would threaten to move on the enemy and be ready to meet or assist Crook. Babcock approved the plan, and so did Grant. Be ready by May 2, Grant told Sigel.[4]

Sigel would be ready, but his men had lost their enthusiasm. He kept himself so aloof and inaccessible that only staff officers could see him. Capable of considerable amiability—he loved to sit and talk about music—he seldom displayed it. Even his good friend Schurz admitted that there was "something reserved, even morose, in his mien, which if it did not discourage cheerful approach, certainly did not invite it." Soon even his staff could not get an audience. Furthermore, he was replacing people known to be "Kelley men" with those friendly to himself and his cronies. With the opening of the campaign only days away, Sigel's administration and morale were a mess.

He had even antagonized Grant. Wanting to have two cavalry regiments returned to his command from the Army of the Potomac, he sent his plea not to Grant, but to a friendly congressman instead. He had become so accustomed to depending on political influences to accomplish his ends that he seems to have thought of no other course. General Halleck, now Grant's chief of staff, intercepted the injudicious telegram and presented it to Grant, whose reprimand was stern. This would not be tolerated; "it is time General Sigel should learn to carry on his official correspondence through the proper channels and not through members of Congress." The rebuke was completely lost on Sigel. He saw not the error of his action, nor any justification for Grant's ire. All he got from the episode was another reason to hate Henry W. Halleck.[5]

As April neared an end, the belief was becoming more and more widespread that Sigel's appointment had been a terrible mistake. Strother, who for a time entertained hopes that his original unfavorable impression was in error, sadly wrote that "Sigel has the air to me of a military pedagogue, given to technical shams and trifles of military art, but narrow minded and totally wanting in practical capacity." He was a "mere adventurer." Halleck was more blunt. On April 29, the eve of the grand campaign, he lamented to Sherman that "It seems but little better than murder to give important commands to such men as . . . Sigel."

But Sigel did have the command, and his regiments were soon on their way to his column's assembly point at Martinsburg. The work of organization began on April 20; four days later he had six regiments of infantry ready, with two more on the way. The last of them, the 18th Connecticut Infantry, came in on April 28. "I expect we are a-going up the Valley," one of its privates wrote home.[6]

Sigel himself arrived in Martinsburg on April 25 to inspect the troops. What he found hardly quieted his fears for the coming advance. While he regarded his artillery as generally good, at least two of the battery captains would soon be under charges of misconduct, one for making menials of his men. The cavalry he found "in a wretched condition" and the infantry not much better. Two regiments, the 116th and 123d Ohio, he believed to be poorly organized and "entirely useless." They had been among those captured with Milroy in 1863 and, though exchanged by the enemy, still lacked many of their officers. As for the newly arrived 18th Connecticut, "I have not much confidence in this Reg't," he wrote. Indeed, the only unit he regarded as good was the 34th Massachusetts Infantry, yet men in other regiments thought the Bay Staters "a lot of barbarians." The soldiers of the 18th Connecticut were delighted when a reorganization took them out of the brigade the 34th was in. Sigel would later lament that he had given better regiments than these to Crook. If so, though, he had no one to blame but himself.

He would do the best he could with what he had. Meanwhile, "that genial gentleman and good soldier, Col. David H. Strother" was made Sigel's aide-de-camp, and Stahel took overall command of all forces at Martinsburg. With departure only a day or two away, Sigel decided to have a grand review of his army on April 27. At 2 p.m. his legions marched out on the parade ground and then, as one soldier put it, "such a time as we had finding our places in the line was never seen before." The confusion was utter; no one knew where to go. It hardly seemed an auspicious start for the campaign.[7]

Even as Sigel drilled, the rumors and fears of a Confederate advance mounted. Confederate deserters reported 7,000 troops and more under Imboden, some said 10,000, and that a raid into West Virginia was imminent. Early was supposedly in the Valley, and Breckinridge with more thousands was on the way. Soon even Lee's chief general James Longstreet was there. Indeed, rumor had every major Confederate in the East facing Sigel except Lee himself. Only one good intelligence report came in, giving a fair picture of the fortifications that he could expect in the Valley and brief evaluations of the principal Confederates. Imboden was "not much thought of by any one," it said, and Echols was regarded much the same, but Breckinridge "is confided in by soldiers & people." Meanwhile, Rebel cavalry and scouts hovered about Martinsburg trying to divine Sigel's intentions. The German's cavalry skirmished with them at Winchester, again near Strasburg, and in the West Virginia mountains. The bluecoats were bested every time.

That was not to be helped now. The last of Sigel's troops came in on April 28, and his little army was complete. Sullivan commanded the one infantry division of two brigades, eight regiments in all. Stahel, nominally still in charge of all forces, would now lead the cavalry division, two small brigades with only three whole regiments and detachments of five others. The five batteries of artillery, under no general commander, reported to whomever Sigel or Sullivan assigned them. The army numbered 9,000 men and 28 guns, and it was ready to go. Orders went out to move at 5 A.M. April 29, and Sigel told Colonel James Washburn of the 116th Ohio to "Turn over your tents and be very ready to march."[8]

They set out the next morning three hours late. Forebodings filled many with apprehension. Strother, fearing disaster, left his cherished diary with his wife in Martinsburg. Others hoped that they would not have to advance too far up the Valley. Some were facetious. They were, said one, "To march on Richmond with six or eight thousand men and attack Lee in the rear, while the army of the Potomac, two hundred thousand strong, held him in check in front." Sigel did not help. Speaking to a Martinsburg audience a few days before, he had said that the war had gone on too long, largely due to "the greatest General of the age, the rebel Robert Lee"! With this ill-advised encomium to spur their confidence, the regiments marched south. A private in the 18th Connecticut spoke for all of them: "We are in for business now."[9]

Those who would have to give Sigel "business" were hardly oblivious to his movements. Imboden and Breckinridge kept watchful eyes turned to the north and west. Indeed, even before the movement of Federal troops to Crook and Averell in West Virginia had begun, Imboden unknowingly prophesied the enemy plan, fearing greatly a combined move against Staunton, Lexington, the Virginia & Tennessee Railroad, and other points at once. Intelligence reports throughout March and April confirmed the impression, and all seemed to agree that Staunton was the principal target. Imboden maintained constant communication with Breckinridge, and on April 18 tersely informed him that "another raid is brewing." The same day, Lee told Imboden that, while he still did not apprehend an advance in the Shenandoah, he hoped that he and Breckinridge could unite to drive one back should it come. Lee would be unable to spare them any aid. They were on their own, yet he charged them with more than just defending the Valley; they must protect as well his left flank. When Grant opened the campaign, Lee would be too busy, and too heavily outnumbered, to guard it himself. An awesome task faced his two men in the Valley, and on Breckinridge, who would naturally command any joint operation, it imposed an especially heavy burden. In his hands might rest the fate of the Army of Northern Virginia. Lee, though he barely knew the Kentuckian, was handing him a trust he had given to no other since the mighty Stonewall.[10]

Preparations to meet whatever should come began immediately, and by the end of April Breckinridge felt his command was nearly ready. The infantry was almost all armed, the cavalry improving, and he now had a six-gun battery with each of his two infantry brigades. Another four-gun battery of horse artillery was in the process of formation. His plans for the department were solely for defense. Echols he kept at Lewisburg, West Virginia, forty miles north of Dublin; McCausland was stationed at Narrows, on the New River, twenty miles north of department headquarters; and cavalry was spread out in Tazewell County, forty miles to the west and far north toward Beverly. The result was a thin, and easily penetrated, defensive line, running nearly 140 miles northeast to south-west, covering almost the whole exposed front of the department. Echols and McCausland stood notified to be ready to move at a moment's notice. Either one could handle an enemy raid singlehanded, he felt, and they were close enough to unite to meet an advance in force. Meanwhile, his cavalry to the north, under Colonel William Jackson, was in communication with Imboden and close enough to cross the Alleghenies to his aid if need be. This was all he could do, Breckinridge felt. "An advance by us at this moment," he told Echols, "is impossible," though he entertained hopes of being able to move on the B&O before long. With Averell coming, he had to defend and was determined to hold all of his department if possible. "I will do all I can short of entire and fatal separation of the troops," he told Echols.

Cheering news came on April 25, when Breckinridge found out that the infantry brigade of Brigadier General Gabriel C. Wharton, 1,000 strong, had been ordered to report to him from another department. Wharton reached Dublin April 30, and Breckinridge immediately ordered him to Narrows to relieve McCausland. Then more good news came when the renowned cavalry brigade led by Breckinridge's old friend Brigadier General John Hunt Morgan, was ordered to him. It would be several days before Morgan arrived, but the prospect for a successful defense seemed definitely improving.[11]

Breckinridge was lucky that it was. On May 1 came a telegram from Lee. There was no doubt any longer: Averell was coming from the Kanawha any day now, his object—Staunton. While Lee's authority did not encompass either Breckinridge or Imboden, he strongly urged them to act in concert against this menace. And they must act alone for, as the general told Breckinridge, "it will be impossible to send any reenforcements to the Valley from this army."[12]

Time and action flew swiftly now. Immediately Echols and McCausland were notified, newly organized cavalry sent out to watch approaches from the west, and fresh intelligence scanned more carefully than ever for any clue to enemy intentions. Many reports indicated that several of those regi-

ments sent out for Averell had recently been seen returning
toward Martinsburg, but the threat, so far as Breckinridge
knew, still remained those forces in the Kanawha. Eleven
regiments of infantry and eight of cavalry were now reported
in Averell's camp at Logan Court House, and Echols' scouts
told him they intended to hit the salt works, the lead mines,
and the bridges of the Virginia & Tennessee.

By May 4 Breckinridge was ready to move out and meet
Averell's advance, wherever it might be found. His three infantry brigades numbered 4,000, his cavalry 2,600, and his
batteries were nearly all armed. He could expect to make a
creditable defense. Additional help was available, too. Two
days before Major General Francis H. Smith, superintendent
at the Virginia Military Institute, communicated with Breckinridge telling him that Lee had authorized him to tender the
services of the Corps of Cadets. Made up of boys from fourteen
to eighteen, it numbered about 250 ready for duty, and one
section—two guns—of artillery. Breckinridge, though doubtful
that he could use the schoolboys, expressed gratification. "This
force will be very effective in assisting to repel or capture destructive raiding parties," he wrote in reply. He had no intention of calling them out.[13]

That evening Breckinridge was at his headquarters at Dublin Depot, getting ready to go personally to the front. Then the
telegrapher handed him a brief message relayed from Richmond. It was from the President.

Richmond, May 4, 1864
General Breckinridge,
    Dublin:
    Information received here indicates the propriety of your
making a junction with General Imboden to meet the enemy
on his movements toward Staunton. Communicate with
General R. E. Lee and General Imboden.
Jefferson Davis

Things had been happening. On the previous day word of
Sigel's move south from Martinsburg reached Richmond and
Lee. The War Department believed that his column numbered

8,000 or more and easily guessed its object as Staunton. Lee, on being informed, expressed to the President the hope that Breckinridge and Imboden could unite to meet Sigel. Davis interpreted this as a request, particularly as Lee expressed as well the wish to concert movements in the Valley with his own, to regard the Shenandoah as officially his left wing. Consequently, he authorized Lee to direct all operations there, at the same time sending to Breckinridge his brief but climactic telegram.[14]

Now the whole complexion of things was changed. On the eve of embarking on one campaign, Breckinridge suddenly found himself faced with meeting two threats, one from Averell which could destroy his department and another from Sigel which could cripple the Shenandoah, even Lee. As if this were not enough, news now came from McCausland that Averell was ready to move from the Kanawha. And from Bragg, his old nemesis now acting as the President's chief military adviser, came an order to send one of his cavalry brigades out of the department to eastern Tennessee, where the enemy was not even moving!

Immediately on receiving Davis' telegram, Breckinridge sent off a hasty wire to Lee asking instructions. He could move to Imboden, he said, but it would not be easy. The only rail connection to Staunton was via the Virginia Central Railroad at Jackson's River Depot, Virginia, some thirty-six miles east of Echols' position and over sixty miles northeast of Wharton's. To march the whole way to Imboden seemed impossible. Lee replied quickly. Sigel was to be stopped if possible. If not, then cross the Blue Ridge to Orange Court House to prevent Sigel's moving against Lee's left. And then Lee took a chance. Himself only hours away from the opening of the campaign against Grant, he gave Breckinridge full responsibility for directing operations in the Shenandoah. Imboden would henceforth report to him. Still Breckinridge seemed uncertain. He wired back to Lee for more information on Federal movements, and proposed that he take Echols and Wharton and perhaps McCausland, with him to the Valley, leaving the bulk of his cavalry and artillery to defend the rest of the department. He would keep the brigade that Bragg had ordered away. The Kentuckian would wait all night for Lee's reply. Then he would make his own final decision.[15]

It was a long night. Couriers came and went. News arrived from several fronts. Imboden reported Sigel at 7,000 strong and still advancing. He had called out the reserves for the emergency. Sigel seemed bent on crossing the Blue Ridge to threaten Lee. He would hold him as long as possible. The hours passed by slowly. In the dim light of the Dublin depot Breckinridge pondered his dilemma. "The situation of affairs in my Department was precarious and nothing but the necessity of preserving Staunton as the left of Gen. Lee's then important line would have justified its temporary abandonment." But was it definitely a necessity? He must hear from Lee.

At 5 A.M. on the morning of May 5, after nine hours of anxious waiting, Lee's telegram arrived. He still could not say for sure that Staunton was the threatened point, but the bulk of those Federal forces originally sent to West Virginia and then brought back appeared to be with Sigel. Meet him, said Lee, drive him back before the German could threaten his left. Even now Grant's legions were across the Rapidan, the campaign opened with some heavy skirmishing in a wooded hell called the Wilderness. Outnumbered two to one in his front by Grant, Lee could not hope to meet an attack from Sigel on his left as well. At this moment, the Shenandoah was more important to him than ever before. It must be held.[16]

Lee's telegram was a relief after the hours of waiting and anxiety. Breckinridge must move swiftly now. There were no more doubts, no more questions. His own words echoed silently in the Virginia mountains: "The hour for action has arrived."

4

"*The Rebs Won't Gobble Us This Time*"

The orders flew. To McCausland, Echols, and Wharton went the same word: Get to Jackson's River Depot fast. Echols, the nearest, would move out at 6 A.M the next morning, May 6. The others would follow. Breckinridge directed transportation for them to be ready at the depot by early on May 7. A morning train would take Echols to Staunton, one that evening would carry Wharton, and another the next day would pick up McCausland. If his transportation did not fail him, he would have 4,500 men and two batteries in Staunton by midday May 8, with Sigel still many miles north of him. Anxious about this, he checked repeatedly by wire with railroad people in Staunton. Would there be enough cars for his troops? Were they on their way yet? He had ordered one week's rations to be ready at Staunton. Would they be ready?[1]

Replies encouraged him as he packed his own saddlebags for the ride north. Then, in the midst of his activity, came word from Imboden. Sigel had reached Winchester. Less than ninety miles separated him from Staunton. With energy, and especially with cavalry at his command, the German could be on its outskirts even as the trains brought in Breckinridge's men. Time was short.[2]

Imboden had been watching Sigel carefully since his march out of Martinsburg on April 29. He sent scouts up to the Federals' very picket lines to discover what they could and actually got a man inside Sigel's lines on May 1 to learn that he intended to go at least as far as Strasburg. Alarmed, Imboden himself broke camp the next day and moved out down the Valley to Mount Jackson with 1,600 mounted and dismounted cavalry to feel enemy strength. Everyone anxiously awaited his report.[3]

Whatever it was, though, Breckinridge could not wait. While organizing his advance, he brought up a pack mule for himself and staff, and set out on the evening of May 5 for Narrows to confer with Wharton. Passing the night at Narrows, Breckinridge's party rode on fifty-two miles to Sweet Springs the next day, and twenty-seven miles on May 7 to reach Jackson's River Depot. Echols' brigade was there to meet him, and so was bad news. The anticipated rail transportation was delayed; his men would have to march all the way to Staunton. Worse yet, Brigadier General Albert Jenkins, whom Breckinridge left to command the department in his absence, reported that an enemy column—Crook—was only twenty miles from Narrows. He expected an attack at any moment. Could not he hold Mc-Causland there for a day or two? Breckinridge, who now found himself kept up nearly all night with orders and planning, assented, painfully cutting his army for its clash with Sigel by a full third. At least, Jones, Jackson, and Morgan should be sufficient to stop Averell, whose advance had approached Wytheville, south of Crook.[4]

Suddenly in a day the whole plan seemed to collapse. On top of it came an anxious telegram from Lee. "The movements proposed in the Valley," he urged, "if made, must be made at once." The words seemed to mock Breckinridge's hopes for the campaign. Unwilling to quit in spite of these setbacks, he started off again early on May 8 for Staunton, riding a little bay given to him by a friend in the Army of Tennessee, Major General Frank Cheatham. The horse's name, coincidentally, was Old Sorrel, but as Breckinridge rode out of the Alleghenies and into the Shenandoah that day, he felt like anything but another Stonewall.[5]

There were others in the Valley by now whose hopes were

much higher. It was a lovely day when Sigel's army marched out of Martinsburg on April 29. The road was good, the weather fine, the men in the best condition they had seen in a year. As they marched south, the people, white and black, lined the pike's sidewalks cheering "God bless you!" It was an auspicious beginning.

Predictably, however, not everything went so well. The Federals were hardly on their way when the good weather worked against them. Used now to months of cold, the sudden warmth took them by surprise. At the first halt in the march men began throwing aside clothing and equipment to lighten their loads. Even at that, it took them eleven hours to cover as many miles to their camp at Bunker Hill. The hard macadam of the Valley Turnpike—often called just the "pike"—left thousands of sore feet in the tents that night.

Sigel, uncertain exactly what he intended to do, let the army stay in camp the next day and, despite an evening rain, the men stayed warm and dry in the little shelter tents they called "dog houses." Reports of enemy activity came into camp. Partisans were supposed to be near Petersburg, West Virginia, moving north, perhaps toward the B&O. Some 1,500–2,000 Confederate cavalry were seen near Woodstock, forty-five miles south of Bunker Hill. Justly cautious, though hardly alarmed, Sigel ordered that no one be allowed near telegraphers' tables for fear that spies might read important wires. Meanwhile, he decided to push on to Winchester.[6]

Despite the sore feet and the heat, the general commanding felt that the army needed more drill and here decreed that whenever it should lie in camp for a day or more, it should have two hours of drill every morning and one hour in the afternoons, with exercises by regiments, batteries, brigades, and divisions. This day, April 30, at Bunker Hill he had the troops out for three or four hours of it, with no fewer than eight different and intricate movements ordered. There were grumblings in the ranks that the army should be marching south to Staunton instead of wasting time on the parade ground.[7]

The next day, May 1, Sigel put the army in motion again for

Winchester, eleven miles south. He sent scouts out in all directions and seemed confident. "We are going up the Valley," wrote one of his privates, "and I think we are strong enough so that the rebs wont gobble us this time."

But disturbing sights met the Federals as they marched this day. All along the pike they saw the graves of men who had gone up the Valley before them, never to return. A soldier of the 12th West Virginia believed that there was "perhaps not a mile of the whole route over which we passed along which there could not be seen a soldier's grave." For those who had been this way before, particularly the survivors of Milroy's disaster of a year ago, the sights of this march were unnerving. Even worse things awaited them when they reached Winchester at 4:30 that afternoon. Passing by the old battleground of June 1863, they saw dead friends and comrades barely covered by earth, many lying where they had been thrown by the hurrying Confederates, with no burial at all. Instead of arousing bitterness in the men, the horrid spectacle left them with a melancholy which was not easily shaken.[8]

On the face of it, a stay in Winchester seemed beneficial. "The weather here has been on the whole very pleasant," wrote Captain du Pont the day after arriving. "This portion of the Valley is very beautiful." The men were not happy, however, when the wagon train delayed coming up for three days with their rations and forage. Their displeasure was passed along to the citizens of Winchester, who found hungry Federals confiscating their sheep and hogs. They had already given the army a cold reception, and these foraging expeditions into barns and pens spurred some to action. Within two days a cavalryman was shot from a house. The assailant was dragged out to watch his home burned before his eyes. This released a spontaneous reaction in the army, and without orders other dwellings soon felt the torch before the men were brought under control. The resumption of daily drill kept the soldiers busy, but not happy.[9]

Most disconcerting of all, though, was the mountain. Here in Winchester they got their first glimpse of it, standing like a silent, brooding, sentinel over the Shenandoah. The northern head of the Massanutten lay before them. Its configuration at this extremity was curious, for it resembled nothing so much as a sleeping dog, lying on its side, its head pointing east. As the mountain ran south, perspective made it appear to taper. Taillike, it led their eyes deep into the Valley that had for so long been a graveyard of Union hopes, until it disappeared. Beyond their sight it continued on to a gap, and New Market.

The mountain was not all that watched Sigel as he lay in Winchester. Imboden was active. On May 2 he had set out from his camp near Mount Jackson and, moving slowly, reached Woodstock four days later. Scouts went out immediately to spy and gather information from citizens. They brought him a good estimate of Sigel's numbers and intentions, and immediately he wired to Lee for reinforcements, which would not come. His signal corps also reported to him Crook's and Averell's movements in West Virginia, and more than ever he feared for Staunton. Sigel must be stopped or delayed to give Breckinridge time to come up from the south, and the more time the better now that rail transportation for Echols and Wharton would not materialize.[10]

Imboden placed his hopes in the partisans. He would have to stay in the Valley, across Sigel's path, until Breckinridge arrived, but they could move at will against the Federal's supply lines. One officer in particular had already achieved a singular fame by his depredations behind enemy lines. Lieutenant Colonel John S. Mosby, formerly of Major General J. E. B. Stuart's cavalry, had organized and operated his partisan rangers in northern Virginia since January 1863, so thoroughly disconcerting Federal movements in the area that it was called by many "Mosby's Confederacy." He had captured one Union general and proved the bane of many others. Now, scouting for Stuart in Grant's rear as the Wilderness operations began, he crossed over the Blue Ridge to harass Sigel. No sooner did the Federals arrive in Winchester than Mosby and a handful of men attacked and captured the eight wagons of Sigel's private train as it traveled south from Martinsburg. Then he hit Sigel's base itself. Mosby and twenty men entered Martinsburg by night, May 1, as the Federals partied. While a few of his men silenced the sleepy guards, Mosby and the rest slipped into the empty officers' tents and lifted their wardrobes, then moved on to the stables and took fifteen horses. Finally, Mosby and one man went into town and carefully studied its fortifications. Their little exploit was not revealed to the Federals until 10 A.M. the next morning.[11]

Even greater things were to come from a guerrilla under Imboden's own command. Captain John H. McNeill and his company of rangers knew the back country of West Virginia as well as any, its passes, mountain roads, and innumerable hiding places. Like all partisan leaders, an independent man, McNeill had only recently antagonized Imboden for refusing to turn over deserters from other commands who enlisted with his own. Brought before court-martial in Staunton, he was released, partly because Imboden needed him in the coming campaign. His daring and resourcefulness would prove indispensable.

In the wake of Mosby's initial successes in annoying Sigel, Imboden and McNeill decided to play for higher stakes. A well-planned and -executed raid deep into Sigel's department could serve a triple purpose. It would afford an opportunity to damage or destroy important stores; a raid, if successful, might slow down Sigel's already unhurried march up the Valley; and, best of all, a strike of proper proportions could dupe the German into diminishing his army by sending off a substantial force to pursue the raiders. The plan had everything to recommend it, and the target could not have been better chosen—the Baltimore & Ohio Railroad, principal trust in Sigel's guardianship.

It was well after nightfall, May 3, when McNeill and sixty men rode out of his camp at Indian Old Field in Hardy County, West Virginia. Moving swiftly, they headed northeast, being joined along the way by Captain John T. Peerce. They turned northwest across Knobly Mountain at Doll's Gap and moved on along the Elk Garden road to pass over the eastern front ridge of the Alleghenies. By dawn of May 5 they had covered over thirty miles, and stood at the crossroads that would take them to Piedmont and Bloomington, in Maryland, the B&O's shop and storage yards. A brief conference followed. Piedmont was McNeill's chief objective, and he ordered its telegraph wires to be cut immediately. Then, apprehending that fortune might chance to bring along one of the many Union troop trains from Ohio and the West that passed by this line through Piedmont at an inopportune moment, he sent Captain Peerce with ten men to Bloomington, one mile west, to stop anything that approached.

Now it was time to move. McNeill stopped the first westbound train that came by, commandeered its engine, and sent Lieutenant George Dolan and two others steaming into Piedmont under flag of truce. They demanded the surrender of the small garrison of the 6th West Virginia Infantry. Reluctant at first, the Federals were soon persuaded when McNeill and the rest of his command rode in behind Dolan and threw a few shots their way. Besides, they knew what McNeill did not. The Confederates' approach had been spotted and word of their coming was telegraphed to New Creek's Federal garrison just five miles south before the wires were cut.

McNeill started the destruction immediately. In all, seven buildings were fired, including the roundhouse, machine shops, and storage sheds. Nine engines standing in the yard were destroyed, and McNeill put six others under full steam and sent them racing south toward New Creek, hoping they might crash into anything on the tracks there. Then he set fire to between seventy-five and eighty freight cars. Within half an hour Piedmont was a blazing hell of flaming wood and red hot, grotesquely twisted, machinery.

The angry column of black smoke rising from the rail yards served as a beacon for the Federal column leaving New Creek. Seventy-five men and one piece of artillery were dispatched as soon as the anxious message from Piedmont came through at 7 A.M., and it did not take them long to reach McNeill's outposts. Putting their field gun in place, they opened fire on the Confederates, and a brief fight ensued, costing McNeill one man killed. Then word came from Bloomington that the line of retreat was clear, and the partisans hastily withdrew. Behind them they left a burning, smoldering ruin.

Actually, the message from Captain Peerce contained more than an assurance of safe retreat. He had done well for himself. While the main force sacked Piedmont, Peerce stopped two freight trains and opened their cars to Bloomington's citizens for looting. Then, advised that another eastbound train was coming, and that it might be loaded with soldiers, he hid his men and waited for it to arrive. There were two carloads of Federals in tow, on their way to Washington, armed but without ammunition. As the train stopped, Peerce mounted his horse and dashed up on the station platform, clattering down the boards to shove his pistol in the face of a captain standing on the rear of a troop car. He demanded their surrender and the 115 surprised Federals capitulated. Notifying McNeill of his success, Peerce set about destroying the trains he had captured. He was still at it when McNeill and his men hurriedly rode up, their pursuers not too far behind. They made an unsuccessful attempt to destroy the railroad bridge across the North Branch of the Potomac, but the Federals were too close. Paroling their prisoners, the raiders rode back into the mountains toward Moorefield.

It had been a spectacular little raid, and it achieved everything that Imboden and McNeill hoped for it. The consternation in Federal ranks proved considerable. B&O officials immediately reported the damage to Secretary of War Edwin M. Stanton and with it sent their hearty complaints for the lack of protection. Stanton was not at all happy and did not mind voicing his displeasure that Sigel had marched off leaving the line so exposed and now was "too far off to do any good." The damage was not irreparable and the road would be open in a day or two, but hundreds of thousands of dollars worth of property had been lost.[12]

Sigel, predictably, adopted a cavalier attitude about it after he received word of the raid late on May 5. It was hardly his fault—though he accepted the responsibility. After all, he had advised West Virginia Governor Arthur Boreman to call out the militia three weeks before to guard the road in his absence. He could not fulfill his part of Grant's plan and defend the B&O at the same time. Besides, he protested, "this affair . . .

seems to me insignificant." Perhaps so, but nevertheless he felt
it important enough to send out 500 men of the 22d Pennsylvania and 15th New York Cavalries under Colonel Jacob Higgins late on May 6. Their mission was to intercept McNeill.[13]

McNeill's daring raid not only reduced Sigel's army marching up the Shenandoah, but also reinforced those reasons for
caution with which the Federal commander augmented his
own natural sloth. It bought the Confederates time, and
Breckinridge needed it desperately now that his brigades were
marching overland to Staunton. Echols had left his camp
south of Lewisburg early on May 6, reaching Jackson's River
Depot the next evening, where he met Breckinridge and the
bad news of no transportation. Left with no alternative, he
marched his men on the next day, hopeful, but not optimistic,
that he could reach Staunton in time.[14]

John Echols was a genuinely impressive figure. A massive
man weighing some 260 pounds and standing six feet four
inches, he dwarfed even the tall Breckinridge. His amiability
was remarkable—somehow a grin seemed always lurking behind his round, mustachioed face. A graduate of V.M.I. and
Washington College in Lexington, he had studied law at Harvard and, by the outbreak of the war, had been practicing for
eighteen years. Echols ardently supported secession and
served as a delegate to the state convention which pulled Virginia out of the Union. Though his natural inclinations did not
include a military career, he volunteered and was elected lieutenant colonel of the 27th Virginia Infantry in Jackson's first
command, the "Stonewall Brigade." He led the regiment in
the First Battle of Bull Run and continued to command it until
severely wounded while fighting under Stonewall at Kernstown in 1862. After recovering he accepted his commission as
brigadier general and led a brigade in Western Virginia, taking command of that department briefly. He was a skillful organizer and a good fighter, though sometimes slow in the field.
The reason for the latter lay probably in his great size, for it
weakened his heart. Within three weeks of the present campaign he would be totally incapacitated. Even now he may
have been feeling the effects of the onset of this "neuralgia of

the heart," but if so, he kept still about it. Unknown to Breckinridge, the fight for time was now against not just a Federal army, but a Confederate heart as well.[15]

Illness or no, however, Echols displayed more than enough energy in the march toward Staunton. In two days out of Jackson's River Depot, his regiments, Patton's 22d, the 23d Virginia Battalion of Lieutenant Colonel Clarence Derrick, and Lieutenant Colonel George M. Edgar's 26th Virginia Battalion, made forty-five miles to Goshen. Staunton was only thirty-five miles away. But the march came at price. His men and horses were almost worn out, and he could not find forage. He needed grain desperately, or else the animals would be totally used up when they finally arrived. However, with or without grain, Echols was determined to reach Staunton.

Echols had far to go, but Wharton had even farther. From his camp at Narrows to Jackson's River it was over sixty miles of mountain marching. His small brigade made eighteen miles the first day, May 6, twenty-two miles the next, and by late on May 9 it went into camp barely a mile from the depot. At first Wharton, too, was told that there would be no transportation for him. His men were also nearly worn out, but his confidence was unshaken. "We will reach Staunton," he wired Breckinridge. His trust was vindicated that same night when, unexpectedly, a train finally arrived to take parts of his units, the 51st Virginia and the 30th Virginia Battalion, on to Staunton. With them too went the four-gun battery of Captain Thomas E. Jackson. The rest had to walk. Captain George B. Chapman's six-gun battery had gone with Echols and, lamentably, the six field pieces of another battery were called back by McCausland just as they were being loaded on flatcars. Still, the matter seemed assured. Breckinridge might only have half an army at Staunton in time, but it would be enough for a fight.[16]

Breckinridge himself reached Staunton on the evening of May 8, after subjecting himself and staff to a grueling forced ride across the mountains. Leaving Narrows early on May 6, they had covered 145 miles in three days. What awaited him was a mixture of good and bad news. Here he first learned of McNeill's handsome success and that Sigel still sat in Winchester. By advancing his own command against the B&O in the wake of McNeill, Imboden believed he could force the Federals to retire. Jubilantly confident, he told the Kentuckian that, together, "we can clear this border in five days." He reported Sigel at 4,000 infantry and 3,000 cavalry. If Breckinridge's troops could all arrive, he felt, the Confederates would not be much outnumbered.

But Breckinridge, not yet settled into his new headquarters, held back a few hours, and events proved him wise. Soon came the report that Higgins—erroneously estimated at 1,300 strong —had gone out after McNeill. Here now was Imboden's task. Intercept Higgins, protect McNeill, and destroy if possible this substantial portion of Sigel's cavalry. If events warranted, he might then move on to the B&O line. Imboden rode out of his camp at Woodstock early May 9 with two regiments and two guns. Behind him, to watch Sigel, he left the 510 men of Colonel George H. Smith's 62d Virginia Mounted Infantry. Imboden hoped to be back within four or five days. He could not be spared longer.[17]

The bad news came from the south. When Breckinridge reached Staunton there awaited him a dispatch saying that Crook was only ten miles from Dublin. Jenkins and McCausland were moving to meet him. McCausland wired to Breckinridge asking for aid, but he could send none. Nevertheless, the Kentuckian's adjutant assured him from Dublin: "We will give them a warm reception here." He was right. In a stiff fight by Cloyd's Mountain, Jenkins gave Crook a hard time, but he took heavy losses, defeat, and a mortal wound himself in payment. McCausland, now in command, was able to save all the stores in Dublin before he had to fall back, though, and now he faced a Crook, superior in numbers, who was in a position to visit devastation on the department. McCausland wired Richmond requesting that Breckinridge be sent back. The ever-meddlesome Bragg got the message. "I have not seen the order which sent Gen Breckinridge away," he noted, "nor do I know the necessity for the move. It is important he should be back if it be possible." Fortunately Secretary of War Seddon saw the telegram, too. Like Bragg, uncertain of what was going on in the Shenandoah or if Breckinridge really needed to be there, he had the good sense to decide that "discretion had better be left to Genl Breckinridge who knows his orders & the chances of movement in the Valley." Thus near calamity was averted. Breckinridge would stay.

And it was good that he did. Even while McCausland and Crook were fighting, a report came in from the signal corps station on the northern summit of the Massanutten. Sigel was marching south from Winchester. The game was on again.[18]

Few generals in either army enjoyed quite the talent for sloth that Franz Sigel could display when he set his mind to it. Day after day his army sat in Winchester, while Breckinridge edged ever closer to Staunton. Of course, he was succeeding in at least one part of his assignment—desperately needed troops were drawn away from southwest Virginia, opening the territory to Crook. But Sigel was also supposed to meet Crook's column for further joint operations. For a general with real drive, there was the tantalizing opportunity to throw a scare into Lee by crossing the Blue Ridge on his flank. But Sigel's initiative lay more in the realm of personal advancement than in movement of armies; that sense of urgency which he felt was not so much for the junction with Crook, as with the continued drill of his weary troops.

Drill they did. Incessantly. Stahel reviewed them, Sullivan reviewed them, Sigel reviewed them. For many it was the first brigade and division drill they had encountered. "These Brigade drills, if such they may be called," Lieutenant Colonel William S. Lincoln of the 34th Massachusetts wrote in his diary, "are full of novelty to us, so different are they from any in which heretofore we have taken part." Particularly novel was the sham battle Sigel planned for May 5.

All the night before the day of the "battle" the regimental officers stayed up studying their manuals. Then came the morning of the fray. Things began badly when Sigel's staff officers, most of them German like himself, proved unable to intelligibly convey orders in English. It did not help that this new kind of drill was unknown to most of the army's regimental commanders. Soon Sigel had every unit in the army advancing, retreating, charging imaginary foes, being charged in turn, and moving with no seeming purpose from one end of the line to the other. The 116th Ohio was ordered to advance first to the right wing, then to the left wing, and then to charge. But Sigel forgot to have them called back. They went so far that they did not hear recall and staff officers finally had to be sent out after them. "It was the funniest farce ever witnessed anywhere," sadly lamented one Ohioan. "Thus endeth the first lesson," remarked the 116th's chaplain. "Yes, by God!" replied its colonel, James Washburn, "and a h—l of a lesson it was, too."

By nightfall the battle was over and the men back in their camps. All, that is, except the 34th Massachusetts. They were still out skirmishing; no one had ordered them back. Finally, Sigel discovered the oversight and had them brought in, long after dark.

This bit of silliness cost Sigel more than a lost regiment or two. It shattered what little respect for him remained in many of his subordinates. "There was never anything seen half so ridiculous," lamented one, "and it bred in everyone the most supreme contempt for General Sigel and his crowd of foreign adventurers." Lincoln found that "our officers, high in place, do not enjoy the full confidence of the command." Colonels August Moor and Joseph Thoburn, the two brigade commanders of infantry, were regarded as "poor soldiers," and Generals Stahel and Sullivan were liked little more. Some officers chafed at the folly of wasting time in Winchester when a campaign was on, and others, cognizant that the enemy's scouts were all about, complained that "Sigel reviewed his troops, and the rebels counted them." When the sham battle farce of May 5 was ordered repeated the next day—with similar results—Colonel George D. Wells of the 34th Massachusetts feigned illness and refused to take out his command. He told Lincoln to take over and do with it as he pleased. "I've lost all interest in it and the service," he said; "*I* won't serve under such fools; and *you* are a fool if *you* do."

Sickness rose in the Union camps, diarrhea becoming commonplace. Worst of all, though, was the hunger. Wagon trains came through, but they did not bring enough, and meanwhile the men could see 250 wagons left standing idle when they could have been bringing supplies. The trouble, as always, was the Confederate raiders Mosby and McNeill. Not content with their previous exploits, they harassed Sigel relentlessly. On May 8 Mosby attacked a Federal guard post near Winchester, taking seventeen prisoners. The "Gray Ghost" captured Sigel's dispatch riders, attacked his trains, and proved himself a master nuisance, equaled only by McNeill. "The bushwhackers bother us some," admitted one Union private. Once again the frequent German-American expression that "a biscuit is worth yust now more den a bayonet" became current. Now safety required that every 100-wagon train from Martinsburg be escorted by at least 400 or more cavalry. The Federal horse stayed in almost constant motion, and Sigel even tried sending out large parties to spread false rumors of his strength and movements. Still the partisans struck. Commanding his reserve division back in Cumberland, Maryland, Kelley was exasperated. "We must kill, capture or drive McNeill out of the country," he told Sigel, "before we can expect quiet or safety."[19]

But the Federals were not in this campaign for safety—none of them, that is, except Sigel, and he would have to move. He had sat in Winchester too long, playing the old game of exaggerating beyond reason the enemy's numbers in his reports to superiors. He even began making plans for withdrawal in case of a reverse. Here was the difference between him and the advancing Confederates. Breckinridge, though outnumbered, was basing his campaign on a plan of attack; Sigel now, started basing his in part on a plan of retreat.[20]

Yet reports from the front made the likelihood of a successful venture seem more promising than he had a right to hope. There seemed to be nothing but a few hundred enemy cavalry between him and Staunton, and his own intelligence was supplemented by Confederate deserters who told him that there were no Confederate units in the Valley, every available man having been sent east to Lee. This decided him in the matter. He would move on up the Shenandoah to "demonstrate against Staunton." If Crook to the south should prove successful in his raid, then Sigel would occupy Staunton and continue on to a junction, and he so notified Washington. On May 8 the orders went out; the command would march south at 6 A.M the next morning. The news came as a relief to the men in the ranks to whom the days spent in Winchester seemed somehow wasted. There were supplies enough gathered to last them until May 15 now, in spite of the partisans. At last the army, and Sigel, were ready to move. But in the tents there were grumblings that "It was the fault of some one that it was not ready before."

That evening Chaplain William Walker of the 18th Connecticut held a Sunday service on the brow of the hill overlooking the camps. He was struck by the great numbers of men from other regiments who attended. There was a particular fervor this night in the song and prayer. "The evening of that day was unusually quiet and solemn," he noticed. The men were lost in thought. Where would they be when the next Sabbath came? Sigel himself felt unsure, unsettled. "We will march farther tomorrow and who knows where to," he wrote to his wife this night. "Farewell my sanctuary."[21]

5

"You Must Judge"

Already a legend was in the making in the Shenandoah. All the trees in the Valley, it would say, came in leaf on May 10, the anniversary of the death of Stonewall Jackson. True or not, this first anniversary in 1864 was to be marked with proper ceremony in Lexington, the principal participants the Corps of Cadets of the Virginia Military Institute.[1]

May 9 had been an ordinary day for them. They drilled for two hours, and then made two sham charges across the parade ground in front of the barracks—a ground where once Jackson had walked—to take a line of pretended breastworks. "It was very exciting," one of them wrote home. Warm weather was coming, they had only a few days before changed to their summer uniforms, and their bedding was still airing out from the winter's use. Then, after the day's drill, came special news. Secretary of War Seddon had received a special flag sent by friends in England to be raised over Jackson's grave. Seddon, in turn, sent it to V.M.I., and now word came from Superintendent Francis Smith that all academic duties would be suspended on May 10 so that the Cadets might have the honor of hoisting the banner in the ceremonies.[2]

A large crowd gathered in Lexington's cemetery that morning as, at 9 A.M., the Cadets formed up. Former governor of Virginia John Letcher addressed them briefly, the flag went up, and the ceremony was over. The rest of the day was their own for the Cadets, until the evening dress parade. They formed on the parade ground, not at all unconscious of the townspeople—and especially the girls—who gathered in the evening cool to watch their exercises. Then, their evolutions and ceremony done, the evening gun boomed forth, the Institute flag came down, and the Cadets marched into the barracks to their supper and their beds.[3]

Many of the boys were still awake a few hours later when, at nine o'clock, the clatter of horse's hoofs came up from the avenue in front of the barracks. Then the drums began beating the long roll for the emergency, and the sleepy Cadets arose, quickly dressed, and assembled. In the darkness they could see a small group of officers gathered about a lantern near the statue of Washington in front of the barracks' archway. They were reading something. Then the adjutant read it to the assembled corps. It was a dispatch from Breckinridge. Sigel was moving up the Valley. He was at Strasburg, probably heading for Staunton. "I would be glad to have your assistance at once," the dispatch said. The order was read amid breathless silence. Then, parade dismissed, the companies broke ranks one by one to make their preparations for the march to Staunton. As they went, wrote Cadet John S. Wise, "the air was rent with wild cheering at the thought that our hour was come at last."[4]

The Cadets had been awaiting their hour for a long time. The Institute, founded in 1839, had already made itself felt in this war. It earned by 1864 the sobriquet "West Point of the Confederacy," and with good reason. Its graduates were fighting the enemy on every front. What little drill and discipline the Southern armies had, they owed largely to V.M.I. men. And there was glory. Seventeen of her sons were or would be general officers. And then there was her former professor Stonewall Jackson, buried in Lexington. With this great war going on all about them, it was no wonder that the Cadets chafed at their inactivity.

What made things worse was that they had come so near to seeing action so many times. In April 1861 the then Major Thomas J. Jackson led them to Richmond to drill newly raised Confederate units. Here many Cadets enlisted with these various units and the Institute, with no corps left, closed its doors until the following January. Reopened, it began with a completely new student body, and then came its next chance when Jackson, now Stonewall, took them with him on his march to victory at McDowell, Virginia, in May 1862. But still they saw no fighting. They spent that summer in chasing deserters in the mountains, and in 1863 took part in three separate expeditions to repel Union cavalry raids by Averell. It was in September of that year that Governor Letcher officially authorized their use in emergencies, but still they saw no action, serving only as wagon guards and escorts. Their frustration knew no bounds.[5]

Thus they had no high expectations over the new campaign that seemed brewing in the Valley in 1864. On April 22 Superintendent (and brevet major general) Smith tendered the services of the corps to Lee, but all that the general said in reply was that Smith should hold them ready to co-operate with Imboden and Breckinridge if necessary. On May 2, with still no indication of anything definite, Smith ordered the corps to be ready to march at an instant's warning. Nothing might come of it, but they would be waiting if needed.[6]

This Corps of Cadets embodied the flower of the South's youth. Cadet James B. Morson was the nephew of Secretary of War Seddon. Robert E. Lee's nephew, George T. Lee, was a Cadet in Company B. Cadet Samuel H. Letcher was the son of the former governor, and John C. Early was the nephew of one of Lee's best fighting generals, Major General Jubal A. Early. Two of the boys, Cadets Robert and William H. Cabell, were cousins to General Breckinridge. The average age was just a week under eighteen, but Cadet John W. Wyatt was nearly twenty-five while Lewis S. Davis had just passed his fifteenth birthday. They were schoolboys much like any other boys. They played pranks, giggled at each other, and resented the rules and strictures of their teachers and superiors, particularly the bespectacled Superintendent Smith, whom they secretly called "Old Specs." But they felt as well a sense of tradition, a pride beyond their years, an elan that bound them to each other and to the Institute. It made them quite remarkable. Intensely mindful of the excellent record already compiled in this war by graduates of V.M.I., theirs was a fierce determination to uphold it and, if circumstances allowed, to enhance it. "From the standpoint of *morale*," wrote one of their sons, himself a future superintendent, "there was, perhaps, not a command engaged in either army in any battle of the Civil War that compared, man for man, with the Corps of Cadets."[7]

Now Breckinridge had called. He needed the Cadets, their two-gun section of artillery, and all the forage and rations they could bring for themselves. Smith wasted no time. He ordered Commandant of Cadets Colonel Scott Ship to have them ready to march by 7 A.M. the next morning, May 11. The superintendent was unwell, though he hoped to join them on the march, but meanwhile he would send with the Cadets two days' rations and over 500 pounds of bacon and beef. He promised Breckinridge that they would be in Staunton by May 12.[8]

There was little sleep that night, even for those not kept up by last minute duties. The anticipation of what might lay ahead kept them awake. By eleven o'clock, as the moon rose in its first quarter, the barracks and grounds of the Institute were a dimly lit sea of activity. Cadets hurried to and fro readying the artillery, filling the caissons and wagons, waking the animals. Inside the barracks the boys attended to a few personal details. Nelson B. Noland of Company C bought two pairs of socks for the march. Another boy sat up sewing buttons on his shirts. As late as 3 A.M. many were still up, writing letters home.[9]

"We surely dwell in the midst of alarms!" Margaret J. Preston of Lexington wrote in her diary the next morning. At 5 A.M. an order came from the Institute impressing her carriage horses to pull the Cadets' two 3-inch iron rifles. Then her cousin, one-armed Captain Frank Preston, tactical officer of Company B, came with two boys for breakfast. Meanwhile, the other Cadets at the barracks ate their morning meal by candlelight, their appetites dampened by their anxiety. There were yet matters to settle. A poll was taken to find those who had been farm boys or had had experience with horses. Thirty-two of them were selected and assigned to the section of artillery. Then came a more onerous duty. Not everyone could go. A guard had to be left for the Institute, and twenty-seven were chosen, twenty-seven very disappointed boys. Francis S. Johnson, the son of former United States Senator Robert W. Johnson of Arkansas, cried unashamedly when left behind, begging to be allowed to go.[10]

Finally at 7 A.M. they were ready to march. The 222 Cadets who would go shouldered their Austrian muzzle-loaders, checked their forty rounds of ammunition, and paraded on the avenue, four companies strong. The artillery section and its complement of boys joined them, as did a fifer and two drummers. At their head rode seven field and staff officers, led by Ship. Once the column was all together, 264 strong, he started them off. As they crossed Woods Creek—derisively dubbed the "Nile" by the boys—they playfully stamped their feet on the wooden bridge to make it sway and rock under them. Then they were off down the pike toward Staunton, Breckinridge, and, they hoped, their destiny.[11]

In Staunton, Breckinridge awaited their arrival anxiously as he marshaled his forces. Reports were in from the east which indicated that Lee was holding well against Grant, but also news of Sigel's advance continued to arrive and it was not encouraging. Citizens claimed that his force numbered 10,000 or more, with 28 guns and more than 200 wagons. It was thought to be an exaggerated figure but this hardly quieted Confederate fears. Breckinridge was still apprehensive of a Union attempt to cross the Blue Ridge to strike Lee's flank. "I want to know at earliest moment any movement towards Grant," he told outposts.[12]

The work of organizing his army went rapidly, thanks in part to the unhappy circumstance that there was not much to organize. The reserves were ready, about 500 of the 1,000 raised being formed in a brigade of four companies, armed with rifles and shotguns and ably commanded by Colonel William H. Harman, a man picked by Imboden in part, perhaps, because he was nearly as unpopular in Augusta County as Imboden himself.[13]

When Breckinridge arrived in Staunton he found another small command waiting leaderless, the 2d Battalion Maryland Cavalry. Its commander had been one of the most dashing partisans of the war, Major Harry W. Gilmor, and among the most troublesome. Handsome after a fashion, possessed of an imposing presence, he was one of many in the Confederate service who fought more out of a love of the glory and romance than for any political reasons. He was the sort of man who received proposals of matrimony from women he did not even know. He had raised his battalion in 1862, and thereafter it proved almost as much a nuisance to the Confederacy as to the enemy. He maintained sloppy discipline, and friends warned him that "there have been indiscretions among your men, & serious ones too." On a raid on the B&O line early in 1864, his men robbed passengers and committed other minor outrages which led to his relief from command and arrest. He went before a court-martial in Staunton in April and won an aquittal, but he still remained under arrest pending Lee's approval of the verdict.

One of Breckinridge's first acts on reaching Staunton was to call Gilmor before him. Despite his irresponsibility, the partisan could be effective when he tried, and the Kentuckian needed every man just now. Breckinridge received him warmly, spoke with him about the court-martial, and then himself reviewed the trial record. While he deliberated, Gilmor looked on. "Seldom have I seen a man," he would write of the general, "who so fully inspired me with admiration and respect as General John C. Breckinridge . . . ; among the general officers in our army I believe [him] one of the most capable." Of course, his opinion may have been influenced by Breckinridge's decision to return him to duty without awaiting Lee's verdict. The general issued a special order restoring Gilmor to his forty-man command, and then directed him to move quickly down the Valley, get in Sigel's rear, harass his supply trains, and delay his advance in any other ways possible so as to give Breckinridge time to gather his forces.[14]

The same day that the general put Gilmor back in the saddle, he sent his message to V.M.I. Superintendent Smith. With the news that his two brigades would not get rail transportation to Staunton, Breckinridge's situation had become desperate. It was only in such straits that he would call on the schoolboys at Lexington. But this same day as well, the first elements of Wharton's brigade appeared on an unexpected train, and by 2 P.M. they were camped just two miles outside the city. The remainder of the brigade would arrive the next day. Despite the distance they had come, his men were still game. Indeed, Company A of the 51st Virginia marched so fast on the mountain roads that Wharton had to put it in the middle of the column to keep it from pulling away from the rest. Echols was doing well, too. Marching hard all the way, his brigade camped within sight of Staunton on the evening of May 11. It seemed miraculous. Where two days before Breckinridge might have despaired of meeting Sigel with anything more than a few hundred raw reserves and Imboden's cavalry, now he had two good but tired brigades and, with them, two batteries. Gilmor was out to annoy the enemy, and the Cadets were on their way; the entire picture had changed, and decidedly for the better.[15]

He let the men rest in camp for a day, May 12, before starting off to find the enemy. They slept, cooked two days' rations, stood for inspection, and looked to their weapons. Meanwhile, Breckinridge saw that his commissary wagons were loaded with the stores he had gathered. That afternoon Scott Ship rode several hours ahead of his command to advise Breckinridge of their coming and confer with him. What the general saw was a young man, just twenty-four, not particularly handsome and a bit overweight. He had graduated from V.M.I. in 1859, fourth in his class, and was regarded as being "oldish beyond his years," a very serious young man. Thereafter he served on the faculty with Stonewall Jackson and, though appointed Commandant of Cadets in the fall of 1861, he saw some combat service with Stonewall at Romney, West Virginia. Anxious for an active commission, he took a leave of absence in 1863 and actually enlisted as a private in the 4th

Virginia Cavalry before returning to the Institute in August. Three months later his rigid personal code led him to attempt to resign over a silly matter of having taken one drink, but he was dissuaded, and fortunately too, for the Cadets liked and respected this stout, straight, but withal amiable commandant.[16]

The Corps of Cadets had marched eighteen miles its first day out, a hard, hot march over the dusty macadamized pike. The walk blistered their feet. Poor Cadet Edward Tutwiler had to fall out at every stream to bathe his sores and then run again to regain his place. Sympathetic to the boys' hardship, their thirty-six-year-old surgeon, Colonel Robert L. Madison, was seen all along the way walking while some tired or footsore Cadet rode his horse. It rained all the next day, turning the road into an "awful *perfect loblolly.*" The Cadets had to "wade through like *hogs.*" But still they covered another eighteen miles by noon and went into camp just a mile out of Staunton. Here was something new to the tired old veterans resting about town, a company of boys nattily dressed in neat gray uniforms, all carrying the same kind of weapon and marching precisely to the even beat of the drummers. This was an organization and uniformity that Confederate units had not known since 1861. As a result, the corps became an item of some curiosity, and derision. The fifer marched them in to the tune of "The Girl I Left Behind Me," but some of the veterans sang children's nursery songs back at them. Perhaps to avoid incidents, Ship restricted the Cadets to their camp for the remainder of the day, but a few slipped into town, spruced and primped, to see girlfriends or steal a few dances. John Wise, his cousin Louis, Beverly "Jack" Stanard, Carrington Taylor, and another boy sneaked into town to Taylor's home for a good dinner. While there, Jack Stanard wrote a letter home, the boys filled their haversacks with goodies, and dried their clothes. Before they left, Taylor's mother asked the other four to take care of her son.[17]

Now Breckinridge's little army was complete. The hard marching had cost him quite a few stragglers—three "lame ducks" from the Cadet Corps would have to remain in Staun-

ton—but still he had a respectable force with which to meet
Sigel. Including the reserves, the Cadets, and a small company
of engineers, his infantry numbered just under 3,500. In addition, two batteries stood ready, to be led by Major William
McLaughlin. One of them, under Captain George B. Chapman, had two three-inch rifled guns and four twelve-pounder
howitzers. The other, whose commander Captain Thomas E.
Jackson had been left behind ill, was led by Breckinridge's
distant cousin Lieutenant Randolph H. Blain, with three
twelve-pounder Napoleons—smoothbores—and one Parrott
rifled cannon. Their crews, added to the two-gun Cadet section, made 248 artillerists and twelve guns. Ahead of them,
down the Valley, lay almost 1,500 cavalry under Imboden,
along with the four three-inch rifles, two howitzers, and ninety-
three men of Captain John H. McClanahan's battery of Staunton Horse Artillery. Once united with Imboden, Breckinridge's
small army would number 5,300 men and eighteen guns. To
be sure, Sigel would still heavily outnumber him, but he would
now have a chance. A chance was all that Breckinridge, Lee,
or the Valley could expect.[18]

All the while that his troops arrived, the Kentuckian received reports from the front on the enemy's movements. Partisan T. Sturgis Davis of Maryland was particularly active,
though his men could no longer penetrate Sigel's line to gather
intelligence and a haze over the Valley prevented observa-
tions from the mountains. Still, he could report that the Federals appeared to number about 8,000. To resist them while
Breckinridge came up, Davis had only his own battalion of
twenty-six men, and the 400 dismounted troopers of Smith's
62d Virginia. Consequently, when Gilmor arrived on his way
to the enemy rear, Davis and Smith implored Breckinridge to
let them keep him until Imboden returned with the main
cavalry force. Already the enemy vanguard was driving in
their pickets north of Mount Jackson, and Imboden should not
be gone long. Indeed, a report appeared on May 11 that he
had defeated a Yankee force the day before, and even then
was on his way back. In fact, he arrived at Mount Jackson that
same night after an eighty-mile ride, leaving his main body to
arrive the next day. When they arrived on May 12, he pulled

his command back three miles before the enemy pickets, to New Market, posting it just south of the road through New Market Gap to Luray, in case Sigel should try to flank him by that route. This place, he felt, or Rude's Hill two miles in his front, offered the best positions in which to meet Sigel's army.[19]

Through the past few days Breckinridge had kept his own counsel as to his plans. For a variety of reasons, it was commonly believed that he would fortify in Staunton and let the enemy come to him. Already outnumbered, he would need the little advantage that standing behind breastworks could afford. Then, too, there was the situation back in his department. Averell had cut the Virginia & Tennessee Railroad. Seddon had turned to Bragg's way of thinking, agreeing now that "I do not think Breckinridges forces could be better employed than in protecting Lynchburg." Even Lee admitted that he might need to return. But the Virginian left the final decision to Breckinridge. "You must judge," he told him.

Breckinridge made his decision, influenced in part by a late report that the Federals were not attempting to cross the Blue Ridge. The game now would be between Breckinridge and Sigel, with the Shenandoah Valley as their field. To save the Valley, he must meet the German and drive him back; to continue to protect Lee's left, he must do so and hold New Market Gap at the same time. "Being convinced that the enemy was advancing in comparative confidence," he reported later, "I determined not to await his coming but to march to meet him and give him battle wherever found." He sent a staff officer ahead to meet Imboden and inform him of his plans and movements and then issued his marching orders. The command would move in the morning, May 13, at 6 A.M. He was confident, and the people of the Valley trusted in him. "If the Yankees come prowling in that direction," wrote an editor a few miles south of New Market, "they will not find the coast entirely clear."[20]

Sigel was trying to stay quiet. As he moved out of Winchester, even those back in his own department knew little or nothing of his movements. Farther north, everyone was in the dark. He did tell Grant what was happening, though, and

when the General in Chief heard that, as of May 8, Sigel was
still in Winchester, he was not at all pleased. This in itself may
not have been a small influence in the German's decision to
move on May 9.

They marched at 7 A.M., preceded by a huge cavalry
screen. The heat wore heavily on them, the dust of the road
parching their throats. The only water to be found on the
march came from springs, some of them sulfur, yet the Federals had to drink it. They lost two men to sunstroke that day.
By 1 P.M., when they reached Cedar Creek, two miles north
of Strasburg, the command was exhausted. They arrived just
in time to catch a party of twenty-five Confederate guerrillas
destroying the bridge over the creek. The Rebels were driven
off, but not before they damaged the bridge sufficiently to
make the Yankees spend the next day in camp while engineers
rebuilt it. As they worked, of course, the infantrymen were
drilled yet again.[21]

The farther south they moved, the more quiet, even sullen,
the Federals found the people of the Valley. It did not help
that they had been stealing citizens' livestock all along the
march. "I pity the 'critter' that is unlucky enough to be right
fat in this country," an Ohio soldier wrote home. "We just pick
them up as we go." While this was going on, though, the Confederates were helping themselves too. Sigel's wagon trains
still presented fat targets, and Mosby's rangers plagued them
continually. Finally, not content with hitting Sigel in his man-
power and his larder, the partisans struck his pocketbook. On
May 9 they captured the sutler of the 21st New York Cavalry,
and with him an $8,000 payroll. Thus harassed, Sigel stepped
up his already excessive precautions. He found out that his
army had not been in Strasburg an hour before news of its arrival was relayed from a Confederate signal station atop the
Massanutten. Henceforward the command would have to
break camp and form without drums or bugles. Meanwhile,
gathering his own intelligence, he received first a false report
of Mosby raiding the B&O, and then some more reliable information that Imboden, and only Imboden, was in his front,
and at least half of the Confederate cavalry seemed to have
gone off after Colonel Higgins' 500-man command in West

Virginia. Still there was no word of whether Sigel had been successful in drawing Breckinridge away from southwest Virginia. Neither did Sigel know Crook's precise whereabouts. There seemed no alternative but to continue the advance, at least as far as Woodstock, and he so gave the orders.

The next morning, May 11, the army marched across a newly repaired bridge and up the pike at 6 A.M. The cavalry, in three detachments, moved on either side and in advance of the main column. They would guard against surprise. In addition, the eastern detachment, 300 men and two mountain howitzers under Colonel William H. Boyd of the 1st New York (Lincoln) Cavalry, was to scout as far forward as Woodstock and, if practicable, proceed to New Market to secure the Luray road through the gap.[22]

Now the march was worse than before. In addition to the heat and dust shots were fired at the column from ambush all along the road to Woodstock. The advance cavalry skirmished nearly all day with Sturgis Davis' little battalion, and by 4 P.M., when the Union army finally marched into Woodstock, the men were bone weary, exhausted from the march and the tension. But Sigel was elated. In taking the town, his vanguard drove out Davis before he could pick up or destroy the documents in the telegrapher's office. As a result, Sigel now had in his hands all of Breckinridge's dispatches from the past week. Now he knew he was coming, knew that he had 4,000 or more with him, and that the Kentuckian was anxious to know of any move toward Grant. The news produced two results in Sigel. First, knowing of Breckinridge's fears, he believed himself justified in ordering Boyd as far forward as New Market, for possession of the gap would afford an opportunity for just such a movement east of the Blue Ridge toward Lee's flank as Breckinridge feared. Second, and predictably, it helped him decide to sit down in Woodstock. He was not strong enough, he felt, to operate here with Mosby and others annoying his flanks and rear. He would advance no farther. However, if Breckinridge came to him, then he would fight.

Here was the essence of Sigel's generalship. He had planned a brilliant lightning raid that could cripple Lee. He was only a day's march from the gap, and he knew Breckinridge was still in Staunton, two days south of it, his army not yet complete. His main objective, drawing the Kentuckian away from Crook, was accomplished. And now, with the opportunity of a lifetime, one such as came to few generals in any war, he decided, was the perfect time to take root in Woodstock. After all, the men needed drilling.[23]

While he waited and drilled, Sigel could at least reflect on the activity of others. The partisans had done it to him again. News of it had come late in the evening of May 10 in a telegram from Kelley at Cumberland. "Rumor says that your cavalry were attacked this A.M. near Wardensville," he said, "by a superior force, under Imboden and McNeill, and were totally routed." Thus came word of the first of what would be several disasters.[24]

Imboden was not one to wait. When intelligence came from his signalmen on the Massanutten that Higgins had gone off on the Moorefield road after McNeill, he decided almost instantly to attack him. At 4 P.M., May 9, he left with the 18th and 23d Virginia Cavalries and two of McClanahan's guns and rode west, over North Mountain and through a dangerous pass called the Devil's Hole. He rode all night, leaving Colonel George H. Smith in command behind him. To prevent Sigel from learning of his plans or movements from Union people in the Valley, Imboden ordered Smith to pass out the word that he had only gone to find a better camp and grazing site. Thus, by the next morning, unknown to the enemy or anyone else, Imboden had covered over twenty miles and was approaching Lost River, in West Virginia.

Since leaving Sigel at Winchester early on May 7, Higgins had made better time than his commanding general. He spent his first night at Wardensville, West Virginia, and by mid-afternoon had come within seven miles of Moorefield. But here, as Higgins' men stopped to water the horses, guerrillas fired on them from a mountainside, killing one man and hitting several horses. Higgins pushed on and rode into town at 4 P.M., only to confront McNeill. The Confederates were grazing and watering their mounts a little southwest of Moorefield, while playfully reading Yankee mail they had recently captured. Suddenly they looked up from their letters to see 500 Federal cavalry outside the town advancing against them.

Immediately, McNeill formed his small command to meet them. The Federals moved at dress parade through the town until, just beyond it, the charge was ordered, but not before one Confederate was captured in a mill, hiding in a barrel of flour. Then it was a race pell-mell up the slope occupied by McNeill. Brandishing their swords and pistols, the Yankees thought for a minute that the Rebels were going to stand. But then McNeill ordered his men to withdraw and, leaving twelve men behind as a rearguard, he fired a volley into the enemy ranks and rode away. After a brief pursuit, the rearguard rejoined Imboden, and Higgins settled down in Moorefield for the night.

The Federals spent the next day in camp, except for a party of fifty who made a circuit southwest to search for McNeill. When they came back that evening, the whole command set out at 9 P.M. for the return to Winchester. Word had been received that Imboden, with 4,500 men, was after Higgins.

Meanwhile, Imboden, with 800, reached Lost River before dawn, May 10, and spread his pickets. It is probable that he had word from McNeill of Higgins' presence in Moorefield, and his own scouts could have discovered without much difficulty that the Federal column was even now on its way through the night, heading toward Lost River. He set up an ambush, putting his men out as mounted pickets to catch Higgins' advance.

Shortly after daylight, an advance company of the 22d Pennsylvania Cavalry, clean and neat in its newly issued uniforms, ran into Imboden's outposts. The Pennsylvanians drove them back with deceptive ease and then Higgins came up and ordered a squad to charge through the gap ahead of them and clear out the Rebels. They rode off "in fine style" for nearly a quarter mile before the Confederates opened a heavy fire on them from the mountainsides, forcing the squad back. The enemy was too strong—they would have to retreat. Higgins and a nine-man escort led the way, riding north toward Romney. "Here," wrote a trooper of the 22d Pennsylvania, "began a ride for life."

Imboden gave them no rest. They "run them all day," a sergeant of the 18th Virginia Cavalry wrote in his diary. North they raced, through Baker and Kirby, on toward Romney. J. J. Lafferty, a Richmond war correspondent, who used the pseudonym "War Path" in the *Sentinel* and *Christian Advocate*, was along for the ride. "Then commenced the hardest, longest race during this war," he wrote, "nip and tuck, head up and tail up."

Higgins' rearguard tried valiantly to stem the gray avalanche coming up behind them, but without much success. Many Federals ran their horses to exhaustion. The wagon train of supplies with the Union column slowed it considerably, but the Confederates slackened their pursuit somewhat, lulling the column into a false confidence. At noon on May 10 the column halted to feed and water the horses. Within ten minutes Imboden came thundering up the road again. The column mounted and prepared to race away, but the wagons had been unhitched, their teams sunning themselves nearby. An attempt was made to get them going again, but the Rebels were too close. Some of the wagons were burned and others abandoned. Apparently some horses were killed to keep the enemy from getting them. Meanwhile, all along the road as they passed, Higgins' men left sabers, pistols, and baggage of every description. It had become an absolute rout.

Finally, on the afternoon of May 10, the panic-stricken column reached Romney, only to learn that McNeill had now joined the pursuit and was barely three miles behind them. Soon afterward the Confederates attacked the town and took it in minutes, driving Higgins back nine miles, across the suspension bridge over the South Branch of the Potomac, to Springfield. The pursuers took several prisoners and reclaimed one Confederate captured earlier in the day just as Higgins' rearguard passed over the bridge. Once past this obstacle, Higgins abandoned his men, riding off to Old Town, Maryland, across the Potomac, to safety. "Why a man like this should command a body of troops," mused one of those he left behind, "will always be one of the queries of the private soldier."

It had been a disaster. By the time what was left of the command staggered into Old Town, it had run nearly sixty miles. The train of wagons lay behind, along with most of the ammunition and forage, and fifty or more casualties, including five dead. Higgins and others immediately exaggerated Imboden's numbers to 3,500 and more, but it could not obscure the magnitude of his defeat. Kelley found Higgins "badly broken down" when he reached Cumberland on May 12, but the man who was really hurt was Franz Sigel. The ineptitude of a colonel had cost him 500 cavalry taken out of action at the very height of a campaign.[25]

News of the defeat only reinforced Sigel's overcautious stand in Woodstock. He let the men dig earthworks and huddle around their fires in the rainy weather. They were silent now. They knew that something was coming, even with a slowpoke like Sigel. "It begins to be lonesome," one of them confided to his diary. Their sense of portent was confirmed when the commanding general ordered everyone to load his rifle. One did not have to be a veteran to know what that meant.

Yet Sigel remained in Woodstock. Among the troops it was generally remarked that "Sigel did not seem in much of a hurry." Even in the North, where almost nothing of his movements was known, it was still feared that he was too slow. "Sigel is at Woodstock," wrote a New Yorker, "wherever that is, and censured for tardiness. It's said that he should have traversed the Shenandoah Valley and been rolling Dutch thunder on Lee's flank and rear a week ago. *Quién Sabe?*"

A chief reason for his slowness was still the remarkable exploits of the partisans plaguing his flanks and rear. His patrols could not stop them. On May 11 a note supposedly from Brigadier General Jeremiah Sullivan's quartermaster was produced, ordering a large train to move back from Woodstock toward Martinsburg. Strangely, no guard was ordered, and the train was well on its way before the quartermaster heard of it and dashed back to return it to safety. In their audacity, Mosby's men were now ordering about Sigel's own trains.

Back in the North the optimism was fading fast. "All the prospect of this campaign is splendid beyond our hopes," mused an observer. "But will it last?"[26]

6

"Now We've Got the D——d Yankees!"

There was no sleepier village in the Shenandoah Valley than New Market. John Sevier, later to be the first governor of Tennessee, was born near this spot, and in 1765 he founded a town there. It was originally called Cross Roads, thanks to the intersection of two old Indian hunting trails. War parties had passed here in precolonial times but after Sevier founded his town only the white man came. Germans and Scots from Pennsylvania migrated up the Valley, settling here in small numbers. They built a race track of sorts and that led to changing the name of the community to New Market, after a well-known track in England. By 1864, a century after its founding, New Market was still only a hamlet, with fewer than 700 inhabitants and a row of houses on either side of the pike at its intersection with the road through the gap.[1]

But the hamlet was not entirely asleep. The people of New Market and the surrounding communities of Shenandoah County watched the approaching armies with more than passing interest. They characterized the Federal leader as "that wily, cautious, crafty, yet energetic Dutch Yankee commander, Gen. Siegle" and estimated his intentions to be the capture of Staunton. He brought six to ten thousand men with him, they believed, but there was little alarm. Breckinridge, "that accomplished and fearless leader," had, they felt, an ample force at hand to take care of them.

As May approached the end of its second week, signs pointed increasingly toward a clash between the converging armies somewhere near New Market. Anticipating some kind of battle, editor J. H. Wartmann of the *Rockingham Register* left Harrisonburg for New Market on May 13, determined to be at the front for whatever happened. What he found when he arrived the same day was a tired but triumphant Imboden resting his command at Rude's Hill again, enjoying what he called "perfect quiet" after his Lost River raid. His troopers had come in the day before, their mounts jaded, the men weary. Now he would sit and watch Sigel and Breckinridge; watch and wait.[2]

Besides the 510 dismounted cavalry under George Smith, Imboden had with him between 800 and 900 troopers of the 18th and 23d Virginia Cavalries. The 18th was something of a family business. Many of its companies had been organized out of Imboden's old 1st Virginia Partisan Rangers, and now it was led by his brother, Colonel George Imboden. Meanwhile, the captain of Company H was another brother, strapping six-foot three-inch Frank Imboden, while James A. Imboden served elsewhere in the regiment as a sergeant major. There was yet a fifth Imboden brother, and he was on the way. Seventeen-year-old Jacob was marching to Staunton as a cadet private in Company B of the V.M.I. Corps of Cadets. General John Imboden's other cavalry unit, the 23d Virginia, was not yet fully organized or mounted. Supporting the cavalrymen were the guns of the big Texan Captain John McClanahan and his Staunton Horse Artillery. His was a company of boys, most of them seventeen to twenty years old, but already they had ridden with Jeb Stuart and seen service with Lee.[3]

These were welcome hours of rest as the men sat in camp on Rude's Hill about four miles north of New Market. The regimental surgeon of the 18th Virginia Cavalry sang to them. Everything seemed peaceful enough. But Major Harry Gilmor was not resting. Happy to be in the saddle again, he was showing unusual activity to please the new general who had restored him to duty after his arrest. He had reached New Market at 1 A.M., May 12, slept for a few hours, and then rode to Imboden's camp at Rude's Hill to inquire for his command, the

2d Battalion Maryland Cavalry. His men were in the advance on picket under Sturgis Davis, Imboden told him. They could not be spared until the 18th and 23d Virginia came in from Lost River that evening.

Around four o'clock that afternoon Gilmor heard firing at the front. Then he saw his men coming in on foot from the picket line. Immediately he mounted them and set off down the pike in column of fours, only to run into Davis rushing back with news that "fully five hundred" Federals were coming. While Davis reformed his own little command behind him, Gilmor and his men charged down the road four miles past Mount Jackson to the vicinity of Red Banks. There he ran headlong into one of Sigel's innumerable reconnaissance forces, Major Charles G. Otis and his 21st New York Cavalry. Gilmor retreated immediately, seeing himself outnumbered. "They ran us handsomely for about two miles," he later wrote, but then, just past Hawkinstown, two miles north of Mount Jackson, the Confederates turned. Otis had let his men get spread out on the pike in his pursuit, and now Gilmor charged his advance. The fight was brief but hot. Several of the Rebels had their horses killed under them, and then Gilmor himself took a painful wound in the back. Barely avoiding capture, he rejoined his men and led them off to the south. Otis showed no inclination to follow any farther, and that evening Gilmor came to Mount Jackson to camp and treat his wounds.

Imboden had more work for the partisan, wound or no. Both he and Breckinridge were still concerned that Sigel might make some move east across the Blue Ridge. But now that Imboden had fallen back to New Market and vicinity, the Federals could make such a move without him knowing it. Consequently, as soon as his main cavalry came in from Lost River, he directed that Gilmor take his command east of the Massanutten toward Luray to watch for the enemy.

Gilmor could not get away until the afternoon of May 13, his painful but slight wound smarting as he rode. He had it dressed at Mount Airy, the home of Virginia militia General John G. Meem, southeast of Mount Jackson at the foot of the mountain, and then rode off across the Massanutten to Caroline

Furnace. Here he learned that Colonel William Boyd's 300 Federal cavalry were barely ten miles north of him at the Burner's Springs crossroads in Powell's Fort Valley, a slight declivity in the northern half of the great mountain. This was the kind of news the Confederates had feared. Determined that he "should be able to give a good account of them," Gilmor rode up the little valley toward Boyd.

He had gone barely two miles when he came across fresh cavalry tracks and learned from a farmer that a force of about 100 had passed that way. Gilmor suspected that they did not number more than fifty, however, and he surmised correctly. Sigel had sent out a detachment of fifty men of the 20th Pennsylvania Cavalry, under First Lieutenant Norman H. Meldrum to find Colonel Boyd's column sent toward New Market and bring it back to Woodstock. Shortly after dark the Confederates stumbled into Meldrum's picket post, but the Federals were so busy making camp that they actually did not see them. Gilmor hid his men in ambush, planning to take the Federals the next morning, when dawn revealed that Meldrum had led his men off by another route. The Confederates pursued, catching the bluecoats off guard in what Gilmor admitted was the "worst managed affair I ever undertook." Nevertheless, the Federals were defeated with no little loss and Meldrum never reached Boyd. Notifying Imboden, Gilmor went into ambush again, this time to await Boyd, unaware that, for the second time in two days, he was laying his trap on the wrong road.[4]

Now the news was definite. Boyd was coming. He might be heading for New Market and Imboden's flank, or he might be only the vanguard of a movement in force across the Blue Ridge. Intelligence from citizens along Boyd's route told Imboden that he intended to meet Sigel at New Market. Whatever his intentions, though, Imboden would now be ready for him.

Federal Scouts were hovering about New Market all day, May 13, and Imboden was forced to keep his men in line of battle continually for hours. In the morning one of Sigel's strong reconnaissance parties drove Imboden's advance from

Mount Jackson, but Imboden wired Breckinridge in Staunton that he would hold his ground at Rude's Hill until the Federals brought up infantry or artillery. Then, however, he would be forced to fall back. When would Breckinridge be up with the main army, he asked? Gilmor's report this day of an enemy column 300 strong moving toward New Market Gap hardly dispelled Imboden's apprehensions.

But by four o'clock that afternoon things looked better. Sigel's advance pulled back out of Mount Jackson. Union prisoners said that the main army still sat in Woodstock and was perhaps even pulling back out of the Valley. Now only Boyd remained an immediate threat. "A few hours will develop their purposes," Imboden telegraphed Breckinridge from New Market. "If he comes on I will fight him here." Then, just as this 4 P.M. dispatch was being tapped out, the telegrapher learned that people in town, looking east at the mountain, could see hundreds of mounted horsemen in the gap. Boyd had arrived.[5]

After leaving Sigel in Woodstock on May 11, Boyd had crossed the Shenandoah River about thirteen miles southeast of Winchester and passed through Ashby's Gap to the east side of the Blue Ridge, the best indirect route by which to approach New Market without being seen. By the morning of May 13 Boyd had led his command back across the Blue Ridge through Luray, where they found and destroyed a considerable quantity of enemy commissary supplies. Then, unaware that Gilmor, having missed his opportunity to ambush Boyd, was moving toward his rear, Boyd took his men up the Massanutten mountain road and into New Market Gap.

Looking down from the Massanutten crest Boyd's men could see New Market and several hundred troops camped north of it. A herd of beef cattle grazed nearby, and what appeared to be a baggage train dotted the pike with its white canvas tops. A column of troops was moving up the pike from Mount Jackson toward New Market. Immediately word was sent back to Boyd, who came galloping up to the front of his now halted column. After scanning the panoramic view before him with his field glasses, Boyd called a conference of his officers. All

believed that the dimly seen troops, their uniforms undistin-
guishable in the gathering evening, were the enemy. All, that
is, except Boyd. Even when it was pointed out that the wagon
train being south of the camped troops, Sigel would thus have
to be moving with his trains *ahead* of his army, Boyd remained
convinced that what lay before him was the van of Sigel's
army. He ordered his advance party, under Captain James H.
Stevenson of the 1st New York (Lincoln) Cavalry, to continue
down the mountain.

Stevenson moved cautiously forward. Soon he saw a section
of artillery and a body of cavalry moving swiftly toward the
base of the mountain south of him. Again he called Boyd forward; but the colonel, though a little disturbed, remained ada-
mant. They must be Sigel's troops, he said; push on. Soon
Stevenson reached the bridge over Smith's Creek. There were
some pickets here dressed in Union blue, but they retired on
Stevenson's approach. The captain sent some men after them
toward town and then spoke again with Boyd. Now they decided to cross the creek and then move north along the stream
until they could reach the pike in the rear of the column they
had seen. Then, if they were friends, all was well; if not, Boyd
could dash north down the pike and make his escape.

Stevenson began the crossing, Boyd following behind, but
they had barely reached the other side when the bluff in front
of them suddenly came alive with yelling horsemen. A shower
of bullets tore into the bluecoats and above them they heard
the triumphant shout, "Now we've got the d——d Yankees!
give 'em h——l!"[6]

The Confederates first spotted Boyd from an eminence just
southwest of New Market called Shirley's Hill, but the oncoming Federals were soon visible from several points in and about
New Market. The men in the camps at Rude's Hill watched
almost calmly as the unexpected visitors moved down the gap.
"The movement was a great surprise to us," recalled an officer
of the 23d Virginia. "War Path" Lafferty wrote five days later
that "we sat and watched as they came down the mountain,
only a couple of miles from our camp." But the Rebels did not

sit for long. Imboden ordered them to saddle and they started up the pike to the crossroads in New Market.

Young Elon Henkel was playing behind his family house on Main Street—the pike—unaware of what was happening. Then he heard an unusual noise and ran to the front of the house to see what it was. Looking north down Main he saw Imboden's two regiments racing "in full swing" up the street, "neck and neck, the horses' hoofs hammering the pike, the scabbards of the sabers rattling, and the cavalrymen giving the Rebel yell." They thundered past Brock's Ham Store, turned left at Strayer's Corner—the crossroads—and pounded eastward toward the Smith's Creek bridge. Little Elon, terrified by the spectacle, ran and hid behind his house, "about the worst scared kid in all Rebeldom."

Imboden laid his plans as he rode. He would take the 18th Virginia Cavalry and two of McClanahan's guns south of the bridge to cross the creek and get in Boyd's rear, cutting off his retreat through the gap. (This was the party which Boyd and Stevenson first saw ride out of New Market.) Meanwhile, Lieutenant Colonel Robert White's 23d Virginia Cavalry would make for a point somewhat north of the bridge to meet Boyd in front and hold him for the 18th to come up behind. Between them they outnumbered the Federals more than two to one; between them they would crush the unsuspecting enemy.[7]

As soon as the Confederates fired on Stevenson, Boyd's men attempted to return their fire and make a stand. They formed and charged the 23d Virginia but it was a half-hearted effort, further hampered by the fire from McClanahan's guns. Thwarted, Boyd turned his men around and charged to the rear. An advance party of about eighty broke through the 18th Virginia, opening the way for the rest of the command to follow. But the retreat was turned into a rout by shells from McClanahan. Most of the men broke and ran for the mountain and the protection of its forest. Stevenson rode to the head of the retreating column and tried to rally the men, but only a few stood. A fence held them up, Stevenson dismounted to tighten the girth of his saddle, and then Boyd raced by shouting that the enemy was right behind him.

Stevenson mounted hurriedly, but was still bent over in the saddle, trying to reach his right stirrup, when a score of Rebels called to him to give up. Pulling his pistol, he fired into them and then spurred his mount toward the woods. A hail of bullets flew around him, striking his scabbard, his blanket roll, and knocking off his hat. Still he managed to escape and, as he rode up the hillside, the scene of panic and confusion about him was terrifying. "As we sped along," he wrote, "our men were seen running in all directions on foot, their horses having given out or got fast among the rocks; while some of the horses rushed along wildly, without riders, the saddles under their bellies."

A heavy downpour began to fall now, soaking the fugitives, making the mountainside slippery and treacherous. With all organization obliterated, it was every man for himself. Only nightfall saved many of them from capture.

That night the frightened cavalrymen hid in the thickets or grouped in little bands of four or five to scurry through the shadows back toward Sigel's army. Boyd, whom many blamed for the disaster, was wholly discouraged. He would rather have been killed than have this happen, he lamented. On through the night they picked their way north, losing men here and there by the wayside. "They are wandering in the mountain to-night," Imboden gleefully reported to Breckinridge, "cut off." Some of Imboden's men pursued through the night and caught up with the remnants of the fleeing Federals the next morning just as they were recrossing the Shenandoah near Woodstock. Right in sight of Sigel's relief party, they captured a few more Yankees, and at least one Rebel captain got so close that he, in turn, was taken.

The proportions of the defeat were extremely gratifying to the Confederates. Though figures varied, Federal casualties in killed, wounded, and missing totaled well over 100. Most important of all, however, another significant enemy column had been destroyed. In four days Imboden had met and defeated completely both Higgins and Boyd, putting over 800 cavalrymen out of the campaign at a cost of only a handful of Confederate casualties. Sigel's flanks were uncovered, his total cavalry for the campaign was reduced by nearly one third, and Imboden still held New Market. All in all, for the Federals it had been a bad Friday the thirteenth.[8] Sigel was, in fact, having more than his share of trouble. His wagon trains were still being attacked with agonizing regularity. Even the weather had turned against the Federals. Despite the now unceasing rains, it was so hot that several men were down with heatstroke, and one had actually died in the road. Strother found that there was "no appearance of a favorable change." The whole countryside was muddy, the back roads nearly impassable, the streams rising so rapidly they might soon be unfordable. Then Sigel made the biggest mistake of the campaign.

With reports coming in that he still faced only Imboden at New Market, Sigel decided to take Mount Jackson and New Market if possible. Yet, unable as always to commit himself entirely, he would send only a part of his army to do the job. Despite the fact that he knew Breckinridge had been in Staunton four days before and now could be approaching New Market himself, Sigel was going to split his army in the face of the enemy. At 9 A.M., May 14, Colonel August Moor, commanding the First Infantry Brigade, was called to Stahel's headquarters. Sigel and Sullivan were present as Stahel asked Moor to take three regiments, one battery and 1,000 cavalry "to feel the position and strength of the rebels under Imboden, reported to be on Rude's Hill." Moor agreed, asking for maps and guides since he was a stranger to the Valley. Nothing was forthcoming. Worse, the regiments he would take were not from his own brigade. "It was a great mistake," he lamented, since he knew his own regiments well but knew nothing of these units now given him.

At 11 A.M. Moor marched out of Woodstock with the 1st West Virginia and 34th Massachusetts Infantry Regiments, four guns of Captain Alonzo Snow's Battery B, Maryland Light Artillery, and two guns of Captain Chatham T. Ewing's Battery G, 1st West Virginia Light Artillery. Colonel John E. Wynkoop, commanding Stahel's Second Cavalry Brigade, came along with detachments of 170 men of the 20th Pennsylvania Cavalry and 130 men of the 15th New York Cavalry. Up ahead at Edinburg the 123d Ohio Infantry would join them, along with Major Timothy Quinn and 600 troopers of the 1st New York (Lincoln) Cavalry, the 1st New York (Veteran) Cavalry, and the 21st New York Cavalry.

In all, Moor's command numbered 2,350 or more of all arms, nearly one third of the Union force. Sigel was sending it off to a point fully twenty miles away from the van of the army. Colonel Strother, already disgusted by the Higgins and Boyd affairs, lamented greatly the German's "sending detachments of his force so far from the main body as to be destroyed in detail." Sigel, he felt, seemed "to court destruction."[9]

The day passed slowly in Woodstock after Moor left. As usual, it continued to rain. The men huddled inside their tents to get out of the wet. Then, at 3 P.M., they heard the distant boom of cannon coming from the direction of Mount Jackson. "By the sound," wrote one foot soldier, "hot work must be going on at the front." The firing continued on through the afternoon, and Sigel sent the 18th Connecticut Infantry to Edinburg to be within supporting distance of Moor. Reaching there, the regiment had a brief skirmish with a party of Confederate pickets, capturing a Rebel captain before driving the pickets out. The Federals could not go much farther up the Valley, the captain warned; "hot resistance" was waiting for them. The men of the 18th Connecticut went into bivouac that night, not at all encouraged by the way Sigel had split his army.[10]

Back in Woodstock, the cannon fire could be heard at intervals until 9 P.M. or later. To give the Federals more cause for anxiety, a Negro man from Lacey's Springs, ten miles south of New Market, came into camp and reported Breckinridge's advance, giving a greatly exaggerated account of his forces. Others, Rebel prisoners and deserters, citizens and refugees, passed by all afternoon reporting Breckinridge on the way with a 15,000-man division and nineteen guns. Already Sigel's cronies believed they could divine the Kentuckian's intentions. He wished to stop Sigel and Crook and pave the way for an advance by Lee down the Valley and into the North. If he failed in these resolves, then Breckinridge would cross the Blue Ridge and take Grant in his flank or rear.[11]

Clearly Sigel was worried by the news of Breckinridge. That night he paced back and forth in his headquarters. A friend found him "as restless as a chained Hyena. His eyes seemed to [be] piercing every object upon which he cast them, and especially as the dispatches from the front were received."

Finally the news turned good. Crook was in Lewisburg and wanted to communicate with Sigel. Good; here was support against Breckinridge if needed, though a long way off. Then came better news. Moor was fighting Imboden around New Market and doing well. He had pushed him back three or four miles and had taken the town. Moor's initial success encouraged Sigel. Mount Jackson, commanding the bridge and the pike's crossing of the Shenandoah's North Fork, was an excellent defensive position. Moor could now hand it to him at no expense. Here was too fine an opportunity to pass up. Sigel issued his orders to General Stahel. The next morning, May 15, at 5 A.M., the army would march for Mount Jackson.[12]

Indeed, it did seem that Colonel Moor had done well enough, and not without obstacles. Sigel regarded him as "a very reliable and experienced officer." The column marched hard as it left Woodstock, and Moor never slowed the pace despite the rain. Soon men of the 34th Massachusetts, in the advance, saw a haggard dismounted Union trooper approaching them, then another. Before long a small procession of scattered cavalrymen, some with worn-out mounts, most on foot, met them. Then they came upon Colonel William Boyd, dismounted, disheartened, discouraged. He told the story of the debacle of May 13, the day before and then moved on toward Woodstock. The news hardly comforted Moor's men, many of them already worried at being sent so far in advance of supports. Then, as they reached Edinburg to pick up the troops there, for the first time the bluecoats could see through the haze to the south a break in the Massanutten—the gap at New Market.

Major Quinn was already well ahead of them. He had left early that morning for Mount Jackson with 600 cavalry. He reached Mount Jackson virtually unopposed and rode down to the Shenandoah bridge to find that Imboden had torn away the flooring planks. At the same time, Imboden's men were in plain view on the crest of Rude's Hill on the other side of the river. Concealing the bulk of his command, Quinn repaired the bridge and then sent across a squad of fifty men. As this first party was driving in the Confederate pickets, Quinn sent sixty more across with orders to take Rude's Hill if possible and hold it for the rest of the command to arrive.

His advance parties found success on the hill, Imboden having only 100 men there to hold it. Soon Quinn brought up the main body and began to press forward. He had gone half a mile when the enemy was seen forming to charge his advance. The attack was repulsed with comparative ease, and the Federals pursued the Rebels nearly two miles until they reached Imboden's main line in front of New Market. By now it was past 3 P.M. Much work remained to be done, and both sides settled into the grim contest for ground by feet and inches.[13]

Imboden had left New Market that morning at 10 A.M., for word reached him that Breckinridge was on the march and would be at Lacey's Springs by noon. Leaving Colonel George H. Smith in command, he rode south to meet his new commander for the first time. Imboden arrived sometime after noon to find the Kentuckian awaiting him. Breckinridge asked the cavalryman to join him at dinner and, as they ate, Imboden reported Sigel's approach to Mount Jackson. Even while they dined, a courier rode in from Smith with the news that Quinn had reached Rude's Hill, George Imboden's 18th Virginia Cavalry falling back before him. The courier said that Smith and Imboden would form a line west of town, probably on Shirley's Hill, and try to hold the Federals there. Then, perhaps an hour later, the two generals heard the distant boom of McClanahan's guns. The fighting was going in earnest now.

Breckinridge ordered Imboden to return and hold New Market until dark, if possible, and then to fall back three or four miles where the Kentuckian would join him during the night. Taking one of Breckinridge's staff with him, Imboden mounted and raced back. Then, at 9 P.M., he sent back word to Breckinridge. The Federals were in the town.[14]

Originally the Kentuckian had intended to march at dawn, May 15, but now his plans changed. He issued orders to move at 1 A.M., "with the intention of attacking the enemy early in the morning." Not knowing that his correspondence had been captured at Woodstock, he still believed that Sigel was unaware of his approach. With the element of surprise seemingly on his side, he decided to make the most of it.[15]

It had been a tough march to Lacey's Springs. Breckinridge's little army moved out of Staunton at 6 A.M., May 13, Wharton in the lead. The Kentuckian's adjutant found the command "all in high spirits." Its elation was dampened somewhat by the heavy drenching showers that fell that day, and for eleven men of Colonel Derrick's 23d Virginia Infantry Battalion things got even worse. Lightning struck the ground so close to his men that some were badly injured and all were put out of action. That Friday the thirteenth was bad for just about everyone but Imboden.

They had moved out at 5 A.M., May 14, in weather more inclement than that of the day before. As they marched along the pike, passing its still-standing toll gates—without paying—the rain softened the leather of their shoes, making the hard macadam of the road seem harder still. Nevertheless, one observer with them saw that the troops "showed the most cheerful spirit from the start." Few things could have cheered them more than, on reaching Harrisonburg, their first sight of New Market Gap in the distance. They might still arrive in time.

When the column reached Lacey's Springs, Breckinridge took up headquarters in an old house. While he waited for Imboden, he ordered the command to cook two days' rations. Lee had already issued a congratulatory order over Imboden's May 13 victory, and the Kentuckian was resolved to give him reason to issue another. He expected to encounter Sigel on the morrow. "If I meet the enemy," he wired Bragg from Harrisonburg, "I will engage him."[16]

In a manner of speaking, the engagement had already begun. At New Market, Smith's 62d Virginia now held the town

—barely—and a well-established line west of it. The 18th and 23d Virginia Cavalry units occupied the village and the ground to the east. They were tired. "They gave us a very hard afternoon's work," one Rebel trooper lamented. Poor Sturgis Davis, whom Smith thought "a very intelligent and efficient officer," had been skirmishing constantly for nearly three days, yet his men too stood in the line. Smith spaced the men at wide intervals to make them stretch from halfway up Shirley's Hill nearly to Smith's Creek in the hope of deceiving the enemy as to his numbers. Meanwhile, he put McClanahan's guns on Shirley's crest, where they commanded a wide field of fire covering the town and its approaches.

Quinn, after making his dispositions to face the enemy in line, continued to advance, and by 5 P.M. stood perilously close to the outskirts of New Market. Then Wynkoop raced up to inform him that Moor was close behind, directing him to fall back on the main column. The artillery of Ewing's and Snow's batteries had already come and reached the line, to see Imboden's men attempting to screen one of McClanahan's guns placed in advance on the pike. Ewing's two-gun section was sent forward to a slight rise and one of them put a shot alongside the Rebel cannon. That was enough to force the Rebels back a few hundred feet, after which Wynkoop ordered a small charge that gained more ground. The skirmishing would continue for two hours yet.

At about the time Wynkoop arrived, McClanahan opened fire in earnest. The dark-haired, gray eyed artillerist from Victoria, Texas, had a good position on Shirley's Hill, and soon he and the Federal gunners were engaged in a regular artillery duel, back and forth across the valley between them. Ewing and Snow had taken position in Strayer's cedars, almost two miles north of Shirley's, on the crest of a rise sometimes called Bushong's Hill. The cannonade between them lasted for nearly two hours, the sound of it guiding Moor as he marched ever closer to the field.

Before long Moor met more than the sound of McClanahan's guns. As his lead regiment, the 34th Massachusetts, came toward Bushong's Hill, enemy shells began to pass the heads of the men. One landed right alongside the road, throwing a shower of mud on the troops. Colonel George Wells, perhaps as much to cover his own anxiety as to bolster his men, cried out comically: "Don't you see how they are firing at me?" By 6 P.M. Moor had his whole command in line, his skirmishers forward, and he began his push for the town. McClanahan tried to aid in meeting the advance by loading his guns with grape, but found that he could not fire for fear of hitting Smith's and Davis' men. Night fell as the blue and gray lines felt each other, and now Imboden arrived back on the field. Following Breckinridge's orders, he decided that it was time to pull out of the town, leaving only his skirmishers on its outskirts.[17]

For the people of New Market, this had been a day like none before it. The constant reports of Imboden's retreat and the Federal advance kept them excited all day long. Men began leaving town early with their horses and carriages. Women and children wept in the street as they recalled exaggerated rumors of Yankee cruelties. Farmers drove their cattle and their Negroes into the countryside to keep them from bluecoat foragers, while the townspeople hid their personal treasures beneath floorboards, taking pigs and chickens into their houses. The final shock came about sundown when, with the rifle and cannon firing already all around them, Imboden's last wagons and squadrons passed out of the town to the Shirley's Hill line. The citizens awaited with closed doors the coming of the Federals.

Mr. S. P. Rupert and his wife, Jessie, loyal Union people at heart, sat at their window watching the Rebel scouts dart up and down the now deserted street. Then they saw no more of them but, from the north, they spied instead the blue-clad advance of Moor's command. One Federal rode cautiously forward and, seeing the Ruperts, motioned for them to come outside. Mrs. Rupert went. The trooper asked for something to eat. Bringing him some bread and tea, she stood beside his horse while he ate, answering his questions about the Rebel scouts. Then a shot rang out and a bullet struck sparks at the horse's feet. Mrs. Rupert jumped back in fright, the horse shied and bucked, and the scout straightened up in his saddle, alert. Another shot was heard, and the Yankee reeled and fell to the ground, his horse galloping away into the twilight. The war had come to New Market.[18]

Going to the summit of Shirley's Hill, Imboden had a full view of Moor's position, the campfires in the rear giving away his location. The Federals were camped on the forward slope of Bushong's Hill, and the advance line appeared to be on a slender rise projecting south almost to Shirley's Hill, separated from it by a depression called New Market Valley which ran directly west from the town. From here it stretched east almost to Smith's Creek.

Imboden did not apprehend that Moor would press his advance farther that night and decided instead to harass him. Since they were of no use in the dark, he sent McClanahan's guns down the hill to the pike and ordered the 62d Virginia Mounted Infantry—now dismounted—forward, leading it personally. It was 8 P.M. now, and Moor's men had enjoyed barely more than an hour's respite between their march and the appearance of Imboden. After only a few minutes, however, Imboden retired, pursued by Federal pickets. Two hours later he led forward another movement, this time a general attack along Moor's line, yet it too was repulsed after ten minutes of heavy fighting. After two attempts, Imboden decided to withdraw to Shirley's Hill for the night. He had given Moor a chance to counterattack if he really wished. Now, convinced that the Federals meant to stay put for the night, he led his men back to their camps. Desultory firing continued until 11 P.M., when the soldiers of North and South finally bedded for the night.[19]

It was a miserable night for everyone. The Federals had to make camp in the mud and rain with no dinner and no fires. The artillery kept its horses hitched and saddled all through the night, fearful of a surprise attack. The men, cold and hungry, could find little comfort. "It was one of the most uncomfortable nights I ever spent," complained a soldier of the 123d Ohio. If it was bad for them, however, how much worse was it for the townspeople of New Market. Terrified mothers put their children in cellars, while the parents barely slept, kept awake by their fear and the necessity to be ready to leave quickly if necessary. "It was a night of horror," wrote Jessie

Rupert, "through which we slept with our garments on, ready
for flight, if driven in terror from our place between the contending armies."[20]

There were those who would not even have the chance to
sleep this night. Breckinridge's army at Lacey's Springs was
getting ready to march once more. No one in his command was
more excited about it than the Corps of Cadets. Few of them
slept that evening. Anticipation kept them wide awake, anticipation and the red glow on the horizon ahead of them. It
had to come from campfires, but whose? Imboden's or Sigel's?
Those who could sleep crept into the old Mount Tabor Church
to escape the rain. Others talked haltingly with a squad of Federal prisoners from the Boyd fight, most of them Germans who
eyed the Cadets questioningly. A few boys sat at the guard
fire. Once the axes of the veterans had stopped ringing and the
firewood was gathered, a cold silence fell over the Cadet camp,
broken only by the monotonous crunching of Colonel Ship's
horse at its fodder. Huddled at a fire, Jack Stanard confided
to his roommate John Wise that he felt a premonition of his
own death.

At midnight a courier from Breckinridge arrived with orders, and the Corps began to form. The boys in the church
were awakened by the noise outside and shortly by the long
roll of the drums. It was an eerie scene in the firelit, stormy
night. "A veil of clouds was drawn across the arch of heaven,"
mused one Cadet, "while the leaping flames of the camp fires
cast fantastic shadows which chased each other into the gloom
beyond." The wind about them seemed to moan. Wise, on
guard, received the order from the courier and immediately
awakened Ship to hand it to him. Rubbing his eyes, the commandant ordered the Corps to move down the Valley at once.
Echols and Wharton were already on their way down the
pike, and the Cadets were to take their place between Echols
and the artillery.

With the command formed and ready, Ship asked Colonel
William Gilham, whom General Smith had sent along as acting
superintendent of the Cadets, to deliver a prayer. However,
Gilham declined, suggesting that the much-liked professor of
tactics, Captain Frank Preston, would be more suitable. With

bowed head, amid the gloom of the stormy night, he asked protection for the Corps. He spoke "of home, of father, of mother, of country, of victory and defeat, of life, of death, of eternity." It was a moving moment, thought Cadet Wise. "It was a humble, earnest petition, that sunk into the heart of every hearer."

The prayer done, Ship detailed litter bearers for the wounded, if any, directing that none but the bearers should stop for those downed by the enemy. Then, at 1:30 A.M., May 15, the Corps took its place in the marching column. As they left, some of the boys tried to break the pall of seriousness that settled on the command. It had been rumored that day that Breckinridge did not intend to use them in the battle unless absolutely necessary. Now one Cadet quipped that "if they are going to pray over us, maybe they think we are going to get into a fight after all." But soon the darkness dispelled any mirth. "I never saw a darker night," Cadet John C. Howard of Company A later recalled. He could see nothing but the man in front of him. Even the mud on his shoes disappeared in the gloom. All that was clearly visible was the red glow on the horizon, a semicircle of blood-red light that appeared to recede before them while they marched, as though they would never reach it. It seemed to portend what lay ahead.[21]

Indeed, the dark hours this early morning, May 15, 1864, seemed full of omens. It was Sunday. All of Stonewall Jackson's great battles had been fought on Sundays. Like Jackson's "foot cavalry" of old, the Confederates had marched with signal speed to meet a sluggish foe. Breckinridge, like Stonewall, rode a mount called "Sorrel." But, as was also usually the case with Jackson, the Kentuckian was faced by a foe considerably larger than himself in numbers. Then, too, this day was Whitsunday in the North, decreed as a "day of public thanksgiving for national victory." Most disturbing of all, though, was something else. Exactly one year ago today the mighty Stonewall had been laid to rest beneath Lexington's sod.

It was, indeed, a portentous day, a day with ominous overtones for great or terrible things. But which would it be and for whom?

7

"We Can Attack and Whip Them Here"

It was sometime after 3 A.M. in the morning of May 15 that General John Imboden was awakened by a lantern-bearing aide. Almost immediately General Breckinridge appeared. His troops were on the way and would reach Imboden's position at Shirley's Hill, south of New Market, shortly before dawn. It was still raining, with no sign of a letup. A bad day for a battle.[1]

Breckinridge's army had marched all night after leaving Lacey's Springs, their only company the mile posts along the pike. It remained a quiet march, but as morning neared the veterans and the boys started once again the playful banter begun in Staunton. As they approached Imboden's line some four or five miles south of New Market, the Cadets encountered the men of Wharton's brigade eating their breakfasts by the roadside. They were, thought Johnny Wise, "merry, nonchalant, and indifferent" to the approaching fight, and so was their general, "smiling 'Old Gabe.'" Then came the teasing. "Don't you want a sugar rag?" called one seasoned Confederate. "Where are your cradles?" "Better go to your mammy." Some veterans came up to the boys inquiring if they wanted their coffins to be of rosewood, satin lined, while one went among them with scissors offering to cut locks to be sent home to relatives after death.

Ship halted his command about dawn to rest and cook its breakfast. Already they could hear up ahead the irregular firing of cavalry skirmishers. Then they heard an uproar. There were hoofbeats, followed by cheering. "We learned its import," wrote Wise, "as Breckinridge and his staff approached, and we joined in the huzza as that soldierly man, mounted magnificently, dashed past us, uncovered, bowing, and riding like the Cid." Wise further writes that Cadet C. C. Randolph called out: "Boys! three cheers for Gen. Breckenridge" [*sic*]. Reining up, the general gracefully raised his hand and complimented the boys on their spirit, but he cautioned that they were near the enemy and should be as quiet as possible. "We have more serious work to do," he told them.[2]

At the front, Breckinridge looked over the available ground. A series of hills ran along the west side of the pike leading to New Market, each sloping down to the road, on the other side of which lay low, largely flat, pasture land sloping down to Smith's Creek. Clearly the anchor of any defensive line would have to be one of the hills, and the general soon selected one. Called Williamson's Hill, it was the highest of the lot, situated directly on the Rockingham-Shenandoah county line, and nearly two miles south of New Market.

At this point Breckinridge planned to fight a defensive battle, letting the numerically superior Sigel attack him in a fortified position. Now he explained to Imboden his plans, ordering the 62d Virginia to act as dismounted infantry for the day and join his main body. Imboden, meanwhile, would take McClanahan's battery and the 18th Virginia Cavalry and form a line to the east, in the marshy ground near Smith's Creek. That was bad country for infantry movement, thanks to the rains, and should be defensible by a thinly spread cavalry line. Feeling that Sigel's attack would come early, Breckinridge set his plans in motion immediately.

Wharton and Echols moved forward down the pike to the appointed line and then filed by the left flank up the slopes of Williamson's Hill, past the still smoldering fires of Imboden's night bivouac. At once the veterans began tearing down fences from the yard in front of Williamson's house and using the rails to construct breastworks, reinforcing them with packed brush and earth. The works would serve a dual purpose: a good line of defense against attack and a ready redoubt to fall back to in case the Confederates advanced and were repulsed. Meanwhile, Breckinridge ordered Colonel Harman's reserves to stay a mile in the rear to guard the wagon train.

Shortly after dawn on May 15 the line was completed. Wharton was on the left, Echols on the right, with Edgar's 26th Virginia Battalion and the Cadets behind the line in reserve. It was, thought Edgar, "the best ground available" for a defensive line. The woods on either end would allow the Rebels to pour an enfilading fire into the flanks of an attacking enemy, and all of the Confederate commanders seemed well pleased with it. As for the men in the ranks, they saw to their weapons and waited; all of them, that is, except Cadet George Lee. With battle imminent, the day that the Corps had awaited for years, he fell asleep behind the breastworks.[3]

Now that he was in place, Breckinridge put the second part of his plan into action—getting the Federals to attack him. Imboden had been out skirmishing lightly this morning. The Kentuckian now ordered him to move forward and attack the enemy and then feign a retreat. Unfortunately, the cavalryman could not lure Moor into a counterattack despite several repititions of his advance and withdrawal maneuver. The German had guessed Imboden's intention. Unwilling to be drawn any farther away from his already distant supports, he stayed put.[4]

This development changed things for the Confederates, and the Kentuckian decided to feel out Moor's position more fully. He ordered Lieutenant Carter Berkeley to take a section of McClanahan's guns forward, behind Imboden, to the crest of Shirley's Hill and open fire on the Federals. Berkeley raced ahead, put his two guns in place, and sent two shells toward New Market. Almost immediately Breckinridge sent Blain with Jackson's battery to support Berkeley, and soon the guns were firing side by side.

Now Breckinridge rode up in person to witness the effects of the shelling. To probe a little deeper, he sent Berkeley's

Major General John C. Breckinridge, the victor. (U. S. Signal Corps photo No. 11-BA-1215, Brady Collection, in the National Archives)

Major General Franz Sigel, the loser. (MOLLUS-Mass. Collection, U. S. Army Military History Research Collection)

igadier General John D. Imboden wed Sigel's advance. (MOLLUS-Mass. llection, U. S. Army Military History search Collection)

Lieutenant Colonel John S. Mosby (shown as a major) plagued Sigel's supply lines. (MOLLUS-Mass. Collection, U. S. Army Military History Research Collection)

tain John H. McNeill led his raiders spectacular raid on the Baltimore & o Railroad. (MOLLUS-Mass. Collec-, U. S. Army Military History Rech Collection)

Captain Harry W. Gilmor, troublesome but effective partisan. (Courtesy of William A. Albaugh Collection)

The Virginia Military Institute as it appeared in 1858. (Courtesy of New Market Battlefield Park)

Major General Francis H. Smith, superintendent of V.M.I. (Courtesy of New Market Battlefield Park)

Colonel Scott Ship, c. 1867. (Courtesy of New Market Battlefield Park)

guns down the hill again to a position just east of the pike. Before he could unlimber and resume firing, Berkeley saw Snow's Maryland guns move out of town to return the Confederates' fire. The artillery duel now begun would continue for two hours or more, but still Breckinridge could not lure Moor from the safety of New Market.[5]

He summoned Imboden to him and together they stood on the summit of Shirley's Hill while the cavalryman explained the lay of the ground spread out like a map before them. Shirley's Hill was by far the most commanding eminence south of New Market. From it all of the town was visible as was the ground eastward to the creek. Immediately north of the hill sat another, slightly lower rise—Manor's Hill—which ran parallel to the pike for nearly a mile, sloping gradually downward as it approached its terminus at Bushong's Hill. This long rise was actually two hills, joined like Siamese twins by a slight elevation in a narrow cut between them known as Indian Hollow, which ran north out of and perpendicular to New Market Valley. The hollow ended in the bluffs above the Shenandoah to the west of town as it made a wide sweep inward toward the pike at Bushong's.

The slopes of the hills facing New Market were mostly clear and under cultivation, offering good room for maneuver. Bluegrass and wheat fields, broken here and there by stone and rail fences, dotted the landscape. East of the pike, the lowland sloped down to the wooded banks of Smith's Creek. It was broken ground, wet and marshy, offering little opportunity for movement of troops. Overlooking the whole scene, seemingly bigger than life, sat the brooding Massanutten to the east. New Market Gap lay to the east directly opposite the town, and the mud pike running through it to the village cut directly across the panorama before Breckinridge.

Breckinridge studied the ground intently as Imboden spoke, and a new plan quickly formed in his mind. The field seemed almost perfect for a battle between small armies. The river on the west and the creek on the east would protect both his flanks. Furthermore, the marshy ground between the town and Smith's Creek would give added protection to his right; he

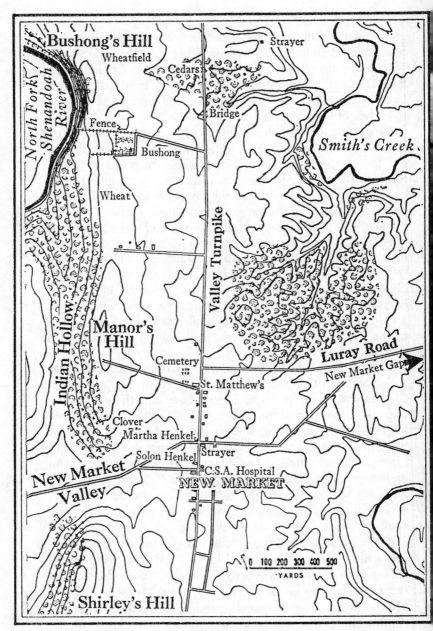

The battlefield at New Market. Contour lines denote 25-foot increments of elevation.

should be able to hold it with a bare skeleton of a line. This would free the bulk of his two brigades to attack west of the pike. Studying the ground along the pike to the north, he thought he saw a succession of good positions for his artillery. They would offer the added advantage of allowing him to co-ordinate the advance of his cannon with his main line of infantry.

In five minutes he had made up his mind, aided perhaps by good news from several fronts. As he was standing here on Shirley's Hill, a message came from McCausland telling him that General John Hunt Morgan had defeated Averell's raiders at Wytheville back in southwest Virginia, and that Crook was no longer a threat to the department. With this heartening information, the Kentuckian also began to get intelligence from Imboden's signalmen stationed up on the Massanutten. They dispatched to him Moor's positions and approximate numbers and almost surely advised him that he faced only a portion of Sigel's army. Finally, he still felt that the Federals were not aware that he had joined Imboden. All this made his decision easy.

One of Imboden's troopers standing with them on the hill watched Breckinridge carefully as he scanned the countryside. "I think he was the handsomest man I ever saw," he wrote later. Then the general took out his watch. It was 10 A.M. There was no more time to wait. "Well," said Breckinridge to Edgar standing nearby, "I have offered him battle and he declines to advance on us, I shall advance on him." Then, his enthusiasm mounting, the Kentuckian turned to Imboden. "We can attack and whip them here," he exclaimed, "and I'll do it."[6]

Moor had no desire to be "whipped," and he had showed good judgment in the matter this morning. As early as 3 A.M. he had much of his line in formation and sent out his scouts and patrols. They brought back word that Imboden had withdrawn from the vicinity of New Market around midnight. Thus, it was a somewhat relieved Moor that had "boots and saddles" and the other morning bugle calls sounded before dawn. Even with Imboden withdrawn there was much to do. Moor ordered the 34th Massachusetts to leave its position by

the town and pull back nearly a mile to the vicinity of Bushong's Hill, apparently thinking to establish a defensive line to
fall back on if necessary. The mud in the fields was so sticky
now that it sucked the shoes from the feet of some of the Bay
Staters as they marched.

At 7 A.M. a reconnaissance party came back into Moor's lines
from the south, reporting that Imboden was posted four miles
up the pike and getting ready to advance. Citizens in the area
said that Breckinridge had joined him. Here was the first news
the Federals had received of the link-up between the two
Confederate forces. Now Moor's situation had become serious
again, and he called the poor 34th Massachusetts forward
once more through the mud to his main line in New Market.
Immediately he sent out skirmishing parties in force and ordered most of what cavalry he had to the east of town to protect his flank.

Sometime before 8 A.M. Moor saw the Rebel line appear off
in the distance on Williamson's Hill. Then Imboden made his
feints. Moor was wise enough not to be fooled into leaving his
defenses and pursuing the enemy cavalry, but he did move out
Snow's guns to a field just south and west of the crossroads.
Before Snow could unlimber, however, two Confederate guns
could be seen advancing toward Shirley's Hill, and soon one
Yankee found that they were "throwing shot and shell exceedingly well upon us."

Moor sent more skirmishers forward, some of them even
moving up Shirley's Hill before the arrival of Blain's guns and
Breckinridge drove them back. Meanwhile, the German sent
word to Sigel to come up; he was needed. In fact, early that
morning Sigel had sent Major Theodore F. Lang to New
Market with a squad of couriers to keep him advised of events.
Reaching Moor, Lang almost immediately dispatched a courier
back to Sigel, conveying the rumored arrival of Breckinridge.
Now, as the Rebel column could be seen advancing in force
from Williamson's to Shirley's Hill, another more urgent message went out. "The enemy advances," it said.

Moor was in a good position, but he could not hold it long
if not reinforced. Then, soon after the rider went, Stahel ap-

peared on the field at the head of the remainder of the Federal cavalry. Immediately he assumed command. Seeing Breckinridge moving up the back slope of Shirley's Hill, Stahel decided that it was time to withdraw the line, to give Sigel time to arrive and to shorten the distance between them. To do this, he would have to abandon New Market.[7]

In the village the few Union people, particularly the Ruperts, had taken some soldiers into their homes for breakfast. Then an officer of the 34th Massachusetts came to the Ruperts' door. The Rebels had been reinforced and even now were forming on Shirley's Hill. "There will be hot work here soon," he warned them. After the officer left, Jessie Rupert asked her husband what should be done and, just then, they heard the opening guns of Berkeley's cannonade from the hill. Almost immediately New Market's streets lay deserted as the artillery duel developed, "and cannon balls and shells rolled and exploded in every direction," Mrs. Rupert later recalled. Some shells exploded in the trees on their lot, their windows shattered, and the house seemed to rock under the concussions. They tore up the flooring to hide their baby son under it, hoping that the house's stone foundation would protect him. And then they awaited the battle. "The air was filled with dust and smoke, and curses and shrieks," Jessie would write, and after that came the staccato thumping of small shot and balls on the fences and houses of the town, a queer symphony of percussion which would last for hours.[8]

Breckinridge had wasted no time in getting his command from Williamson's Hill to Shirley's Hill. About 10 A.M. he deployed the line into column, General Wharton in the advance, and pushed them down the pike the mile and one quarter to the new position. On the march the Confederates first began to feel the enemy shells fall about them, but there was little loss. Meanwhile, the Kentuckian sent up the remainder of Major McLaughlin's artillery command to support Blain and Berkeley, and by the time the vanguard of his infantry began to leave the pike by the left flank in column and trudge up the back slope of Shirley's Hill, twelve Confederate cannon were delivering a rapid fire into the enemy line.

Riding up to Wharton on the pike, Breckinridge ordered him to place his brigade at the left of the new line, running it from the wooded and steep western slope of Shirley's Hill, across the crest and down toward the pike. The Cadets were also assigned to Wharton, as was the 62d Virginia and, attached to the 62d, the dismounted seventy-man Company A, 1st Missouri Cavalry, of Captain Charles H. Woodson. Breckinridge told Wharton he would have to take command of all the line west of the pike.[9]

Finally Breckinridge sent for Colonel Ship, who reached him just as Wharton was setting his line. The Cadets would stay in reserve with Colonel Edgar's 26th Virginia Battalion, the general told him. He did not wish to expose the boys, but he assured Ship that "should occasion require it, he would use them very freely." Ship asked that the Corps not be denied this opportunity. Without committing himself, Breckinridge expressed to him his confidence in the boys, and then ordered Ship to take his place on Edgar's right some 300 yards behind Wharton. When the Corps moved into its assigned spot, some of the veterans of the 26th began giving loud voice to their disgust at being thus "brigaded" with the schoolboys. They called the Cadets "new issue," claiming that they would not fight but would give way at the first fire. The boys bore the insults well. They knew better. Already Johnny Wise and Jack Stanard, with two other boys, had left their posts with the Cadet wagons just for the chance of getting into the battle, the only case of disobedience the Corps would suffer today. Meanwhile the Cadet artillery section under Captain Collier Minge, unable to follow the Corps up Shirley's Hill, was ordered to join McLaughlin's command, and the sight of the V.M.I. guns thundering down the road inspired the boys with renewed confidence.[10]

Within an hour of the time he ordered the line off of Williamson's Hill, Breckinridge's deployment on Shirley's was nearly complete. To his left, on the crest of the hill, was the 51st Virginia. To its right stood Lieutenant Colonel J. Lyle Clark's 30th Virginia Battalion, and then George Smith's 62d Virginia Mounted, with Woodson forming its left company. Smith's regiment stretched almost to the pike, and now Breckinridge ordered Colonel Robert White's 23d Virginia Cavalry to dismount and take a place in Smith's line, forming Smith's right three companies and extending the line just across the pike. The 26th and the Cadets were immediately behind the center of this line, and General Echols was on his way up to extend it to Smith's Creek with his 22d Virginia Regiment and the 23d Virginia Battalion. Poor ailing Echols, clad inconspicuously in a black civilian overcoat, moved with the 23d, but was little in evidence. His illness, it seems, was on him again. Many actually believed that he was not present on the field and that Colonel Patton led the brigade.[11]

It was near 11 A.M. now. Wharton was settled in line and Echols was still on his way. Wharton would form the first line, to the left, while Echols would follow 200 yards behind and to Wharton's right, reaching down to and slightly across the pike. McLaughlin would move more or less on the pike, while the reserve, the Cadets and the 26th, would move in extension of Echols' line to the left, slightly apart from it, behind Wharton.

This done, Breckinridge began to order his units about on the hill in plain sight of the enemy, obviously going to considerably more pains than were required to make a simple readjustment of the line. Colonel Edgar knew what he was doing. Breckinridge, he said, "was playing the old strategic trick of countermarching his men with the view of multiplying their numbers in the eyes of the enemy."

The regiments were moved from right to left and back again, halted in position, then countermarched, and finally thrown into columns of brigades to assume the echelon position Breckinridge really wanted. Edgar and the other officers were much impressed by this first real display of the tricks that this general from one of the South's big armies had at his command. "It impressed me most favorably as to his strategy," wrote the colonel.

The infantry was set. Chapman's guns, four twelve-pounders and two three-inch rifles, stood in place on the crest of Shirley's. Next to them sat Blain's four pieces, and, assigned to Blain, the two Cadet guns.[12]

Breckinridge had special plans for Imboden. Leaving Berkeley and two guns, Imboden would take McClanahan's other four guns and hold the right, east of the pike. But more than this, Breckinridge wanted him to cross the Smith's Creek bridge east of New Market, ride along the east side of the creek toward Mount Jackson, recross the stream well behind the Federals, near the spot where it flowed into the Shenandoah, and destroy the pike bridge over the river. Then, should Breckinridge defeat the enemy here at New Market, the Yankees would be trapped between him and the two rain-swelled streams, with no choice but surrender or destruction. With great hopes for this movement, he sent orders exactly duplicating Imboden's off through the gap to Major Gilmor. He was going to fight the enemy, Breckinridge told the partisan, and "he would whip him." If Gilmor or Imboden could destroy that bridge, he would "capture his whole army, trains and all." It was a bold plan, and if it worked the repercussions of such a smashing defeat could go well beyond the Valley to shake Grant and the entire North.[13]

With Imboden, accompanied by McClanahan's guns, riding off to take his position, it was nearly time to advance. To give the enemy as few conspicuous targets as possible, Breckinridge ordered all mounted field officers to go into the battle on foot. Only he and his staff would stay on their horses. Echols, still tardy, did not yet have all of his troops in position and Wharton, while waiting for him, crept alone down the forward slope of Shirley's Hill to study Moor's positions. Wharton was an excellent officer. Supposedly descended from the Vikings of old, he was the great-grandson of British Major General Sir George Wharton, and he maintained the family military tradition by graduating from V.M.I. in 1847, standing second in his class. Wharton engaged in mining in Arizona territory before the war and then, in 1861, traveled across Texas in company with General Albert Sidney Johnston, on whose staff he served briefly before the Battle of Shiloh. Before joining Johnston, he had organized the 51st Virginia Infantry, being elected its colonel. A handsome, full-bearded man just thirty-nine this May, he had been promoted to brigadier the previous July. It was rumored that President Jefferson Davis did not like him for some reason, which explains perhaps why he never got away from the inglorious western Virginia service.

Crouching under cover of some cedars, Wharton looked out to see that the Federals had now placed a battery—Snow's—in the cemetery behind St. Matthew's Church on the northern edge of town, while another artillery position was set up in a clump of cedars on the right of Moor's line near Indian Hollow. The orchards around New Market appeared to be swarming with Federal skirmishers, while Moor's main line was set behind a low stone fence fronting a road leading west from St. Matthew's up the hill, sometimes called Manor's Hill. It was a fair position, but he believed that his own brigade alone would be enough to force the Yankees out. His only fear was the enemy artillery, which would have free play over his men as they marched down Shirley's Hill. Once they reached the bottom, though, they would be protected by a high rail fence and the fact that the Federal artillery sat back too far on Manor's Hill to fire into New Market Valley. Consequently, returning to his brigade and taking his place with the center of the 51st, Wharton gave instructions for the men not to worry about maintaining formation when they went down the hill, but to rush forward to the fence, where they could reform unmolested. At the same time, he sent back orders to Edgar and Ship to "conform their movements to mine" in the advance down the hill. Then came the word from Breckinridge. It was time to start.

Shortly after 11 A.M. the skirmishers moved first. Company B of the 26th was sent to Wharton's extreme left to move down through the cedars and protect that flank, while most or all of Colonel Clark's 30th Virginia Battalion led in part by Major Peter J. Otey went forward 150 or 200 yards. Breckinridge, whom Otey found the "grandest of men," ordered him in person to drive in the Federal pickets. The 30th moved off, passing down the slope without difficulty, and driving Moor's few skirmishers out of New Market Valley and back to their main line. Then Otey halted his men to reform at the rail fence and await Wharton, only to have McLaughlin's guns start shelling him by mistake. Quickly word of the blunder went back up the hill, and the shelling stopped. Then Wharton's line came out on the crest of Shirley's Hill and started down.[14]

The men in Moor's line, looking out through the now lightly falling rain, could see the Confederate skirmishers creeping and dodging from place to place as they came down Shirley's Hill. Most of them knew what was coming. A skirmish line meant a battle line behind it. Soon they saw what many at first took to be a fence on Shirley's crest, but then it moved and its pickets became bayonets. "A cold chill runs down our backs," wrote one of Ewing's gunners. As the Federals watched, Wharton's line seemed to come down the hill "like a swarm of bees."

Thinking that they were facing only Imboden's cavalry, the Federals were not prepared to see a solid line of infantry coming at them. Some became fatalistic in an instant. With Sigel spread over twenty miles of pike, mused one, "it was easy to comprehend what the outcome was going to be." In the town, where a few errant Yankees were ransacking Dr. Solon Henkel's house, the doctor only saved his case of surgical instruments by cautioning them that before the day was out "it may be that I shall need them for some of you." Seeing Wharton surging down Shirley's Hill, they could believe him.

When Wharton appeared and began his advance, Major Lang at once sent a courier off to Sigel. Soon, when Echols turned up behind Wharton, Lang sent another. Sigel was needed now. Lang would send couriers back every ten minutes from now on. "Finally," he later wrote, "our regiments . . . leisurely began to come into line."

Indeed, the first to appear, coming up after a hard march from Edinburg, was the 18th Connecticut, which actually took its place on the field during McLaughlin's shelling. At first the 18th formed a few hundred yards back from Moor's Manor's Hill line, on the right of Captain Alfred von Kleiser's 30th New York Battery, which had also just come. But then Moor ordered it forward to join the 123d Ohio and Lieutenant Colonel Jacob Weddle's 1st West Virginia in an advance line on the immediate brow of Manor's Hill. They took their position, the 18th on the right, the Ohioans in the center, and the West Virginians on the left supporting Snow's guns, while Wynkoop's cavalry screened the extreme right beyond the 18th. Then Clark and Otey could be seen coming down Shirley's Hill. Major Henry Peale, commanding the 18th Connecticut (and one of only three line officers with the regiment) ordered Captain William Spalding to take Companies A and B forward to skirmish in New Market Valley.

Spalding moved and soon engaged Otey. The fight was small but hot, and one Connecticut man wrote that "we found them too thick and had to fall back." As they began retiring, Spalding was hit in the abdomen after his men repeatedly asked him to take cover. "I am shot," he cried out. His men carried him back to the main line and an ambulance was brought up to take him to the rear. An hour later he asked a surgeon, "Are they driving us?" and then died.[15]

Breckinridge was doing his best to "drive" them. Wharton's men raced down Shirley's Hill "rather pell-mell," thought Otey, but the rush was worth it. Wharton believed he made the move without the loss of a single man. The enemy guns opened on him soon after he appeared, but they were unable to get the proper range before the brigade disappeared into the valley. Then it was time for Echols to move, but there was a delay. With things running smoothly thus far, Breckinridge was perturbed. "Why doesn't Echols move forward?" he asked one of his staff. "He is the slowest fellow." Finally, however, he too moved across the slope of Shirley's and into the valley.[16]

This left the reserve. Behind the crest of the hill, the Cadets had peeled off their coats for action, not knowing or suspecting that once they left, scavengers would steal their haversacks and overcoats. The "rats," first year boys, were sent to fill canteens for the Corps, and then they were ready. Breckinridge rode up to them again. "Young gentlemen," he told them, "I hope there will be no occasion to use you, but if there is, I trust you will do your duty."

Captain Henry A. Wise, tactical officer, of Company A, was

greatly impressed by the general as he spoke to them. "As he appeared on this occasion," Wise wrote, "he was one of the handsomest men I ever saw,—he looked every inch an intrepid soldier, bent on victory and confident of success."

Colonel Ship ordered the advance. "Listen to your officers and obey their orders," he cautioned the Corps. "Battalion forward!" he called, and they were off. From the left of the line Sergeant Major Jonathan Woodbridge ran out to take a place in advance as directing guide "as if we had been upon the drill-ground." Promptly Ship ordered him back. Cadet Sergeant Oliver Evans, color bearer, shook the water out of the Institute's soaked colors and held them aloft. Cadet Lucien B. Ricketts, temporarily attached to Ship's staff, somehow managed to get away with ignoring Breckinridge's order to dismount and rode over the crest and into the gathering battle. The fifer and drummers struck up a tune for the march. To Colonel George Smith of the 62d Virginia, now already in the valley, it sounded somewhat like an old favorite, "Will You Come to the Bower."

The wind was behind them as the Cadets and the 26th Virginia crossed the crest of Shirley's Hill and started down. They marched in perfect order, in quick time, but it was a long way. The enemy had the range now, and at once shells began falling perilously close to them. Echols' line could be seen finishing its hasty movement to the valley, leaving the reserve to face the fury of the Federal guns.

Those below in the safety of the valley looked back to watch the last line come down. Wharton saw that they marched "in beautiful order as tho' going to dress parade. . . . The Cadets acted splendidly, closing up ranks and moving forward in beautiful, military procession and order."

Smith watched them too. "Nothing could have been handsomer than the perfect order in which they moved," he wrote. "Down the hill they move in perfect alignment," Otey would recall. "Their step is as if to martial music." Even some of the townspeople watched them march, intrigued by their natty uniforms and unique flag. One little girl shouted from her doorstep: "The French have come! the French have come!"

The boys had not long been past the crest before a shell passed over the valley to explode near color-bearer Evans, but leaving him unhurt. "The ball opens," muttered one of Otey's men looking back. Wharton began to regret that he had not spoken in person with Ship about the advance. When he sent orders for the reserve line to conform its movements to his, he had intended for them to run hastily down the slope like his first line. But they did not, and now it cost them. No sooner had they passed the first casualties that Wharton left on the slope than Cadet John Howard, looking down the line and wondering if he was any more likely to get hit by artillery fire than any of the other boys, saw a shell explode in the midst of Companies C and D. Captain Govan Hill, tactical officer of C Company, went down with a fractured skull. Cadet Private Charles Read, eighteen years old, was struck over the right eye while a piece of the same shell bent the barrel of his rifle and knocked it to the ground. Cadet Pierre Woodleif of Company B fell with a painful wound. Cadet James Love Merritt of C was hit in the abdomen by a piece of the shell which did not penetrate but "which knocked me about ten feet I thought." He feared it was mortal at first, but then discovered he could walk off the field by himself.

Johnny Wise, just seventeen, was hit. The shell exploded, he said, with "a sound more stunning than thunder. It burst directly in my face: lightnings leaped, fire flashed, the earth rocked, the sky whirled round. I stumbled, my gun pitched forward, and I fell upon my knees. Cadet Sergeant Cabell looked back at me pityingly and called out, 'Close up, men!' as he passed. I knew no more."

In fact, none but Hill was seriously wounded. Veterans of the 26th, seeing some of the boys start to halt to help the wounded, said knowingly, "What did I tell you?" They knew the boys would not stand up under fire. But then Ship called out, "Close up Battalion," and the Cadets obeyed. "Great gaps were made through the ranks," Ship reported, "but the cadet, true to his discipline, would close in to the center to fill the interval, and push steadily forward."[17]

After what seemed an eternity, the boys reached the valley

and the fence. The Confederates rested for half an hour in the little valley, while Breckinridge readjusted his lines. Mc-Laughlin's artillery now came down off Shirley's Hill to go into place on either side of the pike slightly in advance of Breckinridge's line, while Berkeley's two guns pushed a little farther out, well into the southern outskirts of New Market, to try to enfilade Snow's guns in the cemetery.

Ship spoke briefly to his Cadets to calm their excitement and anxiety. They had been blooded now—boys were here detailed to care for the wounded—and there would be more to come. He sought to quiet their anticipation during this rest, but not with complete success. Captain Preston found it "a half hour of intense suspence—the artillery on either side firing—the shot and shell flying and bursting high over our heads—knowing that in a short time we must charge the Infantry, whose dark line we saw drawn up in the woods. What resolutions and vows were made then."[18]

Then Breckinridge passed the order: advance. It would be the last general order that he would give to the command as a whole. Indeed, some units like Smith's 62d, well instructed before the battle, received no more orders at all. To cover his flank and extend the line, Wharton directed that Edgar move the 26th into the front line on his left and advance through Indian Hollow, while Breckinridge ordered McLaughlin's guns to continue down the pike into the town. Then Wharton moved out once again, up the slope of Manor's Hill.

Elon Henkel and his mother had come down into the valley to talk with the Confederates during their rest, and now they saw Wharton's veterans put their rifle butts against the railings of the fence and knock it to the ground on their way up the slope of Manor's Hill. Behind them the Cadets watched, "our nerves were strung and our lips firmly closed, our breath coming short and quick, waiting the crash of musketry which we expected would receive the first line." An officer ran back from the brow of the hill yelling that the Yankee skirmishers were only 100 yards ahead, while a staff officer rode along behind Wharton's line with drawn pistol forcing a few skulkers forward.

Then it was Echols' turn, and finally the Cadets', now on their own with Edgar moving up the hollow. Evans led them up the hill, the Corps banner fluttering sluggishly in the rain until he got the head of the staff caught in the branches of a tree. By the time he got it loose again, the boys were nearly over the top. What met them on the crest was a surprise. The enemy was making barely any resistance at all, with only scattered skirmishing and shelling. Following Wharton, who was 100 yards in their front, they pushed on into ankle-deep mud that slowed them to a laborious walk. Up ahead they could see Smith's 62d Virginia advancing almost unopposed, the only real fighting being on the left where the 51st Virginia faced the 18th Connecticut.

As the Cadets continued, the evidence of the fighting began to move by them. They passed one wounded Confederate lying on the ground, propping himself up on his elbow. As he cheered them, several bullets tore into him at once, killing him instantly. Farther on the boys saw to their left a little group of three injured Confederates who began to encourage them. "Charge them, boys! charge them," cried one. "Give the yankees h——l," shouted another. One tried to raise his hat to wave it. Then a shell exploded in their very midst, and all that remained were parts of bodies that lay quivering in the mire. The boys marched on. If they had thought of it, they might have contemplated with amusement an order issued at the Institute by Ship just eleven days before: on the following Sunday, May 8, it said, and all subsequent Sundays, the Corps would have battalion inspection, and their weapons must be clean enough that a white glove would not be soiled in running over them. The boys were passing another inspection this sabbath, despite their wet and muddy rifles. They had come expecting a battle, reflected Cadet Charles Anderson: "We were not disappointed."[19]

"Nothing could have been finer than their advance," wrote Colonel George Wells of the 34th Massachusetts, who could see Breckinridge emerge from the valley. "The air filled with bullets and bursting shells, and my men began to fall."

Through the now alternating showers and sunshine, the Federals believed they saw three enemy lines coming at them. "I could distinctly see the enemy's movements," reported Stahel, "and finding that his position had the advantage over ours, and seeing too, that he was far superior to us in strength, I considered it wiser to gradually fall back." Indeed, just as he began setting his withdrawal in motion, orders to do just that came from Sigel. Then, only a few minutes later, Sigel himself reached the field to take command.[20]

It had been a difficult morning for the commanding general. It started off badly when he arose at Woodstock before 5 A.M. to find that someone had stolen his brandy flask. Sigel still believed that only a small enemy force opposed Moor at New Market, but he sent Major Lang ahead just in case, to keep him informed. After detaching 250 men of the 12th West Virginia and as many more of the 28th Ohio as a guard for a wagon train going back to Martinsburg—thus further reducing his army in the face of the enemy—Sigel and staff finally set out themselves for New Market.

Soon Lang's couriers began coming back with messages. Breckinridge had definitely joined Imboden, Lang said; Sigel must bring up his entire force. A big battle would be fought soon. Then, after Breckinridge's clever maneuvering on Shirley's Hill, reports came back which showed that the Kentuckian's ruse had worked. The Rebels had 10,000 men, said one report. Another claimed 15,000 were coming, and some men in Moor's line actually believed they faced 20,000 foes. Sigel, doubtful just the same, hurried.

He reached Mount Jackson sometime between 10 and 11 A.M. and ordered Stahel and Moor to fall back to him. As he awaited word from them, he looked for a likely defense line in case he should have to stand and fight here. He knew he had a good position at Mount Jackson, but it would certainly be much better if he could take and hold New Market. Stahel was dragging his feet, Moor wanted to stay in New Market, and his own staff were advising that he push forward. With what he regarded as "good reason and full deliberation," Sigel made his decision: "We may as well fight them today as any day," he said. "We will advance."

Then came a blunder. Four of his infantry regiments were now with Moor, along with almost all of the cavalry and all or parts of three batteries. Two more regiments, the 54th Pennsylvania and what remained of the 12th West Virginia, were moving some distance behind Sigel, another battery with them. But his two other regiments, the 28th and 116th Ohio, along with Captain Henry du Pont's Battery B, 5th U. S. Artillery were far in the rear with General Sullivan and the baggage trains. They were moving forward also, but Sigel, when he first ordered Moor to fall back to Mount Jackson, also ordered Sullivan to move to that place. Now he had changed his plans and was going to New Market, but no orders to that effect went back to General Sullivan and the Ohio units.[21]

Sigel crossed the Shenandoah bridge and rode toward the battlefield. Strother worried at the rain-swollen stream. If the bridge should be burned, the men could never ford the river in a retreat. He had a feeling of being trapped. Despite fears, they reached the outskirts of New Market soon thereafter, amid a brisk cannonade. Leaving his staff at the home of Dr. J. W. Rice a quarter mile north of the St. Matthew's cemetery, Sigel took an orderly with him and, as Lang saw him, "came on the field with a great flourish." Meeting Lang, he continued to make light of Lang's urgent reports, especially as a courier from Moor came to him now with another optimistic dispatch. Immediately the general joined Moor and Stahel on the line.

He arrived just as Breckinridge was moving out of New Market Valley, about noon. "The enemy advanced . . . in excellent order," wrote Strother. "The front line cheered & rushed to the attack at a run." As the Confederates approached, Ewing pulled back his guns, and then the 123d Ohio began to give way without offering any sort of resistance. The 18th Connecticut on the right held out in face of the approaching horde.

Then, before the two lines could close, Sigel gave the order to pull back. Stahel, now commanding his cavalry once again, would cover the movement. The men seemed to move better in response to Sigel's order than they had to Stahel's, and soon the Federals were slowly retreating. They fell back until they came to the 34th Massachusetts and Kleiser's battery. Here they

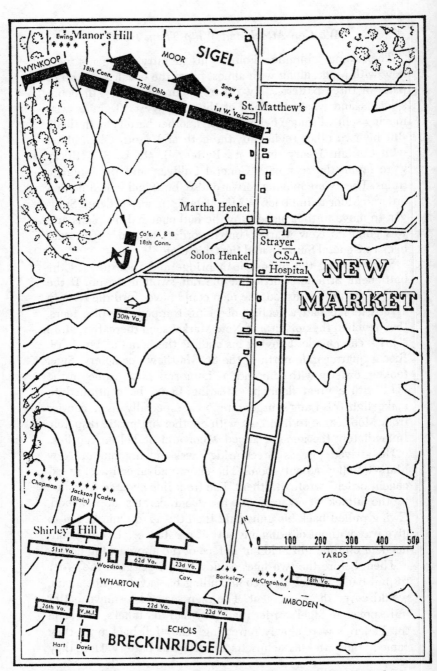

Breckinridge's advance drives Moor back out of New Market,
11:30 A.M.

halted temporarily. Meanwhile, Sigel and staff set about laying out a new line and bringing freshly arrived units into the battle.

Now Sigel began to show some anxiety about Sullivan, and he sent orders for him to hurry one battery and a regiment as fast as possible. Just then, Captain R. G. Pendergast of his escort arrived to say that the head of Sullivan's column was in sight and would be there soon. Feeling secure in the knowledge of reinforcement, Sigel proceeded with the business of readying a new line for battle. He did so despite silent opposition from his own officers. Stahel very much regretted Sigel's decision to stand here when half of his army was somewhere back on the pike. Colonel Lincoln of the 34th Massachusetts was equally disturbed, and Major Lang would later complain of Sigel's "dilatory tactics" and his "absolute mismanagement" in bringing the army up piece by piece. When Sigel first arrived, Lang asked him where the rest of the army was. They were coming, said Sigel. Lang's reply gave full vent to his fears. "Yes, General," he said, "but too late."[22]

8

"I Thought That
All Was Lost"

The smoke from the cannon, held close to the ground by the
pelting rain, enveloped Breckinridge's veterans as they pushed
their advance through New Market's outskirts and down to the
crossroads. Echols' men were slowed somewhat by having to
pass through and around houses and barns while Wharton
had open ground to cross, but Wharton encountered by far the
greater resistance. In any case, the fighting was minor and by
12:30 P.M., "amidst the screaming of shells," the Confederates
had retaken the town.

As they marched through its streets, they saw doors open
as the townspeople came out once more, where "their deliver-
ers were greeted with welcome." Once again a Confederate
army was in New Market. Stonewall Jackson had passed
through here no less than four times, three of them during his
great campaign of 1862, when he stood at the crossroads and
watched his foot cavalry march toward the gap, and history.
Now a new deliverer had come. "O, what a fine-looking soldier
he was!" wrote a girl who watched Breckinridge come into
town. "He rode a fine horse and looked every inch a grand
Confederate general."[1]

The grand general had much to do. First he set up his headquarters in an improvised hospital in the town, while ladies
began baking bread and tearing up their sheets and bedding

for the wounded. The northern end of New Market was still a dangerous place, well within range of Federal gunners and riflemen, but now Breckinridge rode down Main Street to reconnoiter. Bullets struck the road all about him and his staff, "but he came on," wrote a townswoman, "it seemed to me, into the very midst of death."

He stopped at the Martha Henkel home. Introducing himself at the door, he asked to go up on the roof. Two couriers went with him to the housetop, while Breckinridge himself climbed onto the chimney to survey the Federal line. Almost immediately bullets flew so thick around him that he was forced back down. The general mounted his horse again and this time rode on down to St. Matthew's, which sat on a slight rise with a good view of the ground to the north. He was openly exposed here on the edge of town, and shells from Snow's guns soon began hitting the church and falling in the cemetery. Sitting his horse in the middle of the pike, Breckinridge was about to raise his field glasses when one projectile struck a gatepost barely five feet away, sending a shower of splinters over him and his staff. The shell's failure to explode was all that saved their lives. If it had burst, Sigel might have won the battle in one shot.

Looking out to the north where Sigel was reforming his troops, the Confederate general saw "dark lines of infantry with heavy bodies of cavalry on the flank." It was, thought his adjutant, Colonel J. Stoddard Johnston, "an exceedingly strong defensive position." From his position, the ground sloped gently upward to the Federal line. He could see an enemy battery taking its place near the pike, with two or three regiments of infantry forming on its right. Another line appeared several hundred yards to the rear near the crest of Bushong's Hill. Because of the distance and the lay of the ground, it was difficult to make an accurate estimate of Sigel's strength, but he appeared to have about 7,000 of all arms.[2]

To continue his advance, Breckinridge's line needed some readjustments, and to make the necessary time for them, as well as to feel out Sigel's strength and artillery positions, he opened up another cannonade. The gun duel that followed lasted an hour or more but caused few casualties on either side.

Meanwhile, the general set his line. Wharton remained in advance on the left flank, but now Breckinridge moved Echols slightly so that Colonel Patton's 22d Virginia straddled the pike. He sent Captain William T. Hart's little engineer company, thirty-seven men, to Wharton's left and spread Derrick's 23d Virginia Battalion out as a thin skirmish line east of the pike, having to march him clear around New Market on the right to get him in place. Derrick would still move in line with the 22d some 300 to 400 yards behind Wharton in echelon right. Smith's 62d Virginia, now on Wharton's extreme right, would hold his regiment steadily on the left side of the pike during the advance, thus providing a natural guide for the rest of the line as well as for Echols behind him. This might cause Wharton problems for, because of the wide eastward sweep of the Shenandoah on his left, his line could be pinched between the river and the road.

Breckinridge's artillery at first seemed to pose a problem. Because of the gradual slope before him, he could not safely bring his guns up behind his advancing lines to fire over them. But then he saw what appeared to be a series of slight elevations east of the pike and running parallel to it. He could move a battery or two along here, simultaneously with his infantry advance, and fire obliquely to the left into Sigel's line without fear of hitting his own men. This would also have the added advantage of drawing to his guns the enemy's artillery fire, taking their pressure off his advancing infantry. Breckinridge began to sense that his artillery might be the decisive factor on the field. Always a general who fully appreciated the potential of the big guns, he now ordered McLaughlin forward with Chapman, the Cadet section, and Berkeley's section, ten pieces in all. For the rest of the day Breckinridge would spend most of his time with them, personally overseeing their placement and fire. Meanwhile, Blain's four guns would move west of the pike, firing when possible over the heads of his troops.[3]

While Imboden was readying his move to cross Smith's Creek, something new presented itself. Just north of the road to the gap, between the pike and Smith's Creek, lay a dense but reasonably small wood not more than a quarter mile thick. When Breckinridge took the town, Imboden and an aide walked through the trees to the northern edge of the wood to see what force Derrick and Patton would have to face on the east side of the pike. "I was rewarded," said Imboden, "by the discovery of Sigel's entire cavalry force massed in very close order in the fields just beyond the woods." There was a battery with them too, and immediately Imboden sent a message back to Breckinridge. He believed that he could enfilade this cavalry line from a position across the creek, since the stream made an abrupt turn to the west almost behind the enemy troopers. Such a move could throw utter panic into the Yankees.

Breckinridge, without abandoning his original intention to have Imboden destroy the Shenandoah bridge, consented to this move as an alternate objective. "Tell General Imboden," he said to the messenger, "as he knows this ground, and I don't, to make any movement he thinks advantageous, and I will take all the responsibility and consequences." Taking four of McClanahan's guns, Imboden led the 18th Virginia off at a trot down the road to the Smith's Creek bridge.[4]

Sometime before 2 P.M. Breckinridge's line moved forward once more. "The enemy chose their ground, but we joined battle with them," wrote "War Path." The rain became heavy, falling in torrents, but the Confederates pushed forward, their banners bravely trying to flutter in the downpour. As the firing commenced, a flock of sparrows hovered over Wharton's men, frantic with fright, and then flew away.

Sigel opened first with his artillery, the shells passing harmlessly over the Rebels' heads. McLaughlin, now in position on the first rise east of the pike, opened a fire on the enemy flank which, thought Johnston, "seemed to strike them with consternation." The fire from Sigel's line was never heavy, and the Confederates moved relentlessly onward through the mud and knee-high grain.

Breckinridge, after placing McLaughlin's batteries under Chapman and Blain, rode along the moving lines, "steadying them everywhere by his personal presence," thought Imboden as he watched from across Smith's Creek. The Kentuckian was

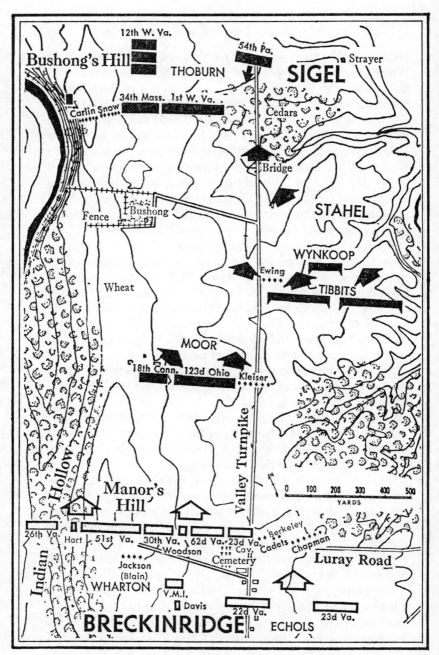

Breckinridge advances on Moor's advance line, 2 P.M., as Stahel withdraws under fire from Imboden (not shown) east of Smith's Creek. Sigel is setting his main line.

The Valley Pike running through New Market, c. 1911. The town has changed little since the battle (Preston Cocke, V.M.I. cadet, 1911, from Turner's *New Market*)

The only known wartime view of New Market, drawn in 1862 by Colonel David H. Strother. New Market Gap in the Massanutten shows clearly in the background. (*Harper's New Monthly Magazine*, XXXIV, March 1867)

The Bushong house and outbuildings around 1880 as viewed from the slope of Bushong's Hill, showing ground over which the V.M.I. Corps of Cadets advanced. (Courtesy of New Market Battlefield Park)

Colonel George S. Patton, whose advancing 22d Virginia regiment helped bolster the stalled 62d Virginia. (Courtesy of Hancock Banning)

Colonel George H. Smith, Patton's cousin barely got past the Bushong house before being pinned down. (Courtesy of New Market Battlefield Park)

Shirley's Hill from the Valley Pike. Brigadier General Gabriel C. Wharton's line formed on the back slope to the left. (Preston Cocke, V.M.I. cadet, 1911, from Turner's *New Market*)

Shirley's Hill view from Colonel August Moor's position in St. Matthew's cemetery, c. 1911. (Preston Cocke, V.M.I. cadet, 1911, from Turner's *New Market*)

New Market Valley seen from the slope of Shirley's Hill. Here Breckinridge re grouped before attacking Moor. Indian Hollow is to the left. (Preston Cocke V.M.I. cadet, 1911, from Turner's *New Market*)

Colonel August Moor, commanding the U. S. First Brigade at New Market on the morning of May 15, 1864. (MOLLUS-Mass. Collection, U. S. Army Military History Research Collection)

The well-worn battle flag of the 1 Connecticut. New Market is inscri third from the left. (Courtesy of Wen W. Lang Collection)

coming to close quarters with the enemy now. His artillery, firing tirelessly, was beginning to tell on the Federals, some shells passing beyond their front line to disrupt troops in their rear. A shell from Berkeley's section disabled a Yankee gun in the battery near the pike. Then the lines closed as the Confederates cheered and charged. As the battle joined, one Federal later recalled, "they came down on our . . . line like an avalanche."[5]

Sigel's skirmishers were driven back almost instantly, and then the musketry began. But nothing, it seemed, could stop the Confederates. A soldier of the 123d Ohio wrote that "they poured in upon us such a storm of shot and shell, so thick that the very air seemed alive with bullets."

Sigel, indeed, had set up two battle lines, thus destroying what little numerical advantage remained to him after his earlier blunders. He first laid out the advance line, assigning it the task of softening Breckinridge's attack before it hit his second, main line. At the same time, he hoped that such an arrangement would slow the Confederates enough to give Sullivan time to arrive. This front line, under Moor once again, was set nearly three quarters of a mile back from the position he occupied in the morning, on a spur of Manor's Hill sometimes called Rice's Hill. Moor placed the troops, in part, behind a stone fence running west from the pike. Next to the road he put Kleiser's six light twelve-pounder smoothbores. On Kleiser's right he stationed the 123d Ohio and, on its right, the 18th Connecticut. Across the pike, north of the wood, sat Stahel's cavalry, with some of his troopers out as skirmishers, and Ewing's battery in support.

Even before the infantry lines met, the Confederate guns were giving Kleiser's battery a good deal of misery. Captain von Kleiser was a young man, just twenty-two, but already he had been two and one half years in the war as an artillerist, in command of the 30th New York Battery since August 1863. His men, like himself, were mostly Germans or other Europeans, as were all of his officers. They found McLaughlin's fire deadly. Horses began falling, men were wounded, and then a shell from one of Berkeley's guns knocked the right wheel completely off a twelve-pounder. Kleiser ordered the gun's crew to hitch up and drag it to the pike nearby, hoping that they might manage to get it back to the rear and the caisson park. Many of the infantrymen to his right believed that he simply abandoned it.

But the infantry had little time to worry about Kleiser's gun. As soon as their skirmishers fell back, it became obvious to all of them that Breckinridge's two lines overlapped theirs on both flanks. The 123d Ohio fired one volley into the oncoming foe and then, seeing themselves outnumbered, fell back without orders. "It was Sigel's way of fighting," claimed one Ohio wag.

They withdrew along a lane to the pike on their left, abandoning the 18th Connecticut. The 18th really did not offer much of a fight either; and before Breckinridge's veterans could reach them, Peale's men pulled back.

As Moor's line fell back in disorder, Kleiser raced back down the pike. The panicked men disrupted portions of the main line as they passed through it. Moor tried to reform it behind Sigel, but with little success. The men of the 123d, knowing they were expected to stop, kept retreating anyhow. "Everybody seemed to be going our way," recalled one Ohioan, and he saw no reason not to keep going with them. Most of the 18th rallied behind Sigel's second line, but even parts of it continued the retreat until they reached Mount Jackson.[6]

Even before Moor's line pulled back shortly after 2 P.M., spent bullets from the Confederates' rifles began falling into Sigel's main line. He had chosen Bushong's Hill, the highest ground available to him. It was a peculiar summit, cresting in the bluffs above the river on the right, and then sloping down evenly eastward so that when it reached the pike, it was almost level. On the other side of the pike the ground was broken by a heavily wooded ravine and a small creek pouring into Smith's Creek. The ground between this line and the Confederates was largely rocky, terribly muddy now, with few trees or buildings to give the Confederates cover in their advance. Furthermore, it was at Bushong's summit that Smith's Creek and the North Fork of the Shenandoah came closest together, their protection of his flanks allowing Sigel to concentrate his troops better than anywhere else on the field.

To anchor the right of his line, Sigel placed the newly arrived Captain John Carlin's six three-inch rifles of Battery D, 1st West Virginia. Carlin, thirty-five, had come forward from Woodstock with Kleiser's battery, but had been slower getting to the field. His gunners only reached their position near the bluff as Moor's advance line was retiring in disorder. On Carlin's immediate left Sigel placed Snow's Battery B, Maryland, six three-inchers, all his guns now being on the field.

Next to Snow, the 34th Massachusetts Infantry, under Wells and Lincoln, went into line, part of it behind a stone fence. One company was sent back and to the right, to a wooded spot where an elbow in the river would allow it to fire across the bluffs to support the right of the line. Meanwhile, another company went forward as skirmishers. Lincoln took his place on the right of the regiment, Wells on the left. Next to them in line was the 1st West Virginia Infantry which, like the 34th Massachusetts, lined up slightly behind the crest of the hill so that they were hidden from full view by the enemy.

Behind these two regiments, in column as a reserve, Sigel put Colonel William Curtis' 12th West Virginia Infantry, a regiment which had never won a battle against the Rebels. By moving the 12th to the right, however, the left of the 1st West Virginia was exposed, and now Sigel brought up the 54th Pennsylvania Infantry to occupy the line between the 1st West Virginia and a point just across the pike. Theirs was the lowest ground held by any of Sigel's regiments, but there was some compensation in a grove of cedars and a fence which gave them some added cover.[7]

Sigel's line east of the pike took its place more through Imboden's unbidden assistance than anything else. After crossing to the east side of Smith's Creek while Breckinridge was still aligning his troops for the advance from New Market, Imboden turned down a road running along the bank of the creek, taking McClanahan's guns up a slight rise which was actually in the rear of Stahel's line, barely 1,000 yards away.

While he sent the bulk of his cavalry on down the creek toward the Mount Jackson bridge and their primary objective, he had McClanahan unlimber his guns and open fire on Stahel as Breckinridge advanced. The first shot set Stahel in some confusion, but soon he collected his units and retired out of range, falling back until even with the line Sigel was setting across the pike. Imboden claimed that his fire totally disrupted Stahel's cavalry. Years later Sigel agreed, calling it a "timely and skillful manoeuvre," but the fact was that it only succeeded in forcing Stahel back where Sigel wanted him anyhow, with little real loss. Imboden then turned his fire on Kleiser's battery at the end of Moor's front line.

It was now 2:15, and Stahel's new line ran from the left of the 54th Pennsylvania almost to the creek, angled backward slightly to take advantage of the high ground overlooking the wooded ravine that an attacking line would have to pass. Lieutenant Colonel Charles Fitz-Simons of the 21st New York Cavalry did not like the position at all. There was, he said, an old rule that cavalry, unless posted where it could charge, "is almost certain to break for the rear." On Stahel's right, near the pike, Sigel placed Ewing's battery, and behind it the rallied portions of Moor's first line.

The only part of Moor's command that reformed in good order for the main line was Kleiser's battery, now five guns. Sigel placed it slightly in advance of his infantry line at the left of the 34th Massachusetts. There was a slight rise here in the slope which led to the main line, and Sigel believed that it offered a commanding field of fire over all approaches to his line. Strother, however, feared that the five guns might be set too far forward for support.[8]

There were a number of officers unhappy with this new line. Campbell of the 54th Pennsylvania believed that Rude's Hill would have been the better position to fall back to. Carlin's battery crews were disturbed over the amount of cover that an advancing line would find in the woods along the bluffs over on the right, while at the other end of the line, in Stahel's cavalry, Fitz-Simons felt that his men were "set up as a conspicuous target for Breckenridge's [sic] well-served artillery."

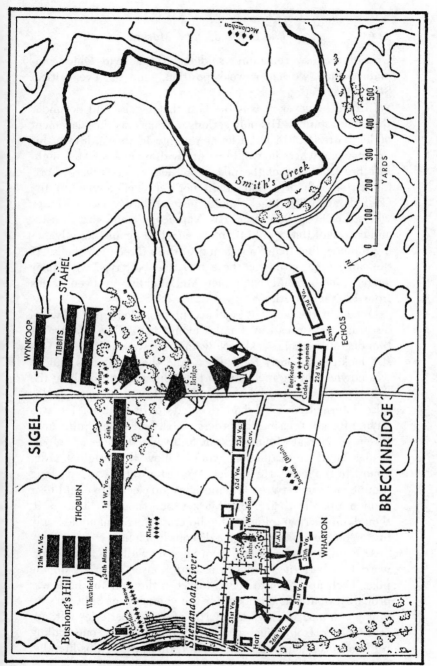

2:45 P.M. Breckinridge fills the gap in his line just as Sigel pre-
pares to charge. Stahel's cavalry charges the Confederate right but
is repulsed with help of Imboden (not shown) and McClanahan.

One of the few remaining soldiers of the 123d Ohio complained that "we had a weak position," and the ever-critical Strother agreed.

In fact, however, it was the best that Sigel could do under the circumstances. His only serious mistake was the placement of his batteries. He put Kleiser roughly in the middle of his infantry line where he would naturally draw most of McLaughlin's fire from east of the pike. Yet Kleiser's guns were short-ranged smoothbores that could not reply effectively to the Confederate rifles. Sigel should, instead, have placed Kleiser where Carlin or Snow sat. His Napoleons could fire canister and case shot that would be more effective against an advancing infantry line than Snow's and Carlin's three-inch shells. At the same time, either of these two rifle batteries, with their longer range, could have met McLaughlin on even terms from Kleiser's position.[9]

Of course, the fact that Sigel accepted battle here at all when his army was spread over miles along the Valley Pike was a blunder on a grand scale. Now that he was in line, he was still looking anxiously for Sullivan and the Ohio units, but he was nowhere in sight. The report that he was approaching the field was obviously erroneous, but largely on the basis of this false information Sigel had decided to risk battle. He was paying for not revising the orders which had called Sullivan to take a position at Mount Jackson. Sullivan, an officer of no particular merit or distinction, would follow this original order almost to the letter. He had left Woodstock at 5 A.M., reaching Mount Jackson between ten and eleven o'clock. He could hear cannon up ahead at New Market but thought little of it, though on his own initiative he did cross the Shenandoah, only to stop on the other side for a half-hour lunch halt.

At noon orders had come from Sigel for Sullivan to send forward two batteries, and Carlin and Kleiser splashed up the pike. Their approach to New Market in the rain and haze was probably what was mistaken for the vanguard of Sullivan's infantry column. Meanwhile, shortly after the batteries left, another order from Sigel came to Sullivan, this one calling for him to come up with his infantry. Interpreting this literally,

Sullivan took only the infantry, leaving du Pont's battery behind, saying he would send for it when he reached the front. But then, about 2 P.M., Sullivan stopped again while still over a mile from Bushong's Hill. He never made his reason for doing so clear, but it is not hard to fathom. By now he was utterly confused.

There are other factors to consider as well. Sullivan was the only non-European in Sigel's high command, and Sigel and his "foreigners" were extremely clannish and suspicious of non-Germans. Sullivan also happened to be the son-in-law of Sigel's enemy General Kelley and, as an outsider in Sigel's court, he may have felt no great love for his commander nor any burning desire to shine on the field for him. In addition, Sullivan was believed by General Crook, among others, to be a coward; "[added] to his many other shortcomings," Crook wrote, "he lacked actual physical courage."

Certainly Sullivan displayed no great anxiety to get into the battle, but blame for this dangerous halt need not all be laid at his feet. Sigel was by now in a state of considerable excitement and, forgetting himself, he was shouting his orders in German, orders which most of his regimental commanders literally could not comprehend. If orders were being sent back to Sullivan in German, or in hasty, garbled translations, it may be a wonder that he got as far as he did.

Sigel, still expecting to see Sullivan any minute, ordered Moor to reform what remained of his first line on the two fresh Ohio regiments supposed to be coming up with Sullivan. Unable to find them, Moor sent couriers back to try to hurry Sullivan. Meanwhile, he continued his efforts to rally the 18th Connecticut and the 123d Ohio. The Rebels were approaching now. "The officers in the line were giving their orders in low tones," reported Colonel Wells of the 34th Massachusetts, "and every man stood, his gun at the ready, his finger on the trigger, waiting to see the face of his foe." Sigel, having overseen some positioning on his right, was riding toward the left. The men of the 54th Pennsylvania were still coming into line. It was about 2:20. Then the enemy appeared and the firing began. "The smoke," wrote one Pennsylvanian, "was so thick I could see nothing in front." The fight was on.[10]

Up to and even during the advance against Moor's front line, the Confederate infantry fired very little. So far the Federal resistance had not required it. About 2:10, however, as Breckinridge looked past Moor's fleeing regiments to the line Sigel was setting on Bushong's, he knew that the time had come for what he called an "ugly effort." Speaking briefly to Otey of the 30th Virginia, he confided that with Sigel well placed in a strong position—and presumably with his army all together in line—he would have to hazard "everything on the one charge." One advantage Breckinridge had was that he would advance in two lines in echelon. It appeared as though Echols' rear line stretched all the way from east of the pike to the rear of Wharton's left thus, in Federal eyes, doubling and even tripling estimates of Breckinridge's numbers. There was no time to think of this now, though. He had to press his attack, and quickly.[11]

Despite the minimal firing thus far, Breckinridge had taken casualties, and those who could, made their way back to New Market, sometimes riding the backs of Federal prisoners. As the doctors and the people worked over the wounded, Breckinridge was doing his best to bring on a fight that would give them more work to do. While his staff stayed mostly with the artillery, the general rode all along his lines cheering on the men, giving what few orders he issued during this part of the battle. Johnston said that "he kept himself in view of his troops and inspired them by his presence." There is no doubt that by staying conspicuous at all times, he greatly added to the confidence of his men. "Breckinridge on his splendid bay that day was indeed superb," said Frank Imboden. Others on the line agreed, and one of the general's aides, Lieutenant James B. Clay, Jr. (grandson of Henry Clay) declared that "Gen Breckinridge is the bravest man I ever saw. He is not afraid to go any where in the world."

The best place for Breckinridge to keep himself in sight of most of his army was near the pike, with the artillery. Mc-Laughlin's batteries had been firing from his position north of town for some time during the advance; but after Moor's retirement and the further forward movement of the Confederate lines, he found he could not keep firing without hitting his own men. Riding back to Chapman's battery, Breckinridge ordered the captain to limber up and "move his guns to the front where they could kill somebody." Chapman thundered off down the pike "at a sweeping gallop," until he came to the next in the series of rises, half a mile from his former position.

Here he went into position on both sides of the pike, being actually somewhat in front of Breckinridge's advancing line, and began sending his shells into the enemy batteries and regiments on Bushong's Hill. Breckinridge stayed with Chapman most of the time now, directing his fire and ordering him to limber up and move forward and then take position and fire again several times as the infantry advanced. Thus he kept the guns always at the front where they could serve him best, "making, as it were," said Johnston, "a skirmish line of artillery."

Meanwhile, Breckinridge moved Blain's battery forward west of the pike, some distance behind the 62d Virginia. "The artillery had a splendid field for operations," Blain's second in command, Lieutenant Micajah Woods, wrote the next day. Breckinridge was quite pleased. With the oblique fire from Chapman's pieces—assisted by Berkeley and the Cadet section—and the frontal fire of Blain's cannon, he was drawing away from his infantry much of the enemy artillery fire. "I succeeded," he reported, "to my entire satisfaction."[12]

The infantry lines were also doing well. Echols' line, yet to encounter resistance east of the pike, moved without difficulty, only halting occasionally to reload as it pushed back Stahel's skirmishers. Wharton also moved well, too, 200 to 300 yards ahead of Echols. The 62d hardly slackened its pace in coming on Moor's advance line and now continued at the same brisk walk. However, the 30th and 51st Virginia to the left, having met more of a fight, ran to catch up and briefly got somewhat in advance of the 62d before coming back into line with it. After passing Moor's position and seeing Sigel's main line some distance ahead, Wharton sent Otey out with the 30th Battalion to skirmish.

Meanwhile, the Cadets continued their advance behind the 62d, and here and there one of them fell, his comrades always closing up the gap and pushing forward. The only real problem with the line was faced by Edgar's 26th Virginia. As the line neared Bushong's Hill, his command came to the abrupt end of Indian Hollow at the bluffs above the Shenandoah. Because of the river's curve, the 26th could not proceed farther, while the march of the 51st on their right began pinching them against the stream.

Now Breckinridge's error in anchoring Smith's right—the dismounted 23d Virginia Cavalry—on the pike became evident. The steady advance forward and the ever greater constriction of the field by the river was forcing the 26th out of the line. Company by company, Edgar dropped back behind the 51st once more until soon the entire battalion marched in its rear. As the ground permitted, he would put a company back in the line, but the unit as a whole never fully regained its place on Wharton's left.

Because of the ground over which they were moving, Edgar's 26th and the left half of Wolfe's 51st could not see the rest of the Confederate line nor did they receive much fire from the enemy. This was due in part to the woods and brush through which some of the men moved, but more important was the slope of the ground. Breckinridge's lines were marching exactly perpendicular to the long saddlelike ridge of high ground that connected Manor's and Bushong's hills. Wharton's brigade, from the middle of the 51st to the pike, were all on the right side of the saddle's crest; Edgar and the rest of Wolfe's men were on the left. There was a rise in the saddle ahead of Wharton where the Bushong barn and outbuildings sat, while the Bushong house was a few hundred feet to its right, out of sight of Wolfe and Edgar. North of the rise, the ground sloped gently down for 200 yards and then began a rapid rise to a high point where the Union batteries of Carlin and Snow sat, about 500 yards directly north of the barn. Just north of the Bushong house stood a small apple orchard and, beyond it, a large shallow depression so muddy and soaked with rain that now the water was standing in it several inches deep in places. Immediately beyond lay the rise in advance of the hill's crest where Kleiser's Union battery was now in position.[13]

The rise at the Bushong buildings served somewhat to protect Wharton's line as it advanced along the saddle. But then Edgar and Wolfe crested the rise and ran into a murderous volume of enemy fire. Sigel had ordered Snow, Carlin, and Kleiser to double-load their guns with grapeshot and canister, and now they turned most of their fire from Chapman's guns to the right half of the 51st and the 30th battalion. The effect was devastating but, in spite of it, Wharton pushed ahead. "My troops advanced with great steadiness in the face of a most galling fire," Breckinridge reported. Soon Ewing's Union battery turned two of its guns east of the pike, to bear on Wharton as well, forcing the men of Sigel's front line to lie down on the soggy ground to avoid the heat and flame of Sigel's cannon.

Still Wharton came on. The general himself was west of the saddle, advancing with Company B of the 51st, and soon moved out in front of the line to shout the charge. It was about 2:40 P.M. The enemy canister was tearing holes in the 51st's four right companies; "but on they came without wavering," wrote one of Carlin's gunners, "and closing up the gaps that four batteries were cutting through them, and yelling like demons."

The four right companies of the 51st slowed down, then stopped several yards in advance of Bushong's north fence. They stood for a few moments, and then a few of the men wavered and started to withdraw. Meanwhile, the companies west of the saddle began to get the fire too, but to a lesser degree. Nevertheless, the halt of the companies on the right forced them also to stop. "Their first line was almost annihilated," wrote one onlooking Federal.

Company by company, the right half of the 51st Virginia began falling back under a fire that Captain David Bruce of Company A thought "seemed to keep the air blue." Telling their men to fire low, Bruce and the other company commanders withdrew to the north Bushong fence to the accompaniment of a taunting cheer in the Federal line in front of them.

Once behind the fence, some of the veterans did not stop. Company A, on the crest of the ridge, remained in its place, but numbers of men to the right began to retreat, mingling with wounded going to the rear in a confused mass. By 2:45, Bruce lamented that "at least half our command was giving way." Those who remained were ordered to lie down behind the fence and commence firing.[14]

This critical situation was not confined to Wolfe's 51st. Otey's men in the 30th found serious trouble as well. The battalion, having come back into position on Wolfe's right after skirmishing, charged past the Bushong house, through a wheat field and the orchard, and across the fence only to be, as Otey put it, "cut up, shattered and scattered" by the enemy canister. Otey himself took a Minié ball which crushed a bone in his right arm, and then the men on his left flank began to fall back as had the right of the 51st. As he lay on the field, the shot and shell flying over him, Otey looked and saw the right of his battalion holding at the fence. But where his left and Wolfe's right once had been, there was now "an ugly gap."[15]

But none of the units in Wharton's line suffered like Smith's 62d Virginia. In moving forward with the advance, it encountered little trouble until it, like the ranks of the 51st and the 30th, ran up against the Federal canister. Passing to the east of the Bushong house, Smith's regiment marched into a slight declivity and then received the full force of Sigel's fire.

That little hollow became a nightmarish hell for the 62d Virginia. In five minutes, five color bearers in succession were felled. Captain Conrad Currence of Company G then picked up the banner, only to be shot dead. The entire color company were either killed or wounded. "The fire," wrote one who lived through it, "was the hottest I was ever under." Of the twelve companies making up Smith's regiment, seven lost their commanding officers. Of the 448 men Smith led into the fight, he lost nearly a hundred in this little ravine. One of his wounded lay stunned on the field after a piece of enemy shell hit him in the side, cut through a plug of tobacco and his diary, gave him a bad flesh wound, and then wound up bouncing into a pants pocket.

It was obvious to Smith, as he puffed on his pipe, that his regiment could not remain isolated in the forefront as it was. He would have to pull back and wait for Echols' line to come up. Standing at the left rear of the 62d, he could see his second-in-command, Lieutenant Colonel David B. Lang, over on the right urging the men to continue the advance. Smith gave the order to retire instead. Lang did not hear him until Smith shouted, "Let the men come back, Col." The regiment withdrew in good order and then reformed on a line with the north Bushong fence. Here they returned the enemy fire as best they could, taking advantage of whatever cover was available. Private B. Orndorf of Company B fired from behind a stump. Turning his back to it, he stooped over to reload when a bullet passed between his legs and burned both his thighs. He fell down kicking his heels in pain and crying out that he had been killed. Private F. D. Kildow grabbed him by the ankles and worked his legs to ease the pain of the flesh wounds. Then Orndorf got back in line and continued firing, while Kildow muttered that he made a "h——l of a fuss for a dead man."[16]

Once his line was settled, Smith reported his movement to Breckinridge, and the general approved. But the 62d still stood in a hot place, receiving a terrible fire from Kleiser's guns. Woodson's company, attached to Smith, was almost right in front of Kleiser, taking the worst of his fire, having advanced slightly ahead on the left of the 62d. He was near the northeast corner of the Bushong orchard and now his Missouri marksmen opened up on Kleiser's gunners.

Woodson's was a unique company, organized in July 1863 as Company A, 1st Missouri Cavalry, when, in fact, it had no official connection with the regular 1st Missouri Cavalry. It was formed in Richmond, Virginia, from Missouri Cavalrymen paroled there by the Federals after their capture at Port Gibson, Mississippi, the previous May. In September the company, mostly dismounted, was assigned to General Imboden in the Shenandoah Valley and enjoyed the distinction of being the only Missouri unit serving with the Confederate army in Virginia. The men liked the Shenandoah service and were voluntarily attached to Smith's regiment. Woodson—"the modest,

gallant Charley Woodson," the journalist Wartmann called him
—was well liked. Nearly six feet tall, the blue-eyed, sandy-
haired young captain was just twenty-one now. His command
went into battle at New Market equipped with a genuine rarity
in the Confederate army—two pairs of socks per man.

By 2:40 P.M. on this day in May 1864 his men were actually
close enough to Kleiser for his officers to fire their pistols at
the gunners. They punished Kleiser's men severely. One can-
noneer fell mortally wounded, four others were put out of
action, and seven battery horses were killed, the highest losses
ever suffered by the 30th New York. One of Woodson's men
later claimed that his company entirely silenced Kleiser's guns.
They did not, but their sharpshooting surely eased the pressure
on the rest of Smith's beleaguered 62d regiment.

It came at a terrible cost. Of the sixty-two men in Woodson's
command, forty were casualties. All of the officers, including
Woodson, were hit. First Lieutenant Edward H. Scott, just
after firing the last round in his pistol, saw Sergeant Will Day
come up to him, blood streaming from his chest. He took Scott's
hand. "Lieut, I am almost gone," he cried. "Please help me off."
Then he died. Then Second Lieutenant J. W. Jones fell dead
at Scott's feet, brains oozing from his forehead. At that instant
Scott was hit in the arm by a shell fragment. He bent over
Sergeant Day, whispering a prayer to him, and had just laid
the dead soldier down when another man came up to him,
blood jetting from a severed jugular, and cried out, "Good-
bye, Lieut. I am killed." That Woodson's losses were largely
Kleiser's work is incontestable. Forty-three per cent of his
wounded, including Woodson himself, were hit by canister or
shell fragments.[17]

While the Confederate line west of the pike was in trouble,
Patton's 22d Virginia and Derrick's 23d Virginia Battalion met
heavy resistance east of the pike. Echols was moving with the
23d Battalion, but he exercised little or no command, leaving
movements almost entirely to his unit commanders. Because of
the difficult ground over which Echols' line advanced, Derrick on the right soon got slightly in front of Patton so that their
line, instead of being parallel with Wharton's, angled some-

what on the left. As they marched, Derrick could catch glimpses of what was happening over on the left. The stall in Wharton's advance worried him. Then, cresting a ridge overlooking the wooded ravine which fronted Union General Stahel's new position, he suddenly saw Federal cavalry drawn up in three lines. Immediately the 23d received such a heavy fire from Stahel that the men were forced to kneel down to hold their position. There were no reserves behind them. Two of Derrick's companies were far off to the right as skirmishers. Seeing a few men on his battalion's left beginning to fall back, he began to fear his ability to maintain his ground. Patton to his left was still moving, but he too felt Stahel's fire and soon became stalled as well.[18]

The situation all along Breckinridge's line looked grim, but nowhere more so than between the 51st and 62d where the gap opened almost in the center of his line. The general was over near the pike with Chapman's battery when his assistant ordnance officer, Major Charles Semple, rode up frantically. Disaster was imminent, he said; surely Sigel would charge when he saw the gap. It must be filled immediately or all was lost. Breckinridge at first said something about contracting his lines toward the center to fill the hole but, pinned down as his men were now, this was out of the question. Then Semple said: "General, why don't you put the cadets in line? They will fight as well as our men."

"No, Charley," Breckinridge replied, "this will not do, they are only children and I cannot expose them to such a fire as our center will receive."

"General, it is too late," Semple cried. "The Federals are right on us. If the cadets are ordered up, we can close the gap in our center."

Would the boys stand, asked Breckinridge.

"Yes," replied the major, "they are of the best Virginia blood, and they will."

Now had come the decision Breckinridge had dreaded since leaving Staunton. He did not want the boys in this fight; he really had not even wanted them in his army, though necessity dictated otherwise. And now that same necessity seemed to demand that he send them into the halocaust that had already disrupted parts of two veteran regiments—the 51st and the 30th—while cutting a third—the 62d—nearly in half. It was a decision that would haunt him periodically for the rest of his life, the most difficult choice he ever faced in this war. But he made it. The members of his staff saw tears in his eyes.

"Put the boys in . . . ," he said, "and may God forgive me for the order."[19]

Semple directed the Corps of Cadets toward the gap which, fortunately, lay almost directly in their front. The Cadets came to the low rise at the Bushong house and were exposed for the first time to the full fury of the enemy. The Institute's banner was riddled with shot and balls, and Sigel's batteries poured forth what Captain Preston called "a terrible fire of artillery." Then a shell exploded in the very midst of Company D. "Suddenly there was a crash in our front," wrote Quartermaster Sergeant Gideon Davenport, "a great gap appeared in our ranks." Three of the boys went down. Two of them—Privates Charles Crockett and Henry Jones—were killed instantly and terribly mangled. The third, First Sergeant William Cabell, was hit full in the chest by the explosion. As the Cadet line hurried on, the boys looked back to see Cabell on the ground clutching and tearing up tufts of grass in his pain, his teeth locked in death agony. Fifty yards farther Private William H. McDowell fell with a bullet in his heart, tearing his jacket and shirt open to expose the wound before he died.

Soon after McDowell's fall, the Corps reached the Bushong house. Here it had to divide, Companies A and B moving around the east side of the house while Companies C and D passed to the west. Private Robert Cousins of Company A, marching alongside the house, heard the heavy, repeated thuds of Federal bullets striking its clapboards, making "a Sounding board upon its sides."

Once past the house, the Cadets moved into the orchard. Now the enemy opened a hot fire on them. "The fire was withering," said Colonel Ship. "It seemed impossible that any living creature could escape." Casualties began to mount rapidly as they crossed the orchard. Jack Stanard fell in the middle of it, his leg broken and badly mangled by a shell fragment. A few feet beyond, Private Thomas G. Jefferson was hit in the stomach. When two comrades ran to help him, he pointed to the front and shouted: "That is the place for you; you can do me no good."

Then Ship, the perspiration standing out in great drops on his forehead, felt himself knocked to the ground when a spent shell fragment caught his left shoulder. He was only stunned, but he lay still for some time and was thought to be mortally wounded. Here the V.M.I. line faltered momentarily, yet the senior tactical officer, Captain Henry A. "Old Chinook" Wise, immediately assumed command and ran the boys forward the last thirty yards to the fence north of the orchard. The gap was closed.

The rails of the fence, which was about four feet high, provided some protection from enemy bullets, but none at all from bursting shells and canister. Now many of the boys discovered that the rain had so soaked their wooden ramrods that they swelled in their clasps and could not be drawn out for reloading. But the Corps was still able to rise on one knee at the command and deliver a volley. An onlooking Federal saw that "a streak of fire and smoke flashed across the field" when the boys pulled their triggers.

Anxiety ran all along the Cadet line. Wharton's first line had been stopped and now stood perilously close to full retreat in its position to their left, while Echols' second line still had not come up. In their present location the Cadets were several yards in advance of Smith's 62d on their right, and a heavy fire on their exposed left flank was causing more casualties. "This was far the most trying time in the whole day," wrote Preston.

Smoke enveloped the Federal line, driven back on it by a light southerly wind, while the rain kept the cloud low, barely two or three inches above the ground in places. The boys could just barely see the legs of Sigel's cannoneers and the wheels of their guns, hardly enough to draw good aim on a target. Meanwhile, the fire from those guns still shook the ground, making the tree boughs in the orchard lean and sway above the boys. Private Nelson Noland of Company C saw bits of paper caught up in the great gusts of air set in motion by the cannon and watched them as they gently floated by spurts across the field.[20]

The decisive moment was at hand. The gap was filled, but Wharton's line was still unsteady, and Sigel's men—what could be seen of them—appeared to be readying themselves to countercharge. Over on the right, Breckinridge could see Stahel massing his cavalry squadrons for a charge up the pike against Patton and Derrick. "The position was very critical," Stoddard Johnston later recalled, "and for a time it seemed doubtful as to which [army] would be the first to give way." Then Captain Preston heard someone shout that the whole Confederate line was about to crumble, "and for a moment," he said, "I thought that all was lost."[21]

9

"*Vare Ish Mein Cavalrie?*"

"I have found Ju Stahel not to be the right man in every respect," Sigel would write to his wife in a few days. "He is much too slow in all his doings." For Stahel's sloth, said Sigel, "I have had to pay."[1]

Stahel was, indeed, slow—slow to think and slow to act. He could see that the Confederate left was stalled and faltering in front of the Federal infantry, and now the enemy right was struggling to hold its position on the rise before him. Yet he delayed making his attack. Part of the trouble may have been his men. "A portion of the cavalry was not good," according to Sigel, and some even sympathized with the enemy. "Heaven thanks I never have hurt a confederate soldier," one of the New York troopers would write, "though I took one prisoner when I could not help it." With men such as this, Stahel might indeed have had second thoughts about a charge even under perfect circumstances.[2]

But soon, even to Stahel it was obvious that the time had come to smite the enemy. Even though disasters with Boyd and Higgins, as well as with several detachments of bridge guards, had reduced his cavalry by fully one third, he still had 2,000 troopers. Massing them now in squadron front, at about 2:45 he gave the order to charge up the pike.

Echols' line was waiting for them. Derrick and the 23d Virginia, on the right, could not tell what was happening west of the pike now. Smoke and trees obscured much of the rest of the field, but he could see the onrushing Yankee cavalry well enough. Clarence Derrick was a handsome six-footer, the only West Point graduate commanding a Confederate unit in the battle. He had 579 men in his battalion, two companies of them far over on the right as skirmishers. Now as Stahel was seen approaching, the companies of skirmishers wheeled to their left to give the Yankees a flank fire, while the men in the 23d's main line grouped together in packs of three and four, backs together, in miniature versions of the "hollow square" formation which could be so destructive against a cavalry charge. Derrick ordered them to wait until the Yankees emerged from the haze of powder smoke and then to fire low.

On Derrick's left, Patton's regiment, the 22d Virginia, straddling the pike somewhat, turned toward the east to give Stahel flank fire on his right. The 22d, numbering 580 men, covered a front of some 250 yards. It, combined with Derrick, gave Echols roughly 1,150 with which to meet Stahel's 2,000.[3]

Of all of the regimental commanders in Breckinridge's little army, Colonel George S. Patton was by far the most talented and the most promising. Born in 1833, he graduated from V.M.I. in 1852, then began the practice of law in Richmond where, in off hours, he delighted in watching the maneuvers of the natty Light Infantry Blues. When he moved to Charleston, Virginia (now West Virginia), in 1856, he organized his own militia company, the Kanawha Riflemen. When war came, his company merged into the 22d Virginia Infantry, of which he was elected lieutenant colonel on July 7, 1861. Later that same year he was promoted and took command of the regiment, which he soon had uniformed in light blue jackets and dark gray trousers with yellow trimmings. Its service up until now had been almost exclusively in western Virginia, yet Patton's conduct in this unsung theater was such that by mid-1863 there was talk of his being promoted to brigadier. "He is an energetic, ardent and most effective friend of the cause," wrote Echols.

Patton's first cousin, Colonel George H. Smith of the 62d

Virginia, knew him even better and wrote more eloquently when he said that Patton "was a man of great gifts as a soldier and otherwise, and of a most noble and loveable character . . . and . . . excited the admiration of every one with whom he came in contact."

Six of his brothers were in the Confederate service. His brother Colonel John M. Patton had commanded the 21st Virginia under Jackson in 1862, while Colonel Waller T. Patton had been mortally wounded leading his 7th Virginia at Gettysburg. Another brother, William, was fourth Cadet sergeant in Company B, now filling the gap over on the left. Thanks to a furlough home some months ago and to what Colonel Patton called "the general effect of the war," his wife was expecting. He, meanwhile, suffered from a chronic cold that had bothered him all winter and spring. Now, of course, he faced Stahel.[4]

Breckinridge had seen Stahel forming for the charge and knew immediately that his best hope of repulsing the attack lay with the artillery. Taking Chapman's battery, Berkeley's section of McClanahan's battery, and Minge's V.M.I. battery, he brought them down the pike to a low stone fence on the right of the road, slightly in advance of Patton's line, and ordered them to double-shot their guns with canister. At the same time, Sturgis Davis' little company, which so far had been moving dismounted behind the Cadets, with no part in the battle, was brought over to the right to help fill a slight gap between Patton and Derrick. General Echols was still with Derrick, apparently, but how much influence he exerted in meeting Stahel's charge is undeterminable. Edgar later claimed that Echols did almost nothing and "was not needed" here at all. "We know, of course," he would tell Smith, "that he [Echols] was not a field man, though an efficient organizer."[5]

As the Confederates watched Stahel ride down on them, they felt uneasy, but held their places. Then Breckinridge gave the Yankees a "simultaneous discharge of canister" from his guns near the pike and almost immediately the enemy charge slowed. The 22d Virginia advanced a little and began shooting down the troopers' horses, while Derrick's two skirmishing companies over on the right began doing the same. By the time

Stahel's men passed a stone bridge on the pike about 300 yards from the Confederate line, they were being hit in front and on both flanks. The artillery was tearing them apart. Besides the guns with Breckinridge, McClanahan's four cannon were still on the other side of Smith's Creek. They began to make themselves felt again. Colonel Strother, looking from the Federal right, could see that the canister "seriously disturbed the cavalry." Meanwhile, after firing an initial volley at the opening of the charge, Ewing's battery did little to support Stahel, but stood back on the pike and delivered about ten minutes of very ineffective fire. Its crew's enlistments would run out in less than a month, and the men may not have been anxious to take chances.

Now the Union charge was almost completely broken and in confusion. Stahel appears to have ordered a withdrawal, but none of his troopers could hear him and vainly tried to ride on in groups here and there. Patton moved the 22d out against them, acting "with distinguished gallantry," wrote a witness. Even the Negro cook of Company H, William Armistead, picked up an abandoned rifle and joined in the fight. The scene was frightening. The sky had turned dark as Stahel's charge began, the rain came down harder, and then came the thunder and lightning. Stahel's poor troopers, many of them unable to distinguish the roar of Breckinridge's guns from the booming in the heavens, began dodging about, trying to duck the thunder. This confusion only added to the deadliness of the Confederate canister.

"Every gun of the enemy was made effective by his use of the smooth ground," wrote an officer of the 21st New York Cavalry, "and by rapid manoeuvring an enfilading fire was kept up most of the time." A trooper of the 1st Maryland Potomac Home Brigade detachment declared that "the Battalion was saved from annihilation or surrender [only] by their desperate courage."

Then, singly and in groups, the Yankee horsemen began breaking for the rear. Colonel Wynkoop tried valiantly to rally them. He was "like a caged lion," said one trooper, but Wynkoop's efforts were to no avail. "Our cavalry behaved badly," lamented a Union correspondent on the scene. Many dropped their guns and surrendered. "I shall never forget the aspect of your infantry attacking," wrote one New York cavalryman to Breckinridge a year later. "The triumphant yell and—my cowardly comrades running back for their miserable life! I was ashamed to be in such an army." When it was over, Stahel's men could be seen streaming back down the pike. "It was a hard Battle," one of Patton's Virginians wrote in his diary, "but we routed them."

Stahel, riding off west of the pike to report to Sigel, could look back and see his command utterly routed, so confused that some units would not reform for several hours as they choked the pike in their panic. The whole movement, wrote disconsolate Colonel William B. Tibbits, commander of the Federal First Cavalry Brigade, "proved a disaster." The affair had taken much of the edge off the Confederates' critical situation, putting them back into the battle. Now Stahel, his division disintegrated, rode up to his commander and exclaimed in his bewilderment: "Mein Gott, General Sigel! Vare ish mein cavalrie?"[6]

The commanding general could see well enough where the cavalry was going, and their repulse could not have come at a worse moment. Up to this time, the fight for Bushong's Hill had gone well for Sigel; Breckinridge appeared hopelessly stalled—even disorganized—in his front. One of Carlin's gunners wrote of the action: "I cannot describe to you the scene, but it was awful; ten [twelve] pieces pouring canister into them at one hundred and fifty yards, and not moving them. At last they wavered, [and] our boys cheered and gave them double charges." Wells of the 34th Massachusetts reported how the Rebel line "staggered" and fell back, its fire ceasing to be effective. Another of Carlin's men felt enthusiastically "that the day was ours."

Sigel was slow, however, to see the inviting gap that opened in the enemy line—at least he was slow to take advantage of it. The smoke from his cannon, which the wind drove back in his face, may have kept him from getting a good clear view of the hole. But when it was clearly revealed to him and one of his staff officers suggested that a cavalry charge here would destroy the Confederates, Sigel had none available. Instead, he ordered Stahel's disastrous attack on the left. Meanwhile, he kept his infantry firing and briefly brought Colonel William Curtis' 12th West Virginia into line, though many of its men could not fire for fear of hitting the 34th in front of them. But the 12th took casualties. Private John A. Christman of Company A joked as the regiment filed into line that "I hope I will be killed today." Moments later, he was the first and only man in the outfit to die, a bullet in his heart.

The 12th gave Sigel trouble now, too, and this surely kept him from the more important task of capitalizing on the gap in Wharton's line. A company of riflemen from the 26th Virginia that Edgar had sent into the woods along the bluff above the river had been able to advance considerably in front of the rest of the line unmolested. They began pouring a destructive fire into the Federal gunners on the crest of the hill. Carlin sent his second in command, First Lieutenant Ephraim Chalfant, to Sigel to ask for some infantry to drive Edgar's men back. Immediately the general ordered two of Curtis' companies to go. "But to my surprise," he would write, "there was no disposition to advance; . . . the men could not be moved an inch."

Finally, about twenty West Virginians went over to Carlin. They were little help, and a gunner complained that "we never had a support through the whole fight."

Then came more trouble. Sigel wanted to ride to his left to see what was happening with Stahel's line. But as he rode, he found that Curtis' troops got up and followed him. Like lap dogs, they would not leave his side, and he felt forced to stay between the 34th and the batteries in order to keep them in place. "In spite of the seriousness of the situation," he later wrote, "it seemed to me almost comical that a major-general commanding a department and an 'army' was condemned to the function of a 'watchman.'" Of course, this watchman work was really the business of Sigel's staff, but for no apparent reason he had ordered most of his staff officers to stay near Kleiser's battery.

Strother tried to remain with the general. Then Stahel rode

The Bushong house and orchard. (Preston Cocke, V.M.I. cadet, 1911, from Turner's *New Market*)

gadier General Gabriel C. Wharton, ose line wavered and nearly broke at e fence in front of the Bushong house. *nfederate Veteran*, XIV, 1906)

Brigadier General John Echols, too ill to take an active part in leading his brigade. (MOLLUS-Mass. Collection, U. S. Army Military History Research Collection)

The Bushong orchard, where Cadet boys became men. (Preston Cocke, V.M.I. cadet, 1911, from Turner's *New Market*)

Cadet Private Gaylord B. Clark, Company D. (Courtesy of New Market Battlefield Park)

Cadet Private Thomas G. Jefferson, Company B, mortally wounded in the battle, aged seventeen. (Courtesy of New Market Battlefield Park)

typical V.M.I. Cadet at New Market. Cadet Captain Benjamin A. "Duck"
lonna. Behind him are the Bushong house and fence. (Courtesy of New Market
ttlefield Park)

The charge of the Corps of Cadets. A rather fanciful painting by Benjamin West Clinedinst. (Courtesy of New Market Battlefield Park)

up with his bad news, and Sigel became more agitated and unintelligible than ever. He seemed, Strother wrote in his diary, "in a state of excitement and rode here and there with Stahel and Moor, all jabbering in German. In his excitement he [Sigel] seemed to forget his English entirely, and the purely American portion of his staff were totally useless to him." Soon Strother gave up and joined the others with Kleiser.[7]

The arrival of Stahel with word of his disaster, combined with his own difficulties with getting supports to counter the destructive fire on Carlin's right, finally decided Sigel. It was nearly 3:00 P.M. He would have to counterattack in order to save Carlin and Snow from Edgar's fire, he believed. He must stop the Confederates' regained momentum from Stahel's repulse. It did not matter that the real moment for a counter-charge had passed several minutes before, nor that in charg-ing now that Stahel was routed, the 54th Pennsylvania would be advancing with its left flank completely exposed. Sigel was suddenly desperate. He seldom thought well as a general even when he was not under pressure; now he did not think at all.

Here he was, about to make a charge which would obviously be a turning point in the battle, for better or worse, the cul-mination of his campaign. He would send three regiments, the 34th Massachusetts, the 1st West Virginia, and the 54th Penn-sylvania, totaling less than 1,700 men between them, while the unmanageable 12th West Virginia stayed as a reserve. To meet them, Breckinridge had the remnants of his Virgin-ians—of the 51st and 30th, Hart's engineers, the Cadets now in line, and Smith's battered 62d, with Edgar's 26th coming up and easily available to fill out the thin spots in the line; in all, some 1,600 to 1,800 men. And Patton and Derrick with their 1,000 were now free to concentrate on the Yankee infantry.

Here was the denouement of Sigel's campaign, the final fruits of his folly. Having begun his march with an army that outnumbered all of Breckinridge's forces almost two to one, he had now mismanaged and maneuvered himself into a position where he was ordering an attack against an enemy that out-numbered *him* by more than three to two. The verdict is clear: Franz Sigel was not just an incompetent; he was a fool.

Sigel gave the order. Colonel Joseph Thoburn, commanding
the Second Brigade comprising the four regiments on Bushong's Hill, rode along the line encouraging the men, telling
them to prepare for the charge. The fire of the Federal artillery had increased in preparation for the movement. The din
was so great that when Thoburn rode past Colonel Wells of
the 34th Massachusetts, he yelled something that Wells could
not hear. Then, when Thoburn rode on to the 1st West Virginia and they immediately started their advance, Wells knew
Thoburn had ordered the charge.

"The men fairly sprang forward," Wells would report, but
one of Carlin's gunners thought differently. "They moved forward," he wrote, "but slowly—not like men who go for victory or death." The mascot dogs of the 34th ran in front of the
regiment, only to be killed in the rain of Rebel lead. Meanwhile, Colonel Jacob Campbell of the 54th Pennsylvania never
got his orders for the charge, but seeing the 1st West Virginia
moving forward, he knew he was meant to follow.

Sigel's delay had given Breckinridge's line time to stabilize.
By the time the Cadets were settled behind the orchard fence,
the men to their left were holding well, reforming behind the
protective rails. Blain's guns were up somewhat to the east of
the Bushong house, while Breckinridge and the rest of the
artillery continued their fire from a new position on the pike,
now well supported by Patton's and Derrick's obliquing line.
The Confederates were more than ready for Sigel.

The 1st West Virginia met the Confederate fire first. Advancing barely a hundred yards into the hail of bullets from
Smith and the Cadets, it was also suffering terribly from the
canister fire of Breckinridge on the pike, and of Blain in front.
Since the 1st had moved out before either of the Union regiments on its sides, its flanks were exposed. The West Virginians
put up very little fight and were already retreating back to
their lines before the 54th Pennsylvania was well into the
charge.

Colonel Campbell and the 54th were having worse fortune.
His men had been somewhat protected from enemy fire by a
slight rise separating him from Smith's right—the 23d Virginia

Cavalry—and Patton's left. But now he crested the rise and almost immediately "sustained a galling and destructive fire" from the Confederates. Campbell made a gallant attempt to stand under the storm, but then saw Patton and Derrick overlapping his left flank almost around to his rear. At the same time, he could see on his right the 1st West Virginia falling back with the Confederates in close pursuit. Obviously, if he remained here any longer, he could be surrounded and destroyed. Reluctantly, and only after he and his regiment had done their duty and more, Campbell pulled away back in good order, ready to make a stand to try to halt the enemy's advance.

This left the 34th Massachusetts, the regiment which would suffer most of all from this ill-advised charge. Smoke hid much of the field again as they advanced, but they yelled and cheered as they ran into the cloud. Then, like Campbell, Colonel Wells saw the 1st West Virginia pulling back, leaving him to go on alone. He shouted to his men to halt; but as one of the men recalled, it was "almost impossible to hear any order from our superior officers."

The regiment kept going in the face of a now-withering fire. In a few short minutes, it suffered 200 or more casualties, nearly half of the outfit. Wells had to run in front of the regiment and take hold of the color bearer, turning him around toward the rear, to get the men to stop and wheel about. The 34th withdrew in steady time and formation, marching all the way while Wells's officers steadied the men, telling them, "Don't run—Keep your line!"

Finally they reached their old position again. Just then Wells's second-in-command, Lieutenant Colonel Lincoln, fell wounded. Looking back toward the now-advancing enemy, Wells saw that "the path of our regiment between our line and the fence was sadly strewn with our fallen." Worse yet, he found that the 1st West Virginia had not halted in its old line in withdrawing but was now streaming back toward the pike and the rear. All he could see was the 54th Pennsylvania, "gallantly holding its ground far to the left."

The Union charge had been an utter failure. Now, at

3:00 P.M., the Confederates, secure in the knowledge that once again they held the advantage, were coming on with a momentum which no one could stop. "We now felt that it would be a desperate struggle for the battery," wrote one of Carlin's West Virginia gunners, "for every man knew that we were whipped."[8]

When the 51st Virginia stood faltering and beginning to break before the Federals' fire at the north Bushong fence a quarter hour before, Captain Bruce had looked to his left to see Edgar's 26th coming up fast to bolster the crumbling line. Edgar, twenty-seven years old, was an 1853 V.M.I. graduate and then a schoolteacher in Florida when the war began. He enlisted as a private in the Confederate army and soon rose to captain of Company D, 59th Virginia Infantry. Discharged, he came to Virginia to raise the 26th Virginia Battalion in May 1862 and was elected its lieutenant colonel immediately. He was a good, reliable officer, rather too much concerned with his record and that of his command, but ever vigilant.

Edgar's alertness paid off for Breckinridge. Marching now mostly to the west of the saddle connecting Manor's with Bushong's Hill, Edgar saw the right wing of the 51st and the 30th stop short under the enemy fire. "I at once ordered my Battalion forward to its support," he reported. Waving his saber above his head, he cried, "Forward, men, forward," and forward they went.

Soon the men from Wharton's front line who had broken began to filter to the rear through Edgar's advancing battalion. "Don't let those men break your ranks," he called to his captains. When it began to look as if the men falling back might seriously disrupt his line, he ordered his company commanders to fall back a few paces, draw their pistols, and shoot if necessary to stop the fugitives. Soon the 26th was right among the men of the 51st and 30th and passing through the broken portions at the top and right of the saddle. "It is due to the Regiment that gave way at the commencement of the action," Edgar would later report, "to state that the officers and men who compose it soon rallied upon the right and left of my Battalion, and fought gallantly."

Edgar's second in command, Captain Edmund S. Read of Company B, a man of strong prejudices, would later claim that after passing part of the 51st he heard someone yell, "Charge Read, Charge—for God sake." Looking to his left, he said, he saw Wharton, alone, crouching behind a tree, the inference being that he was cowering from the Federal fire.

In fact, Wharton was largely responsible for holding together that part of the 51st west of the saddle. A veteran of many fights, Wharton was no coward. He soon had the remaining part of the 51st advancing again in line with, or slightly ahead of, the 26th. The line once again halted at the rail fence, with the men of the 51st and 26th now largely mingled. Meanwhile, Edgar sent Read with his company over to the bluffs to counter the fire from a detached company of the 34th Massachusetts and to begin its very troublesome sharpshooting at Carlin and Snow.[9]

Then came Sigel's charge. But, wrote one Confederate, "the steadiness of our brave troops, was too much for them." Seeing the Federals first waver and then withdraw, the Confederates shouted triumphantly. Then the men of the 34th Massachusetts and the boys of the Corps of Cadets saw something at the same time—something of significance. Sigel's gunners were limbering their guns and pulling away. He was abandoning the line.

Now, said Carter Berkeley of McClanahan's battery, "the most terrible storm I ever witnessed" broke. "A dark and angry cloud hung over the combatants, the forked lightning flashed through the blackness as if heaven were crying out against the horrid work which was going on."

It was 3 P.M. The Cadets, looking to their left, saw Color Sergeant Frank Lindamood of the 51st Virginia march out alone in front of his regiment, waving the battle flag aloft and calling for them to rally on him and charge. A few grouped themselves around him, only to fall under the still heavy fire from the 34th Massachusetts, now back in line, but Lindamood held his ground. A color bearer of the 26th Virginia Battalion did the same and once again Wharton's whole line sprang forward.

Soon Colonel Wells of the 34th could see two enemy banners approaching, and he knew they would not be stopped this time. Wharton himself, setting his sights on Carlin's guns, led the left company of the 51st Virginia in the charge. Fortunately for him and his men, Carlin's gunners were obviously unsteady as they fired their last shots, for their cannon were aimed too low, the balls striking the mud in front of the Confederates. Instead of bounding up and doing some damage, they buried themselves in the ground but, said Wharton, "threw up much mud, at times almost blinding us and covering us from head to foot with mud." And then, halfway to the Federal line, the men of the 51st saw Carlin start to limber his guns to withdraw. The 51st started firing, hoping to kill the horses and force the Federals to abandon the guns.[10]

When Lindamood moved in front of his men, the Cadets sprang from behind the fence, Henry Wise and Frank Preston simultaneously ordering the charge. Wartmann of the *Rockingham Register* was just behind the lines, and he was impressed. "It made our hearts leap," he said, "to see the Cadets from the V.M.I. move forward in the charge upon the enemy's battery. Their step was as steady as the tread of veteran soldiers. They never faltered, but went into the 'harvest of death' as though they had been accustomed to such bloody work."

The veterans had been wrong. Training, discipline, spirit, and tradition were paying well. The Cadets would fight.

By 3:00, the fire from Kleiser's guns had all but stopped as the Corps began its advance, but Federal riflemen were still firing. Some of Woodson's wounded men, lying on the field, rose on their elbows to cheer the boys on, one of them getting to his feet only to be hit again in the face. The Cadets felt the fire almost at once. As some of them tried to avoid enemy bullets, Cadet Charles Randolph called to his comrades: "There's no use dodging, boys, if a ball's going to hit you, it'll hit you anyway." Then Randolph was hit and fell.

Other boys fell, too. Cadet Frank Gibson had a leg shattered just below the knee, while another bullet hit him in the thigh, another in the cheek, and yet a fourth took two fingers from a hand. Cadet John Upshur was seen leaning on his rifle. "Come on, Upshur, close up," someone cried, "no lagging in C Company today."

Upshur tried to take a step and then fell, his right leg smashed terribly. A particular menace to them was the peculiar depression which stood between the Bushong orchard and Sigel's crumbling line. Water was still standing in it, making a patch of sticky, clinging mud nearly fifty yards wide right in the path of the Cadets. Forced to march through it, some of the boys found the mire sucking their shoes and stockings from their feet, in some cases trapping a Cadet for a few seconds before he could extricate his feet. Fifteen-year-old Cadet Samuel B. Adams had one of his shoes sucked off and turned around under fire to pull it out. As the bullets whistled and splashed around him, he recalled, "it seemed to me I was a long time doing it."

Up ahead they could still see Kleiser, some of his guns now moving off the field. The 1st West Virginia to Kleiser's left had retreated now, leaving no doubt as to what the Cadets' objective should be—"we were ordered to charge a battery in front of us," one Cadet wrote home, "which we did." How they ran toward those guns impressed everyone who witnessed their charge. "It was a sublime sight," wrote Wartmann. They were "as brave and chivalrous a command as ever fired a gun." Lieutenant Woods of Blain's battery wrote the next day: "they are glorious boys," and Major Otey of the 30th Virginia agreed, declaring that their advance "surpassed anything that I witnessed during the war." Major Semple, the assistant ordnance officer, later claimed that Breckinridge declared the boys fought "even better, I think, than the oldest soldiers we had."

The enemy, too, took special note of the advance of the Corps of Cadets. Lincoln, lying wounded, saw them come and declared later that he had never really seen discipline until he watched these boys advance. Even the Cadets themselves were impressed. Two days later one of them wrote home: "I never thought that we would have fought so bravely."[11]

To the Cadets' right, Smith's 62d Virginia were also on the

move again. Patton and Derrick still fresh and in good order after repulsing Stahel's charge, came abreast of the 62d and together they continued the advance, starting slightly ahead of the Cadets but marching slower. From now on their charge would not be stopped. Meanwhile, Breckinridge's gunners continued their vital work. "Our artilery Played furiously in the charge," one of Imboden's cavalrymen wrote in his diary. Blain's guns fired 200 rounds or more before and during this final movement, ceasing only when the Confederate line got too close to the enemy.

This was the final charge. Everyone knew it. Smith and Patton advanced together, meeting almost no resistance. "Nor did we ever succeed in getting closer to the enemy," said Smith. The flank movement by the 22d and 23d Infantries did its work well, and at little cost to the Confederates. As Campbell of the 54th Pennsylvania found Derrick and Patton flanking his left, the 1st West Virginia were falling back again from his right, exposing it to the onrushing 62d and the Cadets. He had no choice but to order his regiment to retire. The resistance the Pennsylvanians put up before withdrawing was valiant. Out of 566 men engaged, 254 were killed, wounded, or captured in this, the only part of the battle in which they were engaged, the highest numerical losses of any unit engaged in the battle. Crying "We are flanked," Campbell's men pulled back in some disorder but soon reformed for the retreat. With them went what remained of the rallied portions of the 123d Ohio, its commander, Major Horace Kellogg seriously wounded, the men, by their own admission, "pretty badly shattered."[12]

Smith's left, Woodson and the 62d, and the Cadets enjoyed even greater success. Colonel Ship, coming around after his stunning wound, could see his Cadets going ahead without him. Finally the boys struggled through the muddy "Field of Lost Shoes" and raced toward the crest of the hill, still taking fire from Kleiser and from Carlin and Snow as they sent their last shells toward Breckinridge's guns on the pike. "Though their beloved comrades fell thick and fast by their sides," wrote a witness to the Cadets' advance, "they faltered not, but kept their line well formed and continued to advance upon the enemy's battery."

As they approached Kleiser and the remnant of the fleeing 1st West Virginia, Cadet Captain Benjamin A. "Duck" Colonna ordered one of his privates to fire at the legs of a German officer pointing his pistol at them, but the Cadet aimed slightly higher, no doubt to the eternal dismay of the Federal. Cadet Hugh Fry of Company C called to another Yankee to surrender and, when he did not, shot him in the leg, being too soft-hearted to kill him.

When within a few yards of the enemy line, the Cadets wavered slightly and then pushed to the top. The men of the 1st West Virginia put up a pitifully feeble resistance. "The Yankees broke and ran like sheep," Cadet George Ward wrote home later, before the Confederates even reached them.[13]

This left only Kleiser facing the Confederate charge. It had been a bad day for him. Already one of his six guns had been disabled and was now making its way back on the pike. Then Breckinridge's fire from the pike, combined with Woodson's sharpshooting, repeatedly drove his men from their guns to cover, seriously reducing his fire. He had lost several battery horses during the day, and now the Cadets began firing at his remaining animals. It had been clear from the time that Sigel's charge was repulsed that this Union line on Bushong's Hill must pull back, and Kleiser began limbering his five pieces even before the Cadets started their charge. But there was trouble. Seven horses were dead.

Finally the poor conduct of one of his officers worked against him. First Lieutenant Charles Hausmann, commanding two of the guns, had placed the lead horses of one of his teams so far behind the lines that they could not be reached. Sigel himself found and returned them to Kleiser, only to have one fall dead from a bullet, nearly crushing one gunner against a cannon. (Years later, when Hausmann applied to Congress for a Medal of Honor for his services in the Valley, the nearly crushed gunner remarked to Sigel that the government should, instead, "vote such a gallant Nature a Medal of good Lasting Shoeleather.")

The combination of these circumstances forced Kleiser to make the decision that all artillerists loathed. There were too few horses, too much confusion, no infantry supports, and the Confederates were almost on top of him: he would have to abandon one of Hausmann's guns. There was not even time enough to spike it. Kleiser, whom du Pont regarded as "a most efficient officer and as one particularly noticeable for gallantry," barely got his other four pieces off toward the pike when the Cadets swarmed over his position, exultantly taking possession of a fine twelve-pounder and its caisson.

Nothing could have been more splendid. Here, in their very first battle, the Corps of Cadets had captured an enemy field piece, one of the finest trophies they could have desired. It did not matter that the gun had been left behind or that it was not taken in hand-to-hand combat with the artillerymen. It was a magnificent prize; for most of the boys the high point of their service for the Confederacy and the beginning of a lasting legend and tradition.[14]

There was little time here to exult, however. Almost immediately the right company of the Corps turned toward the 54th Pennsylvania's now exposed right flank, assisting Smith, Patton, and Derrick in forcing it to withdraw. Meanwhile, the Cadets on the left turned to give the 34th Massachusetts an enfilading fire into its left flank, turning the captured gun on them as well. They had taken—or, more correctly, had been given—the center of the Federal line, and now they used their position brilliantly to help put the rest of the Yankee line to flight.

Meanwhile, over on their left, the 51st and the 26th Virginia bore down on Sigel's last remaining regiment, Wells's 34th Massachusetts. The Virginians' charge was unstoppable. Edgar's color bearer, George A. Woodman, carried the flag of the 26th in one hand and fired a pistol with the other. The Federals found the fire too hot to stand. Boughs and leaves from a cedar grove behind their position fell, clipped by Confederate bullets, as though caught in a great storm. In their advance, the Confederates captured the wounded Colonel Lincoln lying on the field and inflicted heavy losses on the 34th. Besides Lincoln, ten other officers felt Confederate bullets, and their flag bearer was hit four times before he could fall from the first wound. Still, the 34th stood its ground as long as it could. "The contest on the right was hotly sustained," Strother would write in his journal, but it had to come to an end. With the withdrawal of the 1st West Virginia, the Cadets were soon firing into Wells's left flank. To his right, parts of the 51st Virginia were getting into a position from which to enfilade his right. There was nothing to do but withdraw. Once again, Wells's men could not hear him for the din of battle, and he had to turn his new color bearer around and order him to follow him off the field. Slowly, and in some disorder, the 34th pulled back down the reverse slope of Bushong's toward the pike, while Wharton's line was still a hundred yards or more from Bushong's crest.[15]

Sigel remained on the right throughout the rough fighting that preceded the 34th's withdrawal. However bad a general he may have been, he proved here that he was a man of courage. He rode back and forth behind the 34th, and Wells would exclaim, "How he escaped is a mystery to me." Even the supercritical Strother was forced to compliment Sigel's bravery. But a general's courage alone could not hold this line. Now that he saw his regiments forced to retreat, Sigel ordered Carlin and Snow to pull out by section, firing as they withdrew. Then he rode toward the pike to see what could be made of the demoralized remnant of his army.

The few men of the 12th West Virginia who were supporting Carlin and Snow received orders to advance through the guns and try to check the enemy long enough for the batteries to limber and get away. As before, they did not obey. The gunners were on their own. Snow limbered first and got away safely, leaving Carlin alone on the hill. "The enemy concentrate their whole fire upon us," a gunner would write three days later, "and it seems impossible to save a single gun."

Carlin ordered all of his guns to retire at once. Immediately the artillerymen began limbering. The men at gun number four barely got started when the Confederates directed their fire at its horses and killed or disabled five of them. There was no time to bring a fresh team. The gun would have to be abandoned. Next to it, three horses of number three fell, but the men were able to get it moving toward the rear. On the other side, a shell broke several spokes of a wheel on number five, broke part of its carriage, and hit its spare wheel. The men started to abandon it when the gun's officer ordered them back. Then three of its horses were hit. Somehow the men kept the animals on their feet and, using whip and spur, got them to pull the gun away. Altogether, Carlin lost seventeen horses on the hill.

No sooner had Carlin abandoned number four and gotten his other guns started than the remaining horses of number three collapsed. With the Confederates so close behind them, the number-three gunner had no choice but to abandon it too. A terrible confusion, already reigning in the fleeing mass on the pike, now possessed the gunners. In their haste to get away, a man was run down by a gun, saved only by the mud which cushioned the cannon's weight upon him. Then, a few hundred yards farther, the already damaged number five gun got stuck up to its axles in the mud and another of its horses fell. Carlin had the team unhitched and the men tried to free the gun themselves, Carlin and Sigel both lending a hand. Failing in this, a fresh team was hitched, only to have more horses fall to enemy bullets. Deciding that it was hopeless, Sigel ordered that this piece, too, be abandoned. Carlin, his battery cut in half, bravely tried to "come into battery"—turn and fire—briefly to slow the advancing Confederates but, his caissons having run off ahead of him, he found he had no ammunition and was forced to limber again and retire.[16]

Carlin's guns were welcome prizes for the Confederates. The final charge of the 51st and 26th Virginia, with some of Otey's 30th participating, had been a rough one thanks to the stubborn resistance of the 34th Massachusetts. Only those companies west of the ridge were spared somewhat from the Federal bullets, but they encountered Carlin's canister instead. Wharton was still over on the extreme left with Company B of the 51st. He could advance somewhat faster than the men east of the ridge. Consequently, Company B was the first to

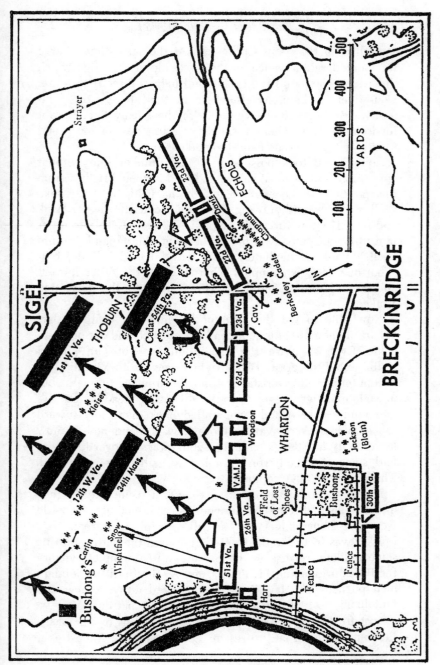

3 P.M. His charge failing, Sigel withdraws from the field.

capitalize on the spoils Carlin left. At the same time, it was the Confederate advance on the west side of the ridge which threatened the 34th's right flank and helped force it to retire. Consequently, here, as elsewhere in this charge, the Confederates never actually closed with the enemy line. Except for isolated cases where a Yankee was too slow or too proud to retreat, there was no hand-to-hand combat.

Company B took possession of gun number four without opposition and then Wharton halted his men briefly. From this position at the extreme left of the field, he could take Wells's slowly withdrawing 34th Massachusetts in the flank and rear. He now turned to Captain William H. Tate to order him to have Company B file to the right oblique and fire into Wells's flank. Immediately Tate was hit and fell dead at Wharton's feet, whereupon Wharton gave the order himself and a volley of Confederate fire tore into the retreating Yankees.

Now able to see the right of his line east of the ridge, Wharton knew that his command was uneven and out of alignment. Even so, with the enemy on the run, he pushed again across the crest. To his right Edgar's 26th Virginia had encountered stiffer resistance from the front of the 34th, but now it, too, swept over the hill, advancing steadily. Carlin's gun number three had been pulled back diagonally toward the pike for several yards before it was abandoned. It now lay directly in Edgar's path. The 26th swarmed over it only to find, some distance beyond, number five still stuck in the mud. This piece, too, they captured.[17]

It was 3 P.M., or shortly after, though it seemed to the men in the ranks that it surely must be later. The minutes in battle were like hours. Sigel was in full, precipitate retreat. New Market was secure to the Confederates and the battle—barring some unlikely reverse in the pursuit—was a complete victory for Breckinridge and his little army. As the tired but jubilant men pushed on after Sigel's demoralized army, a new and tantalizing portent appeared. One year ago that day, May 15, almost to this very minute, the earthly remains of Thomas J. Jackson had been laid to rest in Lexington's soil. Almost as if to mark the anniversary, the Shenandoah had found in Breckinridge another savior. Had a new Stonewall been born? The Federals, for the moment, were more concerned with present emergencies than future Stonewalls. Seeing the Union infantry breaking in panic for the rear, Colonel Strother drew his sword and tried to rally them, others of Sigel's staff doing the same. One officer actually cut down a soldier who refused to halt and stand, and Strother was about to strike another when the man fell, instead, struck by an enemy bullet. "Our position was becoming very hot," Strother wrote in his diary. With the enemy pouring over the crest of Bushong's Hill, he wrote, "Our lines were falling back and were rapidly disintegrating and becoming a rout."

Signal Officer Captain Franklin Town, who soon joined with Strother and the other staff members in an attempt to form a line of the few men who rallied, was more succinct. The retreat, he said, "was at first a panic." Then a Confederate shell struck the ground in their midst without exploding, plowing the ground under Provost Marshal Lieutenant Colonel William C. Starr's horse. At the same instant his horse was hit and fell from under him, and Strother was struck by a spent bullet. While the staff dispersed and headed for the rear, Starr tried to mount a riderless horse nearby, was thrown to the ground, and then run down by a panic-stricken squad of cavalry.

The Federals found the ground turned against them. Whereas the south slope of Bushong's had been gentle but fairly short, the back slope descended gently for more than a quarter mile. Thus, during the Federals' oblique backward trek to the pike, the Confederates constantly had higher ground, and they used it. Carlin's and Snow's guns, meanwhile, had to race straight back into a hollow to escape Breckinridge and would not reach the pike for quite some time after the rest of the army was on it in full retreat.

There were a few initial attempts to stand and halt the Confederate pursuit, particularly by Wells's 34th Massachusetts. Wells had to work assiduously to keep his command moving toward the rest of the fleeing infantry where, he hoped, some rearguard could be formed. About forty Federals rallied behind a barn on Bushong's back slope, but the Confederates soon swarmed over them.

For the rest of the Union men, it was panic. One of Carlin's gunners vividly described the scene in a letter written three days later. "After we reached the road, the scene beggars description. Our infantry was hurrying to the rear, many of them having thrown away their arms. The colors were posted on a knoll, the bugler blowing the assembly, officers riding madly over the field with drawn sabres threatening and coaxing; a line of cavalry in the rear with drawn sabres, all endeavoring to check them, but it was of no use." Years later Randolph Blain would write, "I cannot say that we were much impressed with the bravery of our German friends."[18]

It was only shortly after passing the crest of Bushong's Hill that Wharton got word of a detached company of the 34th Massachusetts over in the cedars by the river bluffs. Cut off from the rest of the Federal line when the Confederates took the hill, it had continued its sharpshooting, while Company A of the 12th West Virginia, sent to the bluffs for the same purpose, ran away. Edgar immediately sent a company of the 26th Virginia, at Wharton's request, to dislodge the Bay Staters. Soon almost the whole company, including its two officers, were captured.

"Then," as Captain Preston wrote, "everything was forgotten but the excitement of the pursuit." An abundance of booty awaited the Confederates as they swept down the north slope of Bushong's Hill over the path of the fleeing enemy. Blankets, oil cloths, saddles, full knapsacks and haversacks, guns, and all manner of prizes lay scattered for the picking. One veteran gathered forty new shirts. Blain's gunners caught Yankee horses to replace their own jaded mounts, and men of the 51st Virginia took Colonel Lincoln's horse and saddlebags, as well as a chestnut horse with Colonel Campbell's overcoat tied on the saddle. Thanks to the light resistance they met, the Cadets were somewhat in advance of the rest of the line in this early stage of the pursuit, and theirs was a large share of the captured goods. They took prisoners, too, between sixty and one hundred, Preston guessed the next day. Cadet Hugh Fry came back with one big German who literally dwarfed him. Cadet Charlie Faulkner alone took twenty-three dejected Yankees prisoner.

Colonels Smith and Patton walked together now, discussing the battle while their regiments ran ahead of them. Within a few minutes after the breakthrough, Breckinridge rode up to them, dismounted, and offered one of them his horse, Old Sorrel. "I do not feel like riding," he said, "when you gentlemen who have borne the brunt of the fight are walking."

When both of them declined, he took the reins in his hand and walked along with them for a while. Smith reported his withdrawal from the advanced position to wait for Patton to come, saying as well that he had lost half of his regiment. Breckinridge approved his movements and then mounted again to ride over to the Cadets. He halted them at once. "Young gentlemen," he said, "I have to thank you for the result of today's operations."

The Corps had lost much of its alignment by now, and fifty-seven of them lay dead or wounded on the field. Breckinridge was proud of them, more than he could say, but they had done enough. He would not expose them more. Around 3:20, ordering them to fall out and rest on the north slope of Bushong's Hill, the general said again, "Well done, Virginians! Well done, men!"

"Then he turned and rode away," recalled Duck Colonna, "taking with him the heart of every one of us."[19]

At the opening of the pursuit just after 3:00 P.M., Smith and Patton of the 62d and 22d Virginia, with Derrick of the 23d on the right, continued their forward advance parallel to the pike, though the mud in the fields slowed many and caused them to open out considerably, mixing the commands. Then the halt of the Cadets opened Smith's left flank and Edgar, moving the 26th obliquely to the right as he marched down Bushong's Hill, soon closed the gap. Despite the seriousness of the affair, the pursuit seemed a lark compared to the hard fighting of only a few minutes before. Jubilantly the men shook hands with each other as they marched at quick time. Captain

Read of the 26th actually started shooting at a rabbit flushed from cover by his advancing company, stopping when he realized the ludicrousness of his act. The battle might be won, but there were still more important things than rabbits to shoot.

When Edgar came abreast of Smith, they found themselves in advance of the rest of the line and halted briefly. Not having seen Wharton in some time nor Echols all day, Edgar, nominally under Echols' command, offered to place himself under Smith's command. Just then Breckinridge rode up again, this time accompanied by Echols. "Colonel," said the Kentuckian to Edgar, "we are mightily scattered, but we are driving them."

He asked Edgar to send someone to the rear to gather and bring up stragglers. Thinking that Sigel might reform down the valley on Rude's Hill and attempt a stand, Breckinridge knew he would need every man, especially if Imboden had been successful in burning the Shenandoah bridge near Mount Jackson. With their retreat cut off, the Federals might find they had some fight left after all, and Breckinridge must be ready for them. He ordered a halt to reform his line and bring fresh ammunition from the train behind Williamson's Hill.[20]

While Edgar and Smith were still advancing toward each other, the Federals finally began to put together some sort of rearguard resistance. "Seeing that our army was falling back," Stahel reported, "I hastened to cover with my cavalry their retreat." The Union cavalry, however, riding wildly without order, did more harm than good, as Provost Marshal Starr could testify. Meanwhile, the 54th Pennsylvania and 34th Massachusetts had found each other and went into a semblance of a line to the west of the pike, retiring slowly in formation and making several stops to send volleys toward the oncoming Confederates. Ewing's guns made a feeble attempt to cover the withdrawal, tying their gun trails to the limbers with ropes so that, in retreating, the cannon were pointed at the enemy and could be fired instantly at a halt without unlimbering.[21]

Then, about 3:30, from his vantage point atop Bushong's

Hill, Cadet Captain Duck Colonna saw something new. The wind had continued to blow the battle smoke northward, which now obscured much of the ground around the pike between the two armies. But through a break in the cloud, Colonna saw two enemy guns line up facing the Confederates and begin "firing furiously." There were no support troops in sight for the guns, and Edgar's advance threatened to overlap and capture the cannon. Still they fired. "I do not see how this section ever escaped annihilation," said Colonna.

"This section" belonged to Captain du Pont. At last he was in the battle. All afternoon, while Sullivan's units went forward, du Pont heard the sounds of the fight ahead. Then his orders finally came and he raced down the pike, only to find the road and countryside crowded with panicked, fleeing men. "I have been anticipating something of the kind all along," he wrote to his father, "as everything has been very much mismanaged in my opinion."

A seeming host of young officers tried to halt him with what he regarded as "the most absurd and contradictory orders with respect to putting the battery in position," but du Pont was his own man and, grasping the situation, knew what needed to be done.

Twenty-six years old now, the son of the wealthy and influential du Ponts of Wilmington, Delaware, the captain had been nearly three years in the army. Ironically, he had applied for admission to the Virginia Military Institute in 1855, only to be rejected because regulations then required all Cadets to be Virginians. Thanks to his family's political influence, du Pont went to West Point instead, graduating first in his class on May 6, 1861, only a few weeks ahead of Clarence Derrick. Thanks to his being stationed in remote assignments since commissioning, New Market was his first battle.

Du Pont had six 3-inch rifles and, in the absence of any general on the field—he saw none until well after dark—he relied on his own judgment. He detached his first platoon, two guns, and sent them dangerously far forward to a position just west of the pike, where their opening fire attracted Colonna's attention. The second platoon he put in place between 500 and 600 yards behind the first, and the third an equal distance to the rear of the second. Thus they were in position for "retiring by platoons." As soon as all of the retreating Federals were well behind du Pont's first platoon, he told its lieutenant "to get out of this." As he fell back, the second platoon opened fire. Thus he continued on through the afternoon, "leapfrogging" his platoons down the pike as the ragged Union rear guard retreated toward Rude's Hill. It was by far the coolest, most daring, and certainly the most able performance from any of the Federal commands during the retreat. Du Pont's fire was stiff enough to cover the routed army, and it proved a factor in Breckinridge's decision to halt in his pursuit for rest and rearming. As a result, it may have saved Sigel from annihilation.[22]

Breckinridge let his weary men rest for nearly an hour as the supply trains came up so they could fill their cartridge boxes. He had no doubt now that Sigel would try to make a stand on Rude's Hill. Accordingly, he set about adjusting his line for another advance. Wolfe's 51st Virginia, finally reunited after its trouble in front of Bushong's house, resumed its place between Edgar's 26th and the remnants of Otey's 30th. Smith's 62d, Patton's 22d, and Derrick's 23d remained as they had been throughout the last of the main battle. The batteries of Chapman and Blain, hauled onto the pike behind the line, were lined up to answer du Pont's salvos.

Then General Imboden appeared, and with him he brought bad news. He and the 18th Virginia Cavalry had been guided north along the east side of Smith's Creek by Walter Newman, a citizen of New Market, only to find the rain-swollen stream too high to ford behind Sigel's lines. In fact, Imboden's attempt to cross had been pitifully feeble, for others would cross the next day over even higher waters. Consequently, the bridge to Mount Jackson was still standing well within Sigel's grasp, and Imboden had returned to the battlefield. Though Gilmor's 2d Maryland Battalion was on its way to the bridge and might actually be able to reach it, they would arrive too late to accomplish their purpose. Thus, the Federals would be able to get away after all. Breckinridge's brilliantly conceived plan to trap and destroy them entirely lay thwarted, and the Confederate cavalry, which had played such a large part by so badgering Sigel that he was ripe for defeat before the battle, proved to be of no use at all in the battle itself. Years later Otey would say that "I haven't spoken of our cavalry as they did nothing." Now Breckinridge ordered Imboden to bring the 18th back to the west side of the creek to aid in the pursuit.

Imboden had found Breckinridge standing with his artillery, his uniform covered to the waist with mud. Briefly the Kentuckian explained the reason for the halt, sent a squad of the 18th back to hunt for stragglers, and then directed that the remainder of the cavalry go into place behind his left, east of the pike. As the two generals spoke, du Pont's shells began to fall perilously close to them, and Imboden urged Breckinridge to move somewhere out of the line of fire. Breckinridge only laughed. He was standing on the only dry ground he could find, he said; everything else was mud, and he would rather risk Federal shot than wade through that infernal mire again. Then word came that the men had finished resupplying. It was time to advance again. At the same time Breckinridge, whom Berkeley found looking "like the very god of war," ordered the artilleryman to take his section and McClanahan's other guns, to the main force, and charge down the pike against du Pont. "I will follow up with the infantry as rapidly as possible," said the general. Berkeley then raced off toward the enemy as the Confederates once again took up the pursuit.[23]

The pike was choked with fugitives, wagons, cannon, and riderless horses as the Federals fled toward Rude's Hill. The twelve-pounder of Kleiser's battery that had been disabled early in the day caused considerable trouble. The axle of the broken wheel somehow got lodged in the stones in the road. Though more horses and men lent their strength to pull it free, they could not drag it farther down the pike. With the obstruction blocking the retreating horde, a cavalry officer—probably Stahel—ordered it thrown into the ditch and abandoned.

With it out of the way, the Federals ran up the slopes of Rude's Hill.

Sigel had attempted to form a line somewhat in advance of the hill, though with little success. Then, looking back, he saw a dark line on Rude's Hill's summit. At last General Sullivan had arrived. Sullivan himself rode forward, missing Sigel but finding Strother, who advised him to form up the batteries of Ewing, Carlin, Snow, and Kleiser on the hill to cover the last of the infantry's retreat. Sullivan, apparently still under the influence of a rather severe fear of responsibility, asked Strother to give orders to that effect. The colonel declining, he did it himself. Then he rode back to Rude's Hill, where Sigel met him. It is a great shame that no account of their first encounter has survived, for Sigel was furious. "I found General Sullivan and with him these two Regiments at a *halt,* the troops in *line of battle* and *lying on the ground,*" he said later, and this despite the fact that he had sent—or later said that he sent—repeated orders for Sullivan to come up to the battlefield. "Sullivan has left me in the lurch," Sigel would complain to his wife, but the fault was as much his own. Moor sarcastically called the whole botched affair a case of "butiful [*sic*] management."

Now, with all three Federal generals present, they set about preparing a new line. Sigel placed the two fresh regiments, the 28th and 116th Ohio, on the right of his line running west from a Dunker church, moving them from their initial position on either side of the artillery Sullivan placed. From this point they were able to cover the rest of what Moor called "disgraceful fleeing masses of cavalry and straggling infantry" until they could be rallied into line behind them. Even these two "fresh" units were tired. The 116th had run nearly four miles to reach the field. The 28th had only five of its ten companies present. Behind the infantry and running east of the pike to the creek he placed what could be salvaged of Stahel's cavalry. In this new line, if necessary, Sigel would meet Breckinridge again.

Once the line was perfected, and before the Confederate approach came too near, Kleiser made a last attempt to save his disabled gun. One of his lieutenants took a limber and

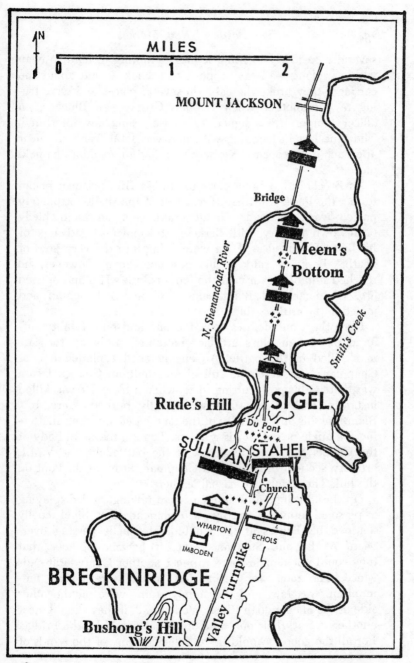

6:30 to 7:00 P.M. Sullivan's fresh units cover Sigel's withdrawal to Mount Jackson. (Symbols are not intended to depict specific units, but rather the position and relative strength of the armies.)

several men to try to bring it in. Attempting to haul it away with a prolonge—a heavy rope with a hook wound about the carriage—they broke the cable in several places and were trying to get another when Captain Gustav von Blücher, an officer temporarily assigned to Kleiser, somehow interfered. The time lost in haggling with him was fatal. With the near approach of the enemy, Kleiser's men had to abandon the field piece.[24]

As Breckinridge came close to Rude's Hill, his men began to feel the Federal artillery fire. Most of the shells fortunately passed over their heads. The general once again relied chiefly on his own artillery, with Berkeley still moving in advance of his line. "It looked as if we were going into the very jaws of death," Berkeley said of his advance. Soon, however, he reached suitable cover near the foot of Rude's Hill and opened fire. Chapman and Blain came up somewhat behind and joined in the artillery duel.

Here the Confederates took the one and only fatality suffered in McLaughlin's artillery battalion, probably the last man killed in the battle. An enemy shell exploded one of Chapman's limber chests full of ammunition. Charles Dixon was there at his post, cutting fuses, when it blew. He was killed instantly, and three others were badly burned. Here, too, Blain took his only casualty of the day, an enemy shell shattering the ankle of one of his gunners. Though the main body of the Cadets had been left back at the battlefield, the V.M.I. artillery section was still with Chapman, firing at du Pont on the hill. They took two casualties here.[25]

On the hill Sigel and Sullivan were talking. Still displaying a personal bravery worthy of commendation, Sigel coolly snapped his fingers at the Confederate shells passing overhead. As he and Sullivan spoke, it became obvious that they could not remain there to meet another Confederate advance. The men were exhausted, losses were heavy, ammunition was low, and the supply trains were on the other side of the Shenandoah River. Worst of all, if they should meet another defeat, their only line of retreat would be the bridge. For all the good it would be to a fleeing army of thousands of

Emboden's position east of Smith's Creek. Beyond the trees lies the ground where Patton and Lieutenant Colonel Clarence Derrick stopped Major General Julius Stahel's charge. (Preston Cocke, V.M.I. cadet, 1911, from Turner's *New Market*)

An imaginative postwar drawing depicting Lieutenant Carter Berkeley's Confederate section of artillery repulsing the Federal cavalry. (John N. Opie, *A Rebel Cavalryman with Lee, Stuart, and Jackson*, 1899)

The position of Sigel's batteries on the crest of Bushong's Hill. (Preston Cocke, V.M.I. cadet, 1911, from Turner's *New Market*)

Lieutenant Colonel George M. Edgar led the brave 26th Virginia Battalion against Sigel's guns. (Courtesy of New Market Battlefield Park)

Colonel Joseph Thoburn was in immediate command of the main line on Bushong's crest. (from Farrar's *Twenty-Second Pennsylvania*, 1911)

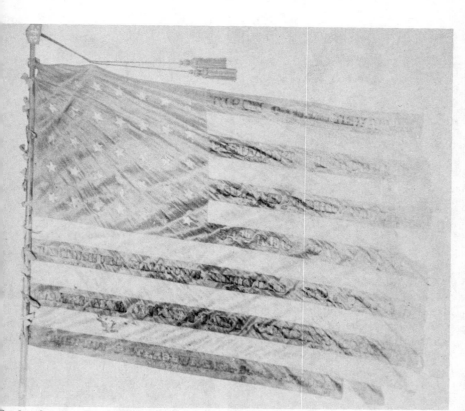

The battle-scarred colors of the 34th Massachusetts, with New Market emblazoned its top. (MOLLUS-Mass. Collection, U. S. Army Military History Research Collection)

Men of New Market. The 34th Massachusetts on parade in 1862. (MOLLUS-Mass. Collection, U. S. Army Military History Research Collection)

Major General Julius Stahel. The failure of his cavalry charge ensured Federal defeat. (MOLLUS-Mass. Collection, U. S. Army Military History Research Collection)

Colonel David H. Strother rendered gallant service in preventing an absolu rout of Sigel's army. (MOLLUS-Ma Collection, U. S. Army Military Histc Research Collection)

Brigadier General Jeremiah C. Sullivan failed to reach New Market in time for the main battle but helped save Sigel from disaster when it was over. (MOLLUS-Mass. Collection, U. S. Army Military History Research Collection)

Captain Henry A. du Pont, whose cannon slowed the Confederate pursuit a bought Sigel time. (Courtesy of Eleut erian Mills Historical Library)

men hotly pursued, it might as well not be there at all. A
further consideration was guerrilla activity in their rear. Two
companies of the 28th Ohio had been roughly handled in a
skirmish near Strasburg when the main battle raged outside of
New Market. Sigel could hardly afford to have the enemy
separate him entirely from his base. Consequently, he ordered
Sullivan to conduct a withdrawal across the bridge to Mount
Jackson. The army would then retreat to Cedar Creek, near
Strasburg, to rest and recuperate.

Leaving du Pont on the pike on top of Rude's Hill and
moving the two new Ohio regiments to either side of it as support, Sullivan and Stahel began overseeing the army's withdrawal. Stahel commanded the over-all movement, while
Sullivan handled the rear-guard action. Here, for a change, he
acted well. Colonel Wells thought his efficiency "conspicuous,"
and even Sigel spoke of the "great skill and promptness" with
which he handled the assignment. Soon the Federals were
strewn out across a flatland called Meem's Bottom, marching
to the bridge, still badly disorganized.

Meanwhile, Breckinridge continued his advance. As he
reached the slopes of Rude's Hill, he was surprised to see the
Federal shelling stop abruptly. Wharton's skirmish line barely
got within a half mile of Sullivan's last line before it pulled out
of sight. Taking possession of Kleiser's abandoned gun, Breckinridge pushed to the summit of the hill, only to see the
remnants of Sigel's army streaming back toward the bridge,
Sullivan in the rear.

Meem's Bottom in 1700 had been the scene of a great mas-
sacre of the Senedos Indians by the Catawbas. Now it witnessed violence again as the Confederate artillery opened up
on the fleeing Yankees. They sent, thought one Federal, "a
perfect shower of shot and shell" into the retreating column.
There was some minor resistance from a few squads of Federal
cavalry, mainly a harassment to slow the pursuit while the rest
of the army crossed the river to Mount Jackson, but no more
real fighting. Breckinridge continued the pursuit, hoping to
catch the Federals before they finished crossing. Meanwhile,
he directed Berkeley to aim his fire at the bridge. "We put in

our deadliest shots as they were packing like frightened cattle across the bridge," wrote the artilleryman.

It was by then too late. Before the Confederate infantry could close up the gap, Sigel's army was all across except du Pont and a squad of cavalry. As du Pont's men prepared to destroy the bridge, he and the cavalry officer tried to outwait each other for the dubious honor of being the last man across. Finally du Pont won, and the bridge finally went up in flames. It was 7 P.M. The Battle of New Market was done.

Sigel did not halt his army until a mile north of the bridge, where he put his guns in place and allowed the men to get their first real rest since early that morning. Meanwhile he ordered Captain Town to erect an observation post to watch Breckinridge's movements on the other side of the river. The men talked of the fight and looked for those who were missing, speaking quietly of those known to be dead. Like one of Carlin's gunners, they accepted defeat manfully. "All I have to say," he declared, "is they whipped us in a fair stand up fight and the only reason that I can give for our defeat is that they fought better than our men."

Sigel was less willing to accept this verdict. At eight o'clock he telegraphed the first word of the battle to Washington. "A severe battle was fought to-day at New Market between our forces and those of Echols and Imboden, under Breckinridge. Our troops were overpowered by superior numbers." He estimated the Confederates at 8,000 to 9,000, adding that his casualties might be as high as 650 killed, wounded, and missing. Whatever the figures, he declared that he could not remain here at Mount Jackson. Enemy guerrillas were still between him and Martinsburg and he feared that Imboden might ride east of Smith's Creek again to head him off somewhere down the Valley. He would have to retreat to Cedar Creek.

The order went out at 9 P.M. The army was to march north for Edinburg. "The manner in which this chaotic mass of wagons, horsemen, artillery, and stragglers moved on . . . was exceedingly fatiguing," Colonel Moor reported. A dejected, tired, hungry Ohio boy wrote home to his mother that "it was a hard old march." The "leg" had skinned Sigel.[26]

The spirit south of the burning bridge could not have been more the opposite. People six and seven miles away could hear the cheers from thousands of victorious Confederate throats. Micajah Woods found Major McLaughlin "in very bright spirits" and as for the rest of the army, he declared that "I never saw troops in better spirits. It is the first time that many of them have ever won a victory, having served under slow coach generals in a slow coach department till Breckinridge handled them."

Stoddard Johnston heard the men giving "cheers of victory such as had not been heard in the Valley since Stonewall Jackson had led them." New Market filled with laughing soldiers, while Breckinridge sent his laconic report to Lee. "This morning two (2) miles above New Market My Command met the Enemy under Gen Siegel advancing up the Valley and defeated him with heavy loss—the action has Just closed at Shenandoah River—enemy fled across North Fork of the Shenandoah burning the bridge behind him."

But it was not a victory without a price, and New Market's doctors and the Confederate regimental surgeons would pass a hard night. Every large building available became a hospital: the Rice house and barn, New Market's Smith Creek Baptist Church which was turned into an operating room and hospital for Federal wounded, and even the Meem home at Mount Airy some miles distant. New Market's surgeons worked almost on their very doorsteps, some of them walking among the dangerously wounded still lying on the field, ministering to them with the aid of many of the town's women as nurses. More than one injured Yankee had cause this night to be thankful that Dr. Solon Henkel's surgical instruments had not been carried away that morning.

Breckinridge walked over the field in the evening twilight, talking with his wounded and with Federal prisoners. He sent his adjutant Johnston to the Cadets to offer his thanks again for their admirable conduct. Then he moved his headquarters to the home of the Reverend Socrates Henkel in order to make more room for the wounded. Like many of the men and officers, Breckinridge would get little rest that night, for when the cheers of victory died, they were replaced by the pitiable cries and screams of the wounded and dying. Colonel Edgar left his bivouac that evening to come into town and look after his wounded. Exhausted, he found a bed close by one of the improvised hospitals and lay down. But as he lay there, he said, "I saw the surgeons at their ghastly work," and he could not stay.

It was still raining. The doctors and nurses continued their work. Jessie Rupert was among them, and she felt what they all felt. "The night passed wearily away," she wrote. "There was no peace in its dark hours." All the glory of victory seemed quickly melted away in the grim aftermath of pain and death.[27]

10

"It Was a Most Brilliant Affair"

Of all the veterans at New Market the day after the battle, none felt quite the exhilaration of the newest "veterans," the Cadets. Their parents, as soon as they heard of the fight, were anxious to know how their boys behaved. The boys told them. "We gained a complete victory," said one. "I am at last a soldier for a little time," another wrote home. They were proud as could be. "The Cadets were in the centre and did nobly eliciting the greatest praise from every one." Then, of course, there were fears to quiet. "By the mercy of God I was not hurt," fifteen-year-old Charles Anderson wrote his mother, but others could not say the same. "We lost good many cadets in the fight," George Ward told his parents. The letters got more sober. "I write you a few lines," James Merritt wrote this day, "to let you know that I was wounded." And to some homes came the inevitable telegram, such as this one: CADET B STANARD WAS KILLED YESTERDAY IN FIGHT WITH SEIGLE [*sic*] NEAR NEW MARKET.

The search over the field for the wounded Cadets after the battle was heartrending. Robert Cabell found his brother William dead, his head split open by his death wound. Lieutenant Berkeley heard a boy moaning as he walked over the ground and found a Cadet crying for help for a fallen comrade whose head he cradled in his lap. The boy was dead.

Charles Anderson came across another of the dead, "lying in a fence corner as if asleep, his musket at his side."

John Wise found poor Stanard still warm after bleeding to death from a horrible leg wound. Duck Colonna and Moses Ezekiel went back over the field after Sigel's retreat looking for their friend Tom Jefferson. They found him lying on the floor of a hut, severely wounded in the chest. Ezekiel walked —shoeless—into town to get a wagon and the boys brought the wounded Cadet to the home of Lydie Clinedinst. There they were given a downstairs room and Jefferson, when laid between the clean sheets, said to Lydie, "Sister, what a good, soft bed."

He remained in that bed in his pain for two days. Then in the evening of Tuesday, May 17, Jefferson asked Ezekiel, a Jew, to read to him from the New Testament—John, Chapter Fourteen. "In my Father's house are many mansions: if it were not so, I would have told you. I go to prepare a place for you."

Then Jefferson's mind began to wander. He thought Ezekiel was his mother, then his sister. Going blind, he asked for light. "It only then dawned upon me," wrote Ezekiel, "that all hope was past and [he was] in his [death] agony." The Clinedinst family gathered, holding lit tapers while Ezekiel took the boy in his arms. "Duncan, come and light a candle," cried the dying, bewildered boy. "It is growing dark." Then he died.

The Confederate dead were brought into town on a limber chest and taken to an empty storehouse while the wounded Cadets found refuge in New Market's homes. Among the wounded were three of the five boys who dined at Carrington Taylor's home in Staunton before the battle, when Mrs. Taylor told them to take care of her son. Stanard was the fourth. Of the five, Taylor was the only one unhurt. General Francis Smith would come from the Institute in a few days for his wounded Cadets, leaving a few to recuperate in New Market while taking the rest back to Lexington. It would be some time before he knew exactly how much the Corps suffered, but it was considerable. Five boys were killed outright, and five more died later of their wounds, one of them, Corporal Samuel F. Atwill, had almost recovered when lockjaw set in.

He "died in the most excruciating agony" on July 20. Besides the dead and dying, forty-seven other members of the Corps felt the enemy's sting, their casualties in all amounting to slightly under 23 per cent of those engaged.

On the morning of May 16, the Corps of Cadets gathered in St. Matthew's cemetery to bury its dead. "It was an impressive and affecting ceremony," wrote a correspondent for the Staunton *Spectator*. As the five boys were laid beneath the sod, the writer mused that now "they rest near where they fell; and their quiet sleep will never be disturbed by the roar of battle in which they went down."[1]

The Cadets were not the only ones who had suffered. The morning after the battle, Breckinridge ordered a return made for all casualties in his army. The results revealed the price he had paid to save Staunton, New Market, and the Valley for a while. While his army for the campaign, including all of Imboden's commands, McNeill, Mosby, Gilmor and the Reserves, totaled 5,300, no more than 4,100 actually took part in the battle. Of that number, at least 531 were casualties, with the figure rising perhaps to 550, altogether slightly more than 13 per cent of those engaged. Nearly fifty men and boys lay dead.[2]

But the Confederates had made Sigel pay. He left ninety-six dead on the field and 225 men were missing, presumably taken prisoner, many of them wounded. As he marched north, he took with him another 520 wounded. In all, 841 Federals became casualties at New Market, and this, of course, did not include the men lost at Moorfield, Lost River, and New Market Gap. Sigel's losses totaled over 1,000 for the campaign. Then there were those five guns (with their ammunition chests) left on the field. Lieutenant Blain's four-gun battery was filled out with two of them, and the others would go to similarly understrength Confederate units. Some 170 horses were taken. They went to replace Confederate battery animals killed and to complete the mounting of White's 23d Virginia Cavalry, which had fought as infantry in the battle. Of course, a wealth of personal items of which the Confederate soldier was so short were left on the battleground. "The men of the army have made great and valuable captures," Lieutenant Woods wrote on May 16. "Many horses were secured and fine saddles. The earth for 7 miles was spotted with capital blankets and oil clothes, knapsacks, haversacks & notions. . . . I have secured a splendid new McClellan saddle—equipments complete—three large gun cloths—two good pairs of shoes— one pair for Bob and one for myself, and a splendid large cavalry overcoat with immense cape and extending some distance below my knees—double breasted and well finished. Some of the men have made their fortunes on the field nearby."[3]

The prisoners Breckinridge sent back to Staunton were to be taken by way of Lynchburg to prisons farther south; but an awesome problem still faced him—all those blue-coated men lying on the field and in his hospitals. "I Rode over the battel field," one of Imboden's cavalrymen wrote in his diary the morning after the fight. "The yankeys lay dead & wond[ed] & dying in abundance."

Many had been robbed during the night by citizens and soldiers alike, and all needed some kind of attention. Jessie Rupert's husband spent the whole night on the field tending the wounded and in the morning sent her a message to ask Imboden for a room somewhere in town to put them. Running through streets crowded with dead and wounded, excited townspeople, (some weeping and some laughing) dead horses, and broken-down vehicles, she found Imboden. He gave her authority to take any vacant place she could find. She located an empty warehouse, but its door was barred and nailed shut. The owner said she could not have it. The whole Confederate army was not strong enough to take it, he said. Seeing a passing squad of Confederates, she explained her plight. Its officer had his command force its way inside the warehouse. Then, after they helped her spread straw from a nearby stable over the floor, her hospital was ready for the Yankee wounded.

They came in all day, filling not only the warehouse, but the Bushong's barn and the Baptist church. New Market's loyal Southerners looked on sourly at these efforts to care for the enemy. Some women cursed Mrs. Rupert as she passed them, and one prominent matron tried to throw scalding water in her face. Food for the wounded was scarce, and medical supplies even more so; but still these Federal wounded would long remember how well they were treated by the Ruperts and others. Indeed, one of them could boast that he was brought back from the dead. Badly wounded, he was taken to the warehouse where the Ruperts gave him up for dead, calling for a cart to come for him. But then he seemed to show a bare sign of life. They gave him whiskey and water and saw "a slight flush, a perceptible breath; and the man opened his eyes." He had already been reported dead by his commander and was well on the road to recovery while his own funeral sermon was being preached at home in Massachusetts.

To aid the Federal wounded in enemy hands, Sigel on May 17 sent back a flag of truce with an ambulance loaded with medical supplies. For the dead, though, it was another matter. The morning after the battle, Breckinridge sent a courier under truce flag to Sigel, asking him to send men back to help bury the Federal dead. The defeated general refused, thus more than doubling the work for the Confederate burial parties. Breckinridge laid his own fallen to rest in St. Matthew's cemetery, along with the dead Cadets, but the townspeople refused to allow the enemy corpses to be placed there. Instead, the Confederates had to bury them outside town along the pike. It rained all day, the ground was muddy, the men were tired, and many of the dead Yankees were covered by only a few inches of soil. In a few days, further rains would wash much of it away, exposing parts of decaying bodies all along the road, and with them the terrible stench of death.[4]

Not all of the first day after the battle was so glum, however. Even while the burial details and the surgeons were at their grim work, a telegram came from Lee shortly after noon. He was still in the grip of tense battle and maneuver at Spotsylvania, but he found time to say to Breckinridge: "I offer you the thanks of this army for your victory over Genl Seigel. Press him down the vally [*sic*] & if practicable follow him into

Maryland." Immediately Breckinridge published the note for his men. The victory, he said, was "due only to them."

The fight of May 15 was one of considerable interest to the people of Virginia. The first accounts of the battle were written the very next day, and they began to appear in the newspapers on May 17, continuing for several weeks afterward. The accolades were everywhere enthusiastic. "We had the pleasure to witness in the fight," Wartmann wrote in his editorial plural, "displays of courage and coolness under a severe fire, which won for those who participated in the conflict immortal honor." A Staunton journal said: "It was quite a glorious little fight." The Richmond papers, of course, affected a more aloof, reserved attitude than those in the backwoods Shenandoah. The *Whig* told its readers that "you can put this down in the usual chapter of our Spring successes."

The plaudits were welcome; but Breckinridge, even with his victory, found that he had little time for them. He was needed elsewhere. Hard upon his congratulatory telegram from Lee came another one. Lee would still prefer that Breckinridge follow Sigel into Maryland to create a diversion which might cause Grant to weaken his army at Spotsylvania. However, should this prove impracticable—and the burning of the Shenandoah bridge effectively cut off an immediate pursuit—Lee could use Breckinridge's infantry and artillery with his own army. With the threat to the Valley checked for the time being, the Kentuckian could organize a guard to stay behind and take his main body east via Staunton and the Virginia Central Railroad.

This, Breckinridge decided, should be his course, and he started on it immediately. After ordering Gilmor to follow the retreating Federals and harass them where possible, he directed Ship to report to Imboden henceforward, stating that he hoped the Cadets could be relieved from further service and sent back to their classrooms. Then late in the afternoon, barely twenty-four hours after he climaxed one campaign in Sigel's rout from Bushong's, Breckinridge got in a buggy with his adjutant, Johnston, and left for Staunton to organize yet another.[5]

Good news came to Staunton on May 17. The Federals had been well repulsed back in his department. "They have utterly failed to accomplish their object," Jackson reported, and General McCausland told him matter-of-factly that "our movements may be considered successful." Averell and Crook were both retiring. This now relieved the other threat to the Valley, which only confirmed Lee's designs for coming east. The Kentuckian determined to move as soon as possible. Imboden would be the Valley guard, assisted by the Reserves. With infantry at a premium, though, he would take Smith's 62d Virginia with him. Echols and Wharton left New Market at 5 A.M. May 17, reaching Staunton the next day.

They had a victory on their records now, and they walked proud of it. Their confidence went with them when they left the Valley. It was a fast march and hard. Patton passed "The Meadows," where his wife and children were staying, coming within fifty paces of her as she watched the column moving toward Staunton. But he could not stop. All he could do was wave his hat and throw her a note. He wrote to her of the battle at New Market and told her with pride that "it was a most brilliant affair."

On May 19 Breckinridge put his army on flatcars at Staunton depot and traveled east to Hanover Junction, north of Richmond. The people of the Valley were saddened at his leaving. Some even questioned the wisdom of his being ordered to Lee after having saved the Shenandoah. They had lost Stonewall Jackson to Lee; why now must their new savior be taken from them? Those like Imboden who understood Lee's needs were more resigned, if not sanguine, at the Kentuckian's departure. "May new honors crown you in all the future, is the sincere hope of myself and little command, whose hearts you have so completely won," Imboden wrote Breckinridge on the day he left New Market. Even greater compliments awaited.

When the general reached Hanover Junction, he found that Lee's veterans cheered him whenever he went. "The celerity with which he had moved and the thoroughness with which he had accomplished the purposes to which he was assigned,"

Johnston would write, "evoked the greatest applause throughout all Virginia."

It came even from Lee himself. On May 22 he came to Breckinridge's headquarters to thank him in person. The Kentuckian had justified entirely the trust and independence given him, and Lee was well pleased. But there was more than compliments to discuss at this meeting. Grant, stymied at Spotsylvania, was sending a corps toward Hanover Junction to renew the fight on new ground. Lee and Breckinridge must be ready. There were more battles to come.[6]

Of all the cheering done in the Valley after the battle of May 15, there was precious little heard between New Market and Cedar Creek. Sigel's retreat in defeat was as painful an experience as anything his soldiers had known. In passing through Edinburg, they learned of Averell's partial success in disrupting rail communications in southwestern Virginia. Strother, as he watched Sigel's precipitate retreat, quipped playfully, "We are doing a good business in this department. Averell is tearing up the Virginia and Tennessee Railroad while Sigel is tearing down the Valley turnpike."

It was a jibe that became popular throughout the Union, but Sigel did not approve. "By gar," he reportedly exclaimed when one of his staff repeated it to him, "I vill not haff beoples zayin' dem kind o' tings! By gar, I pelief dere are beoples on mein staff who are not griefed to zee me dearin' down de 'pike! By gar, Colonel Strodare must not zay dem kind o' tings, or he veel be court-martial!"

Whether he liked it or not, though, there was no doubt that Sigel was tearing down the pike. Indeed, the pace of his retreat was the only speed he displayed in the whole campaign. Where it took him five days to march thirty-two miles from Strasburg to New Market, he now used only twenty-two hours in returning to the same place. He arrived at 5 P.M., May 16, and took his shattered army into camp across Cedar Creek the next morning.

Once safe on the north side of the creek, Sigel told his superiors in Washington that, though beaten when "greatly outnumbered," the troops were in fine spirits and he would be ready to meet the enemy again should he be attacked here. If Breckinridge should withdraw, then he would advance again. Meanwhile, he sent scouting parties in all directions. Some he tried to infiltrate into the Confederate camp at New Market to gather information, but most went out to make sure his line of retreat to Martinsburg was secure. In every campaign, it seemed, Sigel planned his retreat first. Only when he was safe at Strasburg did he send south medical supplies for the scores of his wounded left in enemy hands and those who had fallen out during the withdrawal. "Our wounded were abandoned and left without any surgeons in the enemy's hands," Captain du Pont wrote to his father the day the army reached its Cedar Creek camp, "which is pretty much on a par with everything else under the present regime."

To those few of his wounded that he brought with him, Sigel could offer few condolences. "Boys," he said to them, "we got a little the worst of it this time, but will fight them again."

Opinions varied widely in his broken army as to what had happened to them. All agreed that it had been a tough fight. "I have been present at all the battles in the Valley of Virginia," wrote one soldier, "but this was the hardest fought battle I have yet witnessed . . . it really baffles description."

Sigel himself would later admit that "the battle of New Market was fairly won by the enemy." But there was much discussion among his soldiers about Sigel's own conduct of the campaign and battle. "The soldiers in this command are highly pleased with the Gen'l. Commanding, and all seem glad of an opportunity to *'fight mit Sigel,'*" a man of the 1st West Virginia wrote three days after the fight.

Of course, Sigel's own close supporters said what was expected of them. Michael Graham, one of his lobbyists wrote to a friendly source, "The troops engaged, all speak highly of the coolness of Gen Sigel, and also his consummate bravery, and laud him highly for his watchfulness of every point, and affecting his movements to his present position, and all the time moving in the most perfect order, and at no time losing any part of his organization." The stragglers and disorganized companies that hobbled in to camp at Cedar Creek during the next several days might have disputed Graham's claim.

Most reactions in the ranks were a bit less fullsome in their praise. "We have had another whack at the rebs and found them too strong and had to get back," one Connecticut boy wrote. The search for blame led to several of Sigel's senior officers but, as one soldier said, "thare is so much stuff a Flote thare is no dependance to be put in what you hear."

Still, those in a position to have seen the over-all management of the Shenandoah Valley operations knew the culprit. Some time later Colonel Thoburn, and other officers would claim that "their bad fortune" was due entirely to Sigel's shabby generalship. Strother agreed. "The campaign was conducted miserably by Sigel," he wrote in his diary. "Sigel is merely a book soldier acquainted with the techniques of the art of war but having no capacity to fight with troops in the field. For the rest he is given to detail and littleness and without comprehensiveness and is entirely below the commission which he bears." Moor believed that only the rain and the muddy fields hampering the pursuit saved Sigel's army. Disillusioned soldiers on the retreat back to Strasburg sang a new song, "We fights no more mit Sigel."[7]

Indeed, it began to look as if Sigel would fight no more with anyone. The first reports of the battle reaching the North were sketchy, little better than rumors. On May 18 the New York *Tribune* carried the headline: SIGEL WHIPS THE REBELS AT NEW-MARKET. Then more reliable information came from the Valley, and when the details of the story were known, a new quip, "Who runs mit Sigel?" began going the rounds. However, Union authorities in Washington saw no humor at all in the affair. Major General Henry Halleck, received the first rumors of Sigel's defeat at 10:40 P.M., May 17, and confirmation came shortly thereafter. Only a few hours earlier, Grant had asked Halleck to order Sigel to go on from Woodstock to Staunton, entirely unaware of his advance from Woodstock just two days before. Then, "just when I was hoping to hear of good work being done in the valley," Grant wrote, Halleck sent him the news of Sigel's defeat. "Instead of advancing on Staunton,"

Halleck telegraphed to him near midnight, "he is already in full retreat on Strasburg. If you expect anything from him you will be mistaken. He will do nothing but run. He never did anything else."

Grant was furious. He, Halleck, and Secretary of War Stanton all agreed that Sigel must be replaced. When Halleck proposed Major General David Hunter, Grant replied: "By all means I would say appoint General Hunter, or anyone else, to the command of West Virginia." On May 19 the War Department made it official. Hunter would replace Sigel.

The German received the word at Cedar Creek from friends in Washington that same night: he was out. Two days later, at sunset, Hunter reached Cedar Creek and rode up to Sigel's headquarters at the Hite house. Sigel was absent at the time, but Hunter's cousin, Strother, greeted the new general. While rumors quickly spread through the camps, the two walked arm in arm, discussing the recent past and the operations to come. "I have come to relieve General Sigel," Hunter said. "You know it is customary with a general who has been unfortunate, to relieve him whether he has committed a fault or not." When finally Sigel returned after dark, he found Hunter sitting on the Hite porch. They shook hands and then went inside. At 7 P.M. Hunter assumed command.

In the North the change was received as "a vast improvement on Sigel," and few in the army at Cedar Creek disagreed. Strother was more blunt. "We can afford to lose such a battle as New Market," he said, "to get rid of such a mistake as Major General Sigel."

But Sigel himself was crestfallen. His health had deteriorated since the battle, and this blow had left him stunned. When Strother called on him on May 22, he found that "the tears were standing in his eyes and his lips were quivering. He said it were better to have died on that battlefield than to have suffered this disgrace. . . . The General seems entirely brokenhearted and refused to be comforted." To his wife, Sigel confided that "I have been really miserable."[8]

Hunter found his new command "utterly demoralized and stampeded" in the wake of the defeat, "and the three generals with it, Sigel, Stahel, and Sullivan, not worth one cent, in fact, very much in my way." For the time being, however, he was stuck with them.

To Sigel, entitled to some consideration as an ousted commander, Hunter offered a choice of commands. He could have the cavalry division, the infantry division, or the reserve division back at Harpers Ferry. Sigel did not wish to depose Stahel from his cavalry command, and his relations with Sullivan were still "unsettled" to the point that he did not want to supercede him. So he took the reserve command, a move which, incidentally, bumped Kelley from its command.

Meanwhile, his standing suffered even more as Hunter began uncovering the nefarious financial dealings of the civilian speculators which the German had kept about his headquarters. "I thought," said one of the officers at Martinsburg, "that they were thieves and plunderers." Hunter's new adjutant, Major Charles Halpine, agreed. "The fact is," he wrote, "Sigel appears no soldier, but is entirely in the hands of one Robbins, a citizen trader." This Robbins was exposed now, and would leave with Sigel, soon to be ordered away from the department entirely. Dejected, Sigel wrote to his wife that "I have no enthusiasm for relying on the good words and works of friends. You know certainly how they are and how easily they forget."

On May 23 Sigel and Robbins boarded a buggy and left Cedar Creek for Harpers Ferry. Looking on, Halpine could only "wish to Heaven Stahel were with him." That same day, the Wheeling, West Virginia, press, charging Sigel with gross incompetence, issued its own verdict on the past campaign: "Let us have no more political appointments in this war."

As always, in Sigel's mind the failures of the campaign had not been his. They were the work of his enemies, the same enemies who now tried to lay the responsibility at his feet. But he was confident. "The charges against me will soon be silenced," he wrote his wife, "and public opinion will finally mete out justice to me."

To help public opinion do this, Sigel and his friends began their campaign to vindicate him even before he left

Cedar Creek. A letter-writing assault of considerable proportions went into action, getting results through publication in
several influential newspapers. They stressed what terrible
shape the department was in when Sigel took command,
claiming that the Confederates gained "no advantage of any
kind" from New Market. "The Rebels no doubt, will claim a
victory," Graham wrote for the press, "but in my opinion it
is a victory to the Federals."

The letter writers claimed that Sigel must have battered
Breckinridge badly, else why did the Confederates not pursue?
It seemed to matter little to them that Sigel's burning the Shenandoah bridge made pursuit impossible. Citing Sigel's "consummate skill," one of his cronies even claimed that "his
comprehensive strategic plan was one of the best devised and
most successfully executed of the war."

Sigel himself took a hand. Through the efforts of Captain
Thomas Putnam of his staff, he had hoped to get one of the
officers formerly under his command to write a stirring defense, even trying Strother, who refused. Failing in this, Sigel
wrote it himself in the form of an anonymous letter to the
Congressional Committee on the Conduct of the War and had
a copy of it given to a New York *Herald* correspondent who
was told only that it came from "an officer high in rank." There
followed, in the third person, an extremely laudatory account
of Sigel's management of the campaign, laced with equivoca-
tion and half truths. He claimed that his capture of Breckinridge's telegraphic correspondence at Woodstock decided him
to go on to Mount Jackson to "give him battle," when, in fact,
Sigel had telegraphed Washington after finding the dispatches,
claiming that he was not strong enough to go farther and
would remain in Woodstock. He really did not decide to move
to Mount Jackson until late May 14, after hearing good reports
from Moor. And so it went, right down to his absurd claim that,
after the retreat, he was "ready to fight another battle the next
day." How Breckinridge was supposed to get to him with the
bridge burned remains a mystery. Complaining that his movements had been largely directed from outside the department
and that he had been forced to take a small command in order

to assist his inferior officers, Sigel concluded this incognito defense with the judgment that his defeat was "a misfortune, which was, after all, not principally his own fault."

Sigel sent friends to Washington to lobby and spy for him at the War Department and in the Capitol. One supporter promised to meet with prominent persons, German and American, to speak to every meeting possible, to get the papers to publish "the naked facts," and do anything else necessary. "The reaction *will* take place," he promised Sigel, "& will be in your favor."

Reports came to Sigel that "the grossest misrepresentations of facts" were made and believed in Washington and that Halleck and Stanton seemed to be influencing the people adversely. Trying to shift attention from Sigel, his friends began to accuse others, like Kelley, of disloyalty. Sigel himself, in his desperation, began to believe that even Halleck was a traitor to the Northern cause. "In his very soul an enemy to truly republican and popular institutions," Sigel said of Halleck, he would "*give aid and comfort to our enemies.*"

It might have occurred to many that the best way for Halleck to give aid and comfort to the Rebellion would be to put Sigel in command of another Union army.

The clamor raised by Sigel and his friends kept him afloat awhile longer, but only long enough for him to sink himself. His appointment to the reserve division met little enthusiasm in the army, and it soon became no secret that Hunter did not want him at all. "It seems," Sigel wrote his wife, "that Hunter cannot stand the 'foreigners.'"

When Hunter left at the end of May on his own campaign up the Valley, Sigel was left behind with his reserves at Martinsburg. In July, when Confederate Lieutenant General Jubal A. Early marched down the Valley on his celebrated raid on Washington, he sent an advance force of cavalry toward Martinsburg. On July 3, receiving word of the advance of this party, Sigel panicked. Though, all told, he had nearly 10,000 troops at his command, he began an immediate withdrawal with barely a show of resistance. Behind him in Martinsburg he left huge quantities of stores for the Confederates. It would have galled him to know that the Rebels who occupied the town and feasted on his leavings were the men of the newly formed corps of Early's army, commanded by none other than Major General John C. Breckinridge, who had joined Early at Lynchburg, Virginia, two weeks before. It was, wrote a disgusted Halpine, "beyond any doubt the most disgraceful affair of the war."

When the news of it reached Grant, it was all over for the German. On July 7 Grant wrote to Halleck that "all of General Sigel's operations from the beginning of the war have been so unsuccessful that I think it advisable to relieve him from all duty, at least until present troubles are over. I do not feel certain at any time that he will not after abandoning stores, artillery and trains, make a successful retreat to some place."

That same day the War Department relieved Sigel from field command indefinitely. "My good friends all seem to have hidden themselves away in mouseholes," Sigel wrote his wife. At last the Lincoln administration would put up with no more from him, even at the risk of offending the German element. "We have now paid rather dearly for that 'element,'" lamented Halpine.

Sigel finished out the war in New York and Washington, "awaiting orders" like so many other shelved generals. Finally, on May 4, 1865, he resigned his commission. "We are certainly living," he wrote his wife, "and perhaps we can still enjoy our lives."

In 1867 he moved permanently to New York and took part in an ill-fated land development company before being made a commissioner of the Hudson River West Shore Railroad. He became a vice president of it the next year but resigned to make an unsuccessful bid for secretary of state of New York. In 1871, at the request of President Grant, he served on the commission which investigated the possible purchase of the republic of Santo Domingo. Thereafter, he held a series of minor appointive offices under Republican and then—after he switched his party allegiance—Democratic Presidents.

Meanwhile, Sigel remained a fervent champion of the German-American, lecturing widely. In addition to a few articles on his wartime experiences, he also began work on his autobiography, but it remained unfinished at his death on August 21, 1902. Loyal to him to the end and despite the military shortcomings they had grown accustomed to ignoring, his German friends erected a magnificent equestrian statue of him on Riverside Drive in Manhattan. Many thought it ridiculous that such a failure should have such an effigy but, in fact, it was peculiarly fitting. To all outward appearances, the bronze casting was, like Sigel, grand in appearance, with all the trappings and mannerisms of a great general. Inside, however, it was perfectly hollow.[9]

The aftermath of New Market proved just as hard on many of Sigel's officers in the campaign as it was on him. Captain Ewing was arrested for spreading "rumors." Jacob Weddle, commanding the 1st West Virginia, was dismissed from the service less than a month after his regiment's bad showing at New Market. Poor Captain Kleiser was captured at Buford's Gap, Virginia, on June 20, not to be released until the following March. The War Department tried to levy a judgment of $625 against Kleiser's pay for the disabled gun left on the field in front of Rude's Hill until evidence was obtained showing that he was not to blame. General Sullivan, like Sigel, soon found himself "awaiting orders," until he, too, resigned, living out his days in California. For Colonel Wells of the 34th Massachusetts and his brigade commander, Colonel Joseph Thoburn, death awaited in the Valley. Both would be killed near Cedar Creek in October 1864.

For others, though, the coming years were good ones. Colonels Moor, Campbell, Curtis, and Strother would all receive brevet promotions to brigadier at war's end, while Colonel Tibbits received a commission as a full brigadier general of volunteers. Captain du Pont would win the Medal of Honor before the war's end and later serve two terms in the United States Senate. General Stahel, too, received the Medal of Honor, though that was the only bright spot for him after New Market. Almost immediately Hunter became dissatisfied with him. "It would be impossible to exaggerate the inefficiency of General Stahel," he complained to Halleck.

Still, Stahel was with him on June 5 at the Battle of Piedmont, in the Valley north of Staunton, and, leading a charge while badly wounded, won his medal. But that ended the fighting war for him. Hunter liked him even less than he liked Sigel. A few days after the battle, when Sigel's own relief seemed imminent after the Martinsburg fiasco, Stahel said to him sadly: "Heute dir, morgen mir"—"Today for you, tomorrow for me."

Stahel's relief came on July 12, and thereafter, until his resignation from the army on February 6, 1865, he served on court-martial duty. Halpine felt sorry for the likable Hungarian when he left, but knew it was best for the service: "He has not hair enough." Stahel later won a consular appointment to Yokohama and was somewhat successful in opening new Japanese ports to American trade. He then spent several years at unsuccessful mining in the West, and re-entered the Consular Service to serve in the Orient until 1885, when he resigned as consul-general at Shanghai and returned to New York. He lived there the rest of his life, a confirmed bachelor. In his last years, he was a permanent fixture in his hotel lobby, a sad, lonely, white-haired old man known to everyone as "the general." He died on December 4, 1912.[10]

But bad as things were for some of the Union officers after New Market, they were in some instances worse for the Confederates. The engaging editor of the *Rockingham Register,* J. H. Wartmann, who "'skedaddled' when a shell burst near us" in the battle, continued publishing until Hunter's advancing army took his office in Harrisonburg and broke up his type in June. "An act of premature vandalism," Halpine termed it. Wartmann got the paper in operation again as soon as possible, only to have his office destroyed once more by Federals in October. To his credit, he never quit.

Breckinridge ordered Harman's reserves disbanded in June, but not until after they had performed well at Piedmont under Imboden. Shortly afterward, broken down by typhoid, General Imboden was posted to South Carolina on less strenuous duty, returning to Virginia after the war to begin developing the coal resources of the state's southwestern counties. It was he who first discovered the coking qualities of vast bituminous deposits here, whose main seam would one day be called the "Imboden Seam." He also founded the small coal town of Damascus, where he died, on August 15, 1895.

Colonel George H. Smith served out the war in the Valley and, when the surrender came, joined the thousands of Confederates who moved to Mexico in search of a new home. When his cotton planting dreams failed there, he moved back to Los Angeles to begin a distinguished legal career. A commissioner of the California supreme court and a justice of the district court of appeal, he later won election to the American and British Philosophical Societies. His essays on the theory of the state were credited with helping to turn Great Britain from the "will of the state" to the "higher law" theory of jurisprudence. Smith died, respected and revered, on February 6, 1915.

Another of Imboden's sometime subordinates achieved much greater renown. Colonel Mosby became a living legend in the last year of the war, and in the years to follow, the legend grew. His fellow guerrilla Captain McNeill seemed well on his way to the same fame until October 3, 1864, when, attacking a Union wagon train near Mount Jackson, he took a mortal wound.

Lieutenant Blain landed in a hospital with a shell burn only two weeks after New Market, and the twenty-four-year-old Captain Chapman was killed at Winchester in September. Colonel Wolfe of the 51st Virginia Infantry was killed at Leetown, West Virginia, in July 1864, the regiment later surrendering at Waynesborough, Virginia, in March 1865 after being overwhelmed by Federal cavalry. General Wharton, the brigade commander, escaped the Waynesborough debacle, only to surrender at Lynchburg a few months later. He spent the remainder of his life after the war developing the mineral resources of southwestern Virginia. He died on May 12, 1906, and was buried wrapped in the regimental colors of his old outfit, the 51st Virginia.

Breckinridge's other brigade commander, General Echols, became sick a week after the battle and had to turn his command over to Colonel Patton. Though rarely well thereafter,

Echols still managed to live up to Colonel Edgar's estimate of him as a good organizer by brilliantly putting together an army out of practically nothing to turn back a raid against Saltville in October. Echols finished the war as part of the escort of the fleeing President Davis and afterward put his organizational talents to excellent use in helping found the Chesapeake & Ohio Railroad. He died in Staunton on May 24, 1896.

All Echols' regimental commanders felt the enemy's bite. Colonel Derrick was captured the very day that he arrived at Hanover Junction. Edgar, whom Breckinridge called "a fine little officer," was wounded by a bayonet at Cold Harbor in June and later captured at Winchester.

The capable Colonel Patton, most promising of all of them, almost made brigadier. He had applied for the promotion when he took over command from Echols, and both Wharton and Breckinridge heartily concurred. "Col. Patton is an officer of high merit," Breckinridge told the War Department. Finally, in September, it appears that a commission was issued for him and sent on its way. By the time it arrived Patton was dead, killed by a shell fragment at the Battle of Winchester.

Interestingly enough, Patton's cousin George H. Smith would marry his widow in 1870, to bring up Patton's children proud in the memory of their dead father. One of those children, George, was just nine years old when Patton was killed. When he grew to manhood he, too, would father a son, George S. Patton, who would attend V.M.I., then West Point, to become a full general in command of the Third Army in World War II, a dashing officer and one of the foremost soldiers of modern times. As if to bring the Patton story full circle, the general would have a grandson born on May 15, 1947, the anniversary of an earlier Patton's triumph at New Market.

Captain Woodson, too, came full circle. After the battle, what was left of his cavalry command fought with Breckinridge and Lee for a time, being the only organized body of Missouri troops in the Army of Northern Virginia. Then they came back to the Valley, assigned to serve with Major Gilmor. Woodson did not like riding for the erratic guerrilla, but bore it until the end. Fittingly, this tiny unit, which suffered proportionately more than any other in the battle for New Market, came back to this little Shenandoah town in April 1865 to surrender.[11]

The V.M.I. Cadets? They buried their dead and, three days later, marched back to Staunton, treated royally all along the way. "The people of the Valley of Virginia owe these gallant soldiers a debt of gratitude which they can never repay," wrote Wartmann. Once in Staunton, they finally received their new battle flag, and hard upon it came orders to report to Richmond. With Grant moving on the capital, Lee needed everyone available. The Cadets could guard the city and relieve veterans for the front. More than trenches awaited the Cadets. By the time they arrived, word of their exploit at New Market had spread through Richmond. A resolution of thanks for their "gallant conduct in the battle of the 15 inst." passed the Confederate House of Representatives unanimously on May 23, and the Cadets received in person the congratulations of Governor William Smith of Virginia and President Davis.

After serving in Richmond for a few days, the Cadets went back to the Valley to help stem the new Federal advance under General Hunter. In early June, in the wake of the Confederate rout at Piedmont, Virginia, the Cadets were driven from Lexington and the V.M.I. barracks and other buildings were burned down by Union troops, an act which even Hunter's staff condemned. The Cadets returned to Richmond's lines in September and set up classes in the city's almshouse. They would stay here in the capital until its fall on April 2, 1865, when, for them, the war came to an end.

Colonel Ship made a career of the Institute, changing his name to Shipp, and becoming superintendent in 1890. In his years there he saw the growth and blossoming of the New Market tradition and legend. Shortly after the battle, General Meem kindly offered to donate a piece of his estate near New Market as a burial ground for the dead Cadets, adding that he would put up "a handsome monument" to them at his own expense. But the Institute declined. V.M.I. was a more suitable place for the fallen heroes, but they had to wait for the war's end. In May 1866 a detail of Cadets went to New Market to escort the remains of the five boys buried there to Lexington. Former Cadet Moses Ezekiel, later known as Sir Moses and a world-renowned sculptor, would create a monument, "Virginia Mourning Her Dead," to rest over them. Year after year ceremonies would take place on the battle's anniversary, commemorating the bravery and sacrifice of the ten who died and the rest who fought and bled for the Valley and Virginia. With every passing year the exploits of the Corps of Cadets would grow in the veterans' fading memories and in the burgeoning imaginations of others. Soon it was not just one gun that they captured; it was Kleiser's whole battery. It was forgotten that they were ordered into the gap on Bushong's Hill; their own natural instincts led them into it. Indeed, as time passed, the participation of 5,000 other Confederates in this campaign was almost lost to history. The Cadets seemed almost to have won the battle by themselves. The Richmond *Whig*, a few days after the battle, had exclaimed that "their noble conduct on this occasion will live in history and be immortalized in song." More than that, it would live in legend.

The growth of myths and tales could never cloud the brilliance of what the Corps of Cadets *did* do. They fought like men. They held a critical post in a wavering line and stood their ground, to be in the forefront in the final charge. They did not win the battle, but it could not have been won as it was without them. Even their enemies were impressed. Colonel Lincoln of the 34th Massachusetts and other Federals spoke often around their campfires of the boys' charge. One Pennsylvanian, seeing their charge, resolved to send his son to V.M.I. and wound up sending two. Thirty years after the fight, one of Captain du Pont's lieutenants would come to V.M.I. to hold the chair of military science and tactics. It was du Pont himself, as a United States senator, who sponsored Federal legislation to provide an appropriation to reimburse V.M.I. for the cost of rebuilding the barracks and other buildings destroyed by Hunter and his men.

The Cadet Corps of 1864 passed on a rich heritage. Cadet Robert Cabell, brother of the dead William, became the father of the eminent Southern novelist James Branch Cabell. Cadet

William C. Hardy, first lieutenant of Company A, later became the uncle of General Douglas MacArthur of World War II fame. Cadet Thomas S. Martin one day sat in the United States Senate as Democratic majority leader and authored Joint Resolution No. 1 in April 1917, the declaration of war against the Central Powers. Cadet Ezekiel, of course, achieved worldwide fame as a sculptor; but when World War I caught him in Rome, he set his tools aside to help organize the American-Italian Red Cross. Cadet John S. Wise achieved considerable distinction as an attorney but, in another capacity, left an even more lasting legacy: one of the finest personal narratives to come out of the war. *The End of an Era* was a classic from the date it was first published, in 1899, and remains so, not only as a memorial to the Cadets in their finest hour but also to the Confederate soldier as well, and to the infant nation they fought to preserve.

Every May 15, at V.M.I., certain Cadets are selected for a special duty. Assigned to take the part of the ten New Market Cadets who were killed outright or received mortal wounds in the battle, they stand with the rest of the Corps for the roll call. It is a special roll this day, with ten extra names—Cabell, Atwill, Crockett, Hartsfield, Haynes, Jefferson, Jones, McDowell, Stanard, Wheelwright. As each of these names is called, as though an echo of a roll a century before, one of the ten selected Cadets steps forward two paces, salutes, and makes his report: "Died on the field of honor."[12]

Breckinridge's connection with the Cadets and V.M.I. lasted long after their brief association in the campaign. Brave little Charlie Faulkner served on his staff in later operations in the Valley in 1864. Walter Johnson and Clay Stacker rode with him in the escort he commanded for Jefferson Davis and the Confederate Cabinet as they fled through Georgia in May 1865. During his years of self-imposed exile in Europe, Breckinridge frequently encountered members of the New Market Corps of Cadets and was often asked to tell the story of their fight. In March 1869 he came to Lexington on his return to the United States and spent a few days with General Lee, then president of Washington College. Breckinridge also visited V.M.I., renewing his acquaintance with Ship and General Francis Smith, and viewing an entirely new Corps. They were still fine boys, he said, "and the general demeanor . . . at the Military Institute [appears] to me to be creditable to all concerned."

Late that same year his son Cabell, his aide in the New Market fight, married Sallie Johnson, sister of Cadet Private Francis Johnson who cried and begged to be taken along when he was one of those detailed to stay behind in May 1864 to guard the Institute. Years later the general's grandson, James Carson Breckinridge, married the daughter of Cadet Private Augustus P. Thompson, who had served with Captain Minge's battery during the battle. Their children enjoyed the curious distinction, then, of being descended both from the commander and the commanded at New Market.

It was always with reluctance that Breckinridge talked of the New Market battle and his order to send in the Cadets. "I pleaded with him to tell it to me many times," wrote Colonel Bennett Young of Morgan's cavalry, "and he always did it with reluctance. Invariably, irresistibly, the tear would start in his eye and sadness overspread his face when he recalled the scenes of that memorable day in May, 1864." For the rest of his life, the boys of the New Market Corps remained in Breckinridge's heart and memory as "my cadets."

Yet, reluctance or no, the general could be proud of what he brought about at New Market. His management of the campaign and battle had been masterful. He marched faster and farther than his enemy, kept all of his troops together despite poor transportation and put his full force into action in a battle which he planned in the morning and which—with the exception of the wavering on Bushong's Hill—never left his control for the rest of the day. The brilliant work of Imboden and the partisans played upon Sigel's fears and pared him down by 1,000 men or more, and Breckinridge, though still heavily outnumbered, did the rest.

Despite the later claims on behalf of the Cadets and Colonel Edgar's own claims for the 26th Battalion, there was no one "decisive" unit at New Market. They were all decisive. Without any one of the commands present, east or west of the pike, Sigel's or Stahel's charges would have enjoyed overwhelming chances for success. Breckinridge needed every soldier that he had. Thus, as with the Cadets, while no one regiment or battalion "won" the fight, it could not have been won without any one of them, except the Augusta-Rockingham Reserves whose value in a battle was open to question to the point that the general seems never to have considered putting them into the fray. This is how close he played his hand, and how close he stood to defeat throughout his day-long attack.

Still, if the search for particular credit is persistent enough, it will yield results, and something of a surprise. At the time of the battle, and for a century afterward, chief attention focused on the fight west of the pike—the infantry charges, the hot fighting on Bushong's Hill, and the capture of the Federal artillery. But in fact, the Confederate victory was decided on the pike and east of it, the principal architects of the triumph were Patton's 22d Virginia, to a lesser extent Derrick's 23d Virginia, and Breckinridge with his magnificent guns. Patton's and Derrick's men, spread thin, successfully withstood that most terrifying of assaults to an infantryman, a mounted charge. More than that, they threw it into disarray, turning it into a rout. No matter how strong a position Sigel's infantry had on Bushong's Hill or how weak the Confederate line opposite it might have been, once Stahel's cavalry division was beaten back, Sigel's line was indefensible, as shown when Patton turned and began firing on the exposed flank of the 54th Pennsylvania. Stahel's rout opened the pike to the Confederates, and with it the Federal rear, leaving Sigel no choice but withdrawal.

The ferocity of the fighting in this area east of the pike was intense, despite its short duration. A Confederate walking north on the pike the day after the battle counted more than twice as many dead Federals east of it than there were to the west. Obviously, Patton's flank fire and the double canister from the Confederate artillery did terrible work here, salvaging victory from potential disaster.

Major McLaughlin's artillery, under Breckinridge's personal

supervision during most of the fight, played a more important role in the over-all fight than any other command present. At different times during the battle it seemed to be almost everywhere, and the general's use of it, running the guns up with the advancing infantry and making it, as Johnston said, "almost a skirmish line of artillery," was truly innovative. There is copious testimony from the Federals as to the Confederate artillery's effect. It knocked one Federal gun from the fight, kept the others so occupied that their full force was never turned on Breckinridge's advancing infantry, played a key role in repulsing Stahel's cavalry, and seriously disturbed the left and center of Sigel's infantry in its assault. There was not another battle of this size in the war in which the maneuvering and firing of cannon played so important a part in the outcome.

The men and officers who fought under Breckinridge never forgot the glory the Kentuckian brought them at New Market. "I have always thought," wrote Henry Wise in after years, "Breckinridge deserves great credit for the excellent manner in which he arranged his command and had led his troops in the fight. . . . Breckinridge's confidence, celerity, and pluck, it seems to me, utterly destroyed Sigel's ability to plan his movements and to direct his troops in action."

Edgar agreed. "I have always regarded the New Market fight as the best planned and best managed fight in which I was engaged," he would say. "General Breckinridge had few if any superiors on the field of battle."

General Echols said thirteen years after the battle, "As a hard and desperate fighter, and successful manager of his command when actually engaged in battle, he had few if any superiors in either army."

As for the outcome of the battle itself, the officers were equally emphatic. Lieutenant Woods called it "our glorious and decisive victory." General Wharton regarded it as "one of the most decisive and important small engagements of the war," and General Imboden declared that "there was no secondary battle of the war of more importance than that of New Market." The somewhat partisan Stoddard Johnston claimed, "It was not excelled by any feat of the war," and others agreed. "Breckinridge had gained, all things considered, the most brilliant victory of the war," Gilmor wrote barely more than a year after the battle.

It seems that their enemies agreed with them. Major Lang would always speak of "the splendid handling of the entire force of the Confederates." Indeed, it was so splendid that one Federal cavalry officer, Lieutenant Francis Wyneken, disgusted at the rout of his comrades at New Market, secured his discharge from the Federal service and later asked Breckinridge for a place on his staff if the South should ever renew its fight for independence!

Authorities in Richmond recognized the value of the triumph. Secretary of War Seddon declared it a "signal victory," and Lee told Breckinridge that his success was "of great importance." Clearly, no one doubted that the Kentuckian had earned his $400-a-month major general's pay for May.[13]

New Market did, in fact, have far-reaching impact on the war in Virginia, an importance much beyond what the numbers involved might seem to indicate. Most immediately, it saved the Valley, and particularly Staunton, for the Confederates for three weeks—tremendously important weeks. It allowed enough time to begin the harvest of the Valley wheat crops that Lee needed to feed his army. They were weeks when Lee was so hard pressed by Grant that he could not also withstand an enemy attack from Staunton nor the disruption of his communications with the Valley via the Virginia Central Railroad. Most important, they were weeks during which, had Breckinridge been defeated and the Shenandoah left wide open to the invader, no troops could have been spared from the Army of Northern Virginia for its defense. However, by the end of those three weeks, when a new Federal threat to the Valley appeared, Lee was in a position to send reinforcements. Finally, by sending Sigel tearing back down the pike, Breckinridge freed his own two brigades to go east to join Lee, where they would be instrumental in early June at Cold Harbor in repulsing the heaviest infantry assaults ever made by Grant.

Speaking of the victory at New Market, one of Sigel's officers declared that it was "within bounds to say that it made a difference to General Grant . . . of over twenty thousand men"—the army routed at the battle, the men lost fighting Breckinridge's additional troops with Lee, and the reinforcements necessary to send Hunter up the Shenandoah Valley. "Seldom," wrote Douglas Southall Freeman, pre-eminent student of Lee and his army, "did a small victory have so large an effect."

Inevitably, Virginians got around to making comparisons. Breckinridge had shown "unflagging energy," they said, " 'old Breck' was most gallant," "Breckinridge has been at work," and so on. It was only a short step, and two days, before they sought in him a reincarnation of their gallant champion, Stonewall Jackson. "Stonewall Jackson and Turner Ashby [who commanded Jackson's cavalry] had made that beautiful valley famous enough for Yankee races," wrote the Richmond *Whig* on May 17, "but the gallant Kentuckian has added to its celebrity in this respect."

This started the ball rolling. Two days later came the Richmond *Daily Dispatch* with: "Gen Breckinridge, in celerity of movement, has proved himself a worthy successor of Jackson." The next day the Richmond *Enquirer* added its voice, saying that "celerity of movement, as well as vigor of action, did not desert our cause when Stonewall Jackson died."

The Confederate soldiers agreed. Johnston found that "everybody hailed Breckinridge as the new Jackson, who had been sent to guard the Valley and redeem it from the occupation of the enemy." Two weeks after the battle, a war correspondent in Staunton found that "Gen Breckinridge, by the way, is a universal favorite here and with the soldiers of his army. They say his manoeuvering in the battle with Sigel was masterly, and that the energy of his movements reminds them of Jackson."

There was more than wishful thinking behind the comparisons. Of course, it can be argued that just about any general in the Confederate Army could have beaten Sigel, and it is a valid argument. But the same can be said of the men Stonewall

Jackson faced in his great Valley campaign of 1862. The Union put stars on the shoulders of few men who enjoyed less talent as soldiers than John C. Frémont, James Shields, or Nathaniel P. Banks. Yet the fact remained that, talent or no, the armies that they led so outnumbered Jackson's that if any of the three had been able to bring his full force to bear, Stonewall could have been overwhelmed by sheer force of numbers, all generalship aside. The same was the case with Sigel and Breckinridge.

The manner in which the Kentuckian defeated Sigel is the real test. Of course, there are the obvious comparisons. Breckinridge was fighting on a Sunday, like Jackson, and he rode a very propitiously named sorrel. But there were items of more substance. Jackson, in his Valley campaign, established a marching speed which became legend and led to his infantry calling themselves "foot cavalry." In his forty-eight marching days of the campaign, he averaged fourteen and one tenth miles per day. Breckinridge two years later moved Echols from near Lewisburg to New Market, 143 miles, in eight marching days, seventeen and nine tenths miles a day. Those portions of Wharton's brigade that took the train from Jackson's River Depot to Staunton averaged two tenths of a mile less per day. That part of his brigade that had to march the full 187 miles from Narrows, via Jackson's River to Staunton and on to New Market, did it in eight marching days, an outstanding twenty-three and one half miles per day. Jackson would have been proud of them.

Like Jackson, once Breckinridge reached his destination after his rigorous march, he had his entire army up and ready for the fight. Meanwhile, Imboden, like Turner Ashby of old, had so harassed the enemy that his numbers were severely reduced before he reached the field. Once ready for battle, Breckinridge took the initiative and never relinquished it through the rest of the day. His attack was almost constant, and he used every reliable unit at his command so that, like Jackson, he was actually able to equal or outnumber Sigel's infantry in line despite the nine-to-five advantage the Federals enjoyed at the opening of the campaign.

Once the battle began, the Kentuckian showed the same versatility in his tactics that he displayed in his campaign strategy. Whereas Sigel's division of his army was intrinsic to his plan of battle, Breckinridge's division of his force into two lines was a deception, and one which worked. Breckinridge's use of his artillery was most imaginative, and the orders to Imboden and Gilmor for a wide flank move to cut off Sigel's retreat and trap him were truly reminiscent of Jackson's brilliant flank march at Chancellorsville. It is significant that throughout the war, Jackson, Breckinridge, and Jubal Early were the only generals whom Lee left to fight entirely at their own discretion in protecting his vital left flank in the Shenandoah.

Of course, the comparison can go only so far. Breckinridge was not Stonewall Jackson, nor did he ever pretend to be. His Valley campaign was much shorter than Jackson's, and Breckinridge might not have been able to sustain a campaign as long as Jackson with the limited resources available. He did not possess Jackson's consuming drive nor quite that touch of the peculiar about himself which Jackson displayed and which played a significant part in holding together Jackson's "army of the living God." But still, this Kentuckian was satisfactory enough for the people of the Valley. It had been a year since Jackson's death, and this new man from the Western army seemed to fill his shoes well enough. Indeed, among all of the Confederacy's major generals this spring, there was no other who could fill them better.

For these reasons, the Valley people viewed Breckinridge's departure soon after New Market with dismay and, following subsequent Confederate disasters in the Valley, with undisguised anger. A few days after the Piedmont defeat, one question was heard throughout the Shenandoah and even on Richmond's street corners: "Who ordered Gen. Breckinridge to leave the Valley after his defeat of Sigel?"

Many concurred in the opinion that "a more egregious blunder had not been committed during this campaign." In Lynchburg the press believed that "if Breckinridge had been retained in the Valley after the defeat of Siegel [*sic*], as he should have been, the prestige of his success and the spirit of his troops would have prevented our late disaster." After the Kentuckian returned to the Shenandoah Valley under Early and then had to leave again, the outcry was even greater. If Breckinridge had commanded in the Valley instead of Early, the Federals "would have found it far more difficult to drive our army out," declared Edgar. "I was sorry for his leaving the Valley," wrote Gilmor, "and every officer and man of us united in admiring his soldierly qualities." Young Faulkner wrote to the general: "It is useless for me to express how much I, as well as all the Valley people regret your not being in that department." But they lost him nevertheless.

Once with Lee after New Market, Breckinridge led his brigades in the battles on the North Anna and at Cold Harbor where, on June 4, an enemy shell struck Old Sorrel and ended the career of the horse that Breckinridge thought bore a charmed life. The general was injured in the fall and was at first thought dead. He recovered, however, and a few days later, still bedridden, he led his command back to the Valley again to try to repel Hunter. Unable to walk, he still managed to organize the defenses of Lynchburg and delayed the Federal attempt to take that city until Jubal Early's Second Corps arrived to relieve him and launch the raid on Washington in June. Breckinridge commanded one of the two corps that Early formed in organizing his Army of the Valley, and with it he took Martinsburg, West Virginia, from Sigel on July 4. Five days later, the Kentuckian had one of his division commanders, Major General John B. Gordon, execute a successful flanking maneuver in the Battle of Monocacy which decided the fight and, on July 11 and 12, Breckinridge stood on the heights at Silver Spring, Maryland, and looked out upon the spires and domes of the capital where once he sat as senator and Vice President.

When Union reinforcements moved into Washington, Early retreated into the Valley but, in a brief offensive planned by Breckinridge, he moved against the Federal forces of General Crook at Kernstown—scene of one of Stonewall Jackson's fights —and defeated him. The plan of battle was New Market all

over again—an infantry attack on the Federal right while
cavalry went on a wide sweep around the Federal left to cut
off retreat. Thereafter, Breckinridge stayed with Early until
the Battle of Winchester on September 19, the first clash of the
Confederates with the new Yankee general in the Valley,
Philip H. Sheridan. Early was beaten, and shortly afterward
Breckinridge received orders from Richmond to return to the
Department of Southwestern Virginia. There he repelled two
enemy raids, led one of his own into east Tennessee that almost reached Knoxville, and thereafter fought to hold together
a crumbling territorial command through the terrible winter
of 1864–65. Then, in January 1865, he was called to Richmond
where, on February 6, President Davis appointed him Secretary of War.

His new job was a hopeless one. Realizing now that the
Confederacy was doomed, he bent all his efforts toward a con-
clusion of the war with honor, with as little damage to the
South as possible and to the successful escape of Jefferson
Davis and his Cabinet. When Richmond fell on April 2,
Breckinridge organized the evacuation of the city, conferred
briefly with Lee, who was retreating to Appomattox, and sat
as an adviser to General Joseph E. Johnston in his negotiations
with General William T. Sherman for the surrender of the
Army of Tennessee at Durham Station, North Carolina, April
26. He directed Davis' attempted escape and then, after the
President separated from him, effected his own flight down
through Georgia and Florida by horse and boat, and across
the straits to Cuba.

Under indictment for treason in the United States, Breckinridge spent the next three and one half years in exile in
England, the Continent, and Canada, his only hope being to
be allowed to return to Kentucky and live out his days under
the flag he never really wanted to leave. In February 1869,
under the terms of a general amnesty, he finally came home
again and returned to his law practice in Lexington, Kentucky.
It was commonly acknowledged that Breckinridge could have
had any political office in the state that he wished, merely for
the asking, but he eschewed politics completely and devoted

himself to rebuilding what the war had destroyed. He directed an infant railroad, served as president of a life insurance company; and on those rare occasions when he spoke publicly, he called for peace and harmony and reconciliation. His only harsh words after the war were for the Ku Klux Klan, and contemporaries credited him with singlehandedly disrupting the Klan in Kentucky for decades by the simple force of his opposition.

The rigors of the war and the heartbreak of exile, however, proved fatal to his constitution. In 1875, when just fifty-four, he contracted what he and those around him knew would be his final illness, and on May 17 he passed quietly from a life that had been filled with as much drama and romance as any of his era. The nation united in mourning his death and, as one Northern journal said, "There is now no north and no south."[14]

But one principal in the New Market drama remains, one that suffered more than all the others and which, yet, outlived them all—the Shenandoah Valley itself. Its people were a little smug after the victory. "No apprehension, we imagine, need be entertained of the advance of Sigel's whipped Yankees as high up as New Market," claimed one newspaper.

But Imboden believed that the New Market triumph "proved in the end a great calamity to the people of the Valley." His reason was simple. It led to the replacement of "that gentlemanly and brave German" Franz Sigel. Hunter was only slightly better as a general, but he possessed a ruthlessness which Sigel could never approach, and the Valley paid in the destruction of homes and public buildings. His advance, unlike Sigel's, was steady until he reached New Market, where he spent three days reburying the Federal dead, many of whose bodies were protruding from the ground. Living comrades, seeing the remains of their friends, declared that the seeming mistreatment of the dead "can neither be forgotten nor soon forgiven." When they went into battle at Piedmont on June 5, Hunter's cavalrymen charged, crying: "New Market!"[15]

Following his victory at Piedmont and subsequent failure at Lynchburg, Hunter withdrew into the Appalachian Mountains while Early moved on Washington. Little happened in the Shenandoah after that, aside from occasional skirmishing and the fight at Kernstown, until August, when Sheridan replaced Hunter. From that time on, the Valley would know little peace. Early was beaten at Winchester and again, two days later, at Fisher's Hill. More maneuvering followed, and then Sheridan gave the Confederates a third beating at Cedar Creek in October. This effectively ended major operations in the Valley for the winter, as both Early and Sheridan joined the main armies now locked in battle around besieged Petersburg. When spring approached, they went back and, on March 2, 1865, the Federals virtually destroyed Early at Waynesborough, capturing much of his little army. There was no more disputing Federal control of the Valley but by this time it mattered little. The once fruitful Valley lay devastated, owing to the Federals' policy of burning crops and buildings and destroying anything else that might aid the Confederates. A fertile "paradise" had been turned into a wasteland.

After Appomattox, and with remarkable speed, the Valley recovered. The crops were planted anew, the homes were rebuilt, the schools reopened, often like V.M.I. in temporary quarters. The veterans—among them Robert E. Lee—settled once more between the Alleghenies and the Blue Ridge and joined with the widows and orphans in the work of reconstructing their lives. It seemed suddenly that the Valley was green again. The pastoral, if not immediately prosperous, granary of the South found itself once more on the road to peace and happiness. Wheat and corn were seeded in fields which for four years had known only bullets, and a hundred little villages like New Market continued to thrive in their small way. New homes and towns grew up in the Valley until, in the swift passing of the decades, many of the battlefields were lost and almost forgotten. Museums and markers were erected on a few, and aging veterans in ever-decreasing numbers gathered on anniversaries to recall what they had done so many years before. Finally, the inevitable time came when there were no veterans, and many old fights found themselves relegated at last solely to the dusty shelves and antiquarian memories.

But not New Market. It was a battle that would not dim or die in recollection. While the other fights faded, it has stayed alive in the minds and hearts of the Valley's people. It seems to have some special claim—perhaps because of the Cadets, perhaps because of the fact that it was the last Confederate victory in the Shenandoah. Whatever it is, New Market lives as the Valley's best known action of the war. It is celebrated, even re-enacted, and now memorialized in a beautiful battle-field park donated, fittingly, by a loyal alumnus of the Virginia Military Institute. It is an appropriate tribute to the courage of the men who fought there, to the boys who became men there, to the struggle of all the Valley's people for the "lost cause," and most of all to that enduring, almost ethereal, quantity that Major Halpine called "the romance of the war."

Appendix A

Strength of Commands in the New Market Campaign

Since no comprehensive field reports of numbers for the units involved were made—or are known to survive—for either of the two armies engaged, it has taken considerable research and evaluation to arrive at the figures given below. They are, of course, open to question, particularly if new sources overlooked should come to light. But barring new information, they are as accurate as can be hoped for and have been relied on throughout this book.

When speaking of numbers "engaged," only commands taking part in the main battle are included. Thus du Pont's Battery B, 5th U.S. Artillery and the 28th and 116th Ohio, along with the 18th Virginia Cavalry, etc., are not included in this column.

Unit	Campaign Strength	Engaged	Remarks
FEDERAL ARMY—MAJ. GEN. FRANZ SIGEL			
First Infantry Division—Brig. Gen. Jeremiah C. Sullivan			
First Brigade—Col. August Moor			
18th Connecticut	350	350	7 companies
—Maj. Henry Peale			engaged
28th Ohio			
—Lt. Col. Gottfried Becker	700	—	not engaged
116th Ohio			
—Col. James Washburn	800	—	not engaged
123d Ohio			
—Maj. Horace Kellogg	700	700	
First Brigade total	2,550	1,050[1]	

Unit	Campaign Strength	Engaged	Remarks
Second Brigade—Col. Joseph Thoburn			
1st West Virginia			
—Lt. Col. Jacob Weddle	700	700	
12th West Virginia			
—Col. William B. Curtis	929	929	
34th Massachusetts			
—Col. George D. Wells	500	500	
54th Pennsylvania			
Col. Jacob M. Campbell	566	566	
Second Brigade total	2,695	2,695[2]	
First Infantry Division total	5,245	3,745	

Unit	Campaign Strength	Engaged	Remarks
First Cavalry Division—Maj. Gen. Julius Stahel			
First Brigade—Col. William B. Tibbitts			
1st New York (Veteran)			
—Col. Robert F. Taylor	—	—	no figures available
1st New York (Lincoln)			
—Lt. Col. Alonzo W. Adams	750	500	250 were lost May 13
1st Maryland Potomac Home			
Maj. J. Townsend Daniel	50	—	no figures available
21st New York			
Maj. Charles C. Otis	—	—	no figures available
14th Pennsylvania			
—Capt. Ashbel F. Duncan	104	—	no figures available
First Brigade total	figures insufficient		
Second Brigade—Col. John E. Wynkoop			
15th New York			
—Maj. H. Roessler	130	130	
20th Pennsylvania			
—Maj. R. B. Douglas	170	170	
22d Pennsylvania			
—1st. Lt. Caleb McNulty	88	—	not engaged
Second Brigade total	figures insufficient		
First Cavalry Division total	3,035	2,000[8]	

Artillery
Battery B, Maryland Light
—Capt. Alonzo Snow 100 100 6 3-inch rifles
30th Battery, New York
—Capt. Albert von Kleiser 156 156 6 12-pounder
Napoleons

Battery D, 1st West Virginia
—Capt. John Carlin — — 6 3-inch rifles;
no figures
available on
strength

Battery G, 1st West Virginia Light
—Capt. Chatham T. Ewing — — 4 3-inch rifles;
no figures
available on
strength

Battery B, 5th United States
—Capt. Henry A. du Pont — — not engaged
(6 3-inch
rifles) no
figures avail-
able on
strength

Artillery total	660	530[4]	22 guns
ARMY TOTAL	8,940	6,275	

CONFEDERATE ARMY—MAJ. GEN. JOHN C. BRECKINRIDGE
Infantry Division
First Brigade—Brig. Gen. John Echols
22d Virginia
—Col. George S. Patton 580 580
23d Virginia Battalion
—Lt. Col. Clarence Derrick 579 579
26th Virginia Battalion
—Lt. Col. George M. Edgar 425 425
First Brigade total 1,584 1,584[5]

Second Brigade—Brig. Gen. Gabriel C. Wharton
30th Virginia Battalion
—Lt. Col. J. Lyle Clark 347 347
51st Virginia
—Lt. Col. John P. Wolfe 700 700
62d Virginia Mounted

Unit	Campaign Strength	Engaged	Remarks
—Col. George H. Smith	448	448	detached from Valley cavalry; fought as infantry
Co. A, 1st Missouri Cavalry —Capt. Charles H. Woodson	62	62	attached to 62d Virginia; fought as infantry
Second Brigade total	1,557	1,557[6]	
Attached commands Hart's engineer company —Capt. William T. Hart	37	37	fought as infantry
Augusta-Rockingham Reserves —Col. William Harman	500	—	not engaged
Davis' Co. Maryland Cavalry —Capt. T. Sturgis Davis	27	27	fought as infantry
23d Virginia Cavalry —Col. Robert White	315	315	fought as infantry
V.M.I. Cadets —Lt. Col. Scott Ship	229	226	3 boys left ill in Staunton, May 13
Attached commands total	1,108	605[7]	
Infantry Division total	4,249	3,746	

Cavalry, Valley District—Brig. Gen. John D. Imboden

18th Virginia —Col. George W. Imboden	615	—	not engaged
2d Maryland Battalion —Maj. Harry W. Gilmor	40	—	not engaged
McNeill's Company, Partisans —Capt. John H. McNeill	60	—	not engaged
43d Battalion —Lt. Col. John S. Mosby	20	—	not engaged
Cavalry total	735[8]	—	

Artillery–Maj. William McLaughlin			
Chapman's Battery			
—Capt. George B. Chapman	123	123	4 12-pounder howitzers; 2 3-inch rifles
Jackson's Battery			
—1st. Lt. Randolph H. Blain	93	93	1 Parrott rifle; 3 12-pound Napoleons
McClanahan's Battery			
—Capt. John McClanahan	93	93	4 3-inch rifles; 2 howitzers
V.M.I. section			
—Cadet Capt. C. H. Minge	32	32	2 3-inch rifles
Artillery total	341	341[9]	18 guns
ARMY TOTAL	5,335	4,087	18 guns

Appendix B

Casualties in the Battle of New Market

Figures on losses at New Market are as troublesome as those for numbers engaged, if not more so. Fortunately, for the Federals an official report of casualties for each unit engaged was made out on May 22, 1864, but somehow it never found its way into the *Official Records,* nor is it to be found in the National Archives. However, the New York *Tribune* published it in full on May 27, 1864, and this is the source of most of the Federal figures below. Confederate losses are more difficult to come by, though a few scattered reports exist. For the purposes of this list, only casualties of those units engaged in the main battle are listed; losses suffered before or after that are not included.

Unit	Killed	Wounded	Missing	Total	Percentage loss of total engaged
FEDERAL ARMY—MAJ. GEN. FRANZ SIGEL					
First Infantry Division—Sullivan					
First Brigade—Moor					
18th Connecticut —Peale	1	31	24	56	16%
28th Ohio —Becker	not engaged				
116th Ohio —Washburn	not engaged				
123d Ohio —Kellogg	5	33	37	75	10.7%
First Brigade total	6	64	61	131	12.5%

Second Brigade—Thoburn

1st West Virginia					
—Weddle	4	54	18	76	10.9%
12th West Virginia					
—Curtis	1	27	12	40	4.3%
34th Massachusetts					
—Wells	30	131	54	215	43%
54th Pennsylvania					
—Campbell	32	180	42	254	44.9%
Second Brigade total	67	392	126	585	21.7%
First Division total	73	456	187	716	19.1%

First Cavalry Division—Stahel

First Brigade—Tibbitts					
1st New York (Veteran)					
—Taylor	12	26	9	47	not known
1st New York (Lincoln)					
—Adams	—	—	—	—	not engaged
1st Md. Potomac Home					
—Daniel	—	—	1	1	not known
21st New York					
—Otis	2	12	—	14	not known
14th Pennsylvania					
—Duncan	—	6	2	8	not known
First Brigade total	14	44	12	70	not known
Second Brigade—Wynkoop					
15th New York					
—Roessler	2	3	11	16	13.3%
20th Pennsylvania					
—Douglas	1	5	15	21	no figures
22d Pennsylvania					
—McNulty	—	—	—	—	
Second Brigade total	3	8	26	37	
First Cavalry Division total	17	52	38	107	approx. 5%

Artillery

Battery B, Md. Light					
—Snow	—	4	—	4	4%
30th Battery, New York					
—Kleiser	1	4	—	5	3.2% 2 guns
Battery D, 1st W. Va.					
—Carlin	4	3	—	7	not known; 3 guns

Unit	Killed	Wounded	Missing	Total	Percentage loss of total engaged
Battery G, 1st W. Va.					
—Ewing	1	1	—	2	not known
Battery B, 5th U.S.					
—du Pont	not engaged				
Artillery total	6	12	—	18	3.4% 5 guns
ARMY TOTAL	96	520	225	841	13.4%[1] 5 guns

CONFEDERATE ARMY—MAJ. GEN. JOHN C. BRECKINRIDGE

Unit	Killed	Wounded	Missing	Total	Percentage loss of total engaged
Infantry Division					
First Brigade—Echols					
22d Virginia					
—Patton	4	29	—	33	5.7%
23d Virginia Battalion					
—Derrick	2	75	2	79	13.6%
26th Virginia Battalion					
—Edgar	3	21	—	24	5.6%
First Brigade total	9	125	2	136	8.6%[2]
Second Brigade—Wharton					
30th Virginia Battalion					
—Clark	1	45	—	46	13.3%
51st Virginia					
—Wolfe	2+	90+	—	103	14.7%
62d Virginia Mounted					
—Smith	11	81	—	92	20.5%
Co. A, 1st Missouri					
Cavalry—Woodson	5	35	—	40	64.5%
Second Brigade total	19+	251+	—	281	18%[3]
Attached commands					
Hart's engineer company					
—Hart	—	10	—	10	27%
Augusta-Rockingham					
Reserves—Harman	not engaged				
Davis' Co. Md. Cavalry					
—Davis	—	—	—	—	not known
23d Virginia Cavalry					
—White	4+	36+	1+	41+	13%+
V.M.I. Cadets					
—Ship	10	45	—	55	24.3%
Attached commands total	14+	91+	1+	106+	17.5%[4]
Infantry Division total	42+	467+	3+	523+	14%

Cavalry, Valley District—Imboden
   18th Virginia

—Imboden	not engaged				
2d Maryland Battalion					
—Gilmor	not engaged				
McNeill's Company,					
Partisans—McNeill	not engaged				
43d Battalion					
—Mosby	not engaged				
Cavalry total	not engaged[5]				
Artillery					
Chapman's battery					
—Chapman	1	4	—	5	4%
Jackson's battery					
—Blain	—	1	—	1	1%
McClanahan's battery					
—McClanahan	—	—	—	—	
V.M.I. section					
—Minge	—	2	—	2	6.1%
Artillery total	1	7	—	8	2.3%
ARMY TOTAL	43+	474+	3+	531+	13%[6]

Documentation and Notes by Chapter

Chapter 1

1. Charles G. Halpine to "My Dearest Love," May 29, 1864, Charles G. Halpine Collection, Henry E. Huntington Library, San Marino, Cal.

Chapter 2

1. Roy P. Basler, ed., *The Collected Works of Abraham Lincoln* (New Brunswick, N.J., 1953), VI, p. 93n.

2. Cincinnati *Commercial*, February 27, 1863; New York *Times*, August 22, 1902; Basler, *Lincoln*, VI, p. 217n.

3. Basler, *Lincoln*, VII, pp. 129, 244n; Franz Sigel to Elise Sigel, March 4, 1864, K. N. Whaley to Sigel, January 31, 1864, Schuyler Colfax to Sigel, February 8, 10, 17, March 1, 7, 1864, Franz Sigel Papers, New-York Historical Society, New York, N.Y.; Wheeling *Daily Intelligencer*, February 29, 1864; Margaret B. Paulus, comp., *Papers of General Robert Huston Milroy* (n.p., n.d.), I, p. 348; Cecil D. Eby, Jr., ed., *A Virginia Yankee in the Civil War: The Diaries of David Hunter Strother* (Chapel Hill, N.C., 1961), p. 213 (hereafter cited as Strother, *Diaries*).

4. U. S. War Department, *War of the Rebellion: A Compilation of the Official Records of the Union and Confederate Armies* (Washington, D.C., 1880–1901), Series I, Volume 33, pp. 618, 664 (hereafter cited as *O.R.*, with series, volume, part, and page numbers given as *O.R.*, I, 37, 1, p. 100); David H. Strother, Journal of Military Events &c in the Department of West Virginia, I, March 11, 1864, Franz Sigel Papers, Western Reserve Historical Society, Cleveland, Ohio (hereafter cited as Strother Journal); Strother, *Diaries*, pp. 213–14.

5. Henry A. du Pont to Louisa du Pont, March 19, 1864, Winterthur Manuscripts Collection, Eleutherian Mills Historical Library, Greenville, Del.; Jacob Campbell to Sigel, May 1, 1867, Sigel Papers, Cleveland; William Ellis to Mary Ellis and Mary Phillips, March 20, 1864, William Ellis Papers, Norman Daniels Collection, U. S. Army Military History Research Collection, Carlisle Barracks, Pa.; Charles Fitz-Simons, "Sigel's Fight at New Market," *Military Order of the Loyal Legion of the United States, Illinois* (Chicago, n.d.), III, p. 61; Wheeling *Daily Register,* March 23, 1864.

6. Strother Journal, I, March 11–12, 1864, Sigel Papers, Cleveland; Wheeling *Daily Intelligencer,* March 1, 1864.

7. Strother Journal, I, March 14, 1864, Sigel Papers, Cleveland; William Hewitt, *History of the Twelfth West Virginia Volunteer Infantry* (Steubenville, Ohio, 1892), p. 99.

8. Sigel to Lorenzo Thomas, March 24, 1864, Sigel Papers, Cleveland; *O.R.,* I, 33, pp. 674–75.

9. *O.R.,* I, 33, pp. 634, 654–55, 675, 683, 719.

10. Strother Journal, I, March 26, 28, 1864, diagrams of commands, Sigel Papers, Cleveland; Franz Sigel, "Sigel in the Shenandoah," in Robert U. Johnson and C. C. Buel, *Battles and Leaders of the Civil War,* (New York, 1884–87), IV, p. 487; *O.R.,* I, 33, pp. 679, 703; Wheeling *Daily Register,* March 29, 1864; Strother, *Diaries,* p. 219.

11. Campbell to Sigel, May 1, 1867, Sigel Papers, Cleveland; Wheeling *Daily Intelligencer,* March 31, 1864; *O.R.,* I, 33, p. 720; Basler, *Collected Works,* VII, p. 263n.

12. Basler, *Lincoln,* VI, pp. 55, 79–80; Julius Stahel, Report of Service, October 23, 1874, Records of the Adjutant General's Office, RG 94, National Archives, Washington, D.C. (hereafter cited as NA); *O.R.,* I, 33, p. 739; Wheeling *Daily Register,* March 23, 1864; Strother, *Diaries,* pp. 217, 223.

13. Strother Journal, I, March 19, 24, 26, 30–31, 1864, Sigel Papers, Cleveland; *O.R.,* I, 33, pp. 716, 767, 797; Wheeling *Daily Register,* March 26, April 1, 1864.

14. *O.R.,* I, 51, 2, p. 820; James B. Clay, Jr., to ?, April 23, 1905, in possession of Mrs. John M. Prewitt, Mount Sterling, Ky.

15. *O.R.,* I, 33, pp. 1198, 1203, 1210, 1211, 1269; J. Stoddard Johnston, "Sketches of Operations of General John C. Breckinridge," *Southern Historical Society Papers,* VII (June 1879), p. 258.

16. George S. Patton to Susan G. Patton, March 18, 1864, George S. Patton Papers in possession of Ruth Ellen Patton Totten, South Hamilton, Mass.; *O.R.*, I, 33, pp. 1231, 1246, 1250, 1269–70; Richmond *Enquirer*, March 29, 1864; James Z. McChesney to Lucy Johnson, April 12, 1864, James Z. McChesney Papers, Confederate Collection of Stanley E. Butcher, Andover, Mass.

17. Patton to Susan Patton, March 18, 1864, George S. Patton Papers; *O.R.*, I, 33, pp. 1215, 1236, 1243; George P. Kane to Harry Gilmor, April 1, 1864, Harry Gilmor Papers, Maryland Historical Society, Baltimore.

18. John D. Imboden to "Dear Major," April 25, 1864, John D. Imboden Papers, King Library, University of Kentucky, Lexington.

19. *O.R.*, I, 33, pp. 309, 1192; [Henry Corbin], "Diary of a Virginia Cavalry Man, 1863–4," *Historical Magazine*, Third Series, II (October 1873), pp. 212–13; Staunton *Spectator*, April 12, 19, 1864; Staunton *Vindicator*, April 29, May 6, 1864; William Couper, *History of the Shenandoah Valley* (New York, 1952), II, p. 924.

20. Patton to Susan Patton, March 18, 1864, George S. Patton Papers; *O.R.*, I, 33, pp. 1215, 1291.

Chapter 3

1. Sigel, "Sigel in the Shenandoah," p. 487; *O.R.*, I, 33, pp. 697, 758, 765; Strother Journal, II, April 21, 1864, Sigel Papers, Cleveland.

2. *O.R.*, I, 33, pp. 799, 858, I, 32, 3, p. 246; U. S. Grant, *Personal Memoirs of U. S. Grant* (New York, 1885), II, pp. 131–32; U. S. Grant, "Preparing for the Campaign of 1864," *Battles and Leaders*, IV, p. 112.

3. Franz Sigel, "A Campaign in May, 1864," Sigel Papers, Cleveland; *O.R.*, I, 37, 1, p. 526, I, 33, p. 893.

4. Sigel, "Sigel in the Shenandoah," p. 487; *O.R.*, I, 33, pp. 901, 911, 964.

5. Strother, *Diaries*, pp. 216–17, 219, 221; Carl Schurz, *Reminiscences of Carl Schurz* (New York, 1907–1908), II, p. 350; *O.R.*, I, 33, p. 734.

6. Strother, *Diaries*, p. 222; *O.R.*, I, 34, 3, p. 333, I, 33, pp. 929, 964; David Cushman to Caroline Cushman, April 14, 1864, David Cushman Papers, American Antiquarian Society, Worcester, Mass.

7. Sigel, "Sigel in the Shenandoah," p. 487; Statement of troops at Harpers Ferry, April 13, 1864, Sigel Papers, Cleveland; *O.R.*, I,

33, pp. 965, 988, 1006; Cushman to Caroline Cushman, April 14, 24, 1864, Cushman Papers; Theodore F. Lang, *Loyal West Virginia from 1861 to 1865* (Baltimore, 1895), pp. 106, 111; Jacob Campbell Diary, April 27, 1864, Jacob Campbell Papers, West Virginia Collection, West Virginia University, Morgantown; Thomas F. Wildes, *Record of the One Hundred and Sixteenth Regiment Ohio Infantry Volunteers* (Sandusky, 1884), p. 82.

8. Wheeling *Daily Register*, April 9, 13, 15, 25, 1864; Strother Journal, II, April 17, 21, 1864; Sigel Papers, Cleveland; *O.R.*, I, 33, pp. 913, 936, 942, 986, I, 37, 1, p. 77; William S. Lincoln, *Life with the Thirty-fourth Mass. Infantry* (Worcester, 1879), p. 252; David Cushman Diary, April 28, 1864, Cushman Papers; Campbell Diary, April 29, 1864; Wildes, *One Hundred and Sixteenth Regiment*, p. 82.

9. Campbell Diary, April 29, 1864; Strother, *Diaries*, p. 221; Lynchburg *Daily Virginian*, June 4, 1864; Lincoln, *Thirty-Fourth Mass.*, p. 260; William C. Walker, *History of the Eighteenth Regiment Conn. Volunteers in the War for the Union* (Norwich, 1885), p. 212; Charles H. Lynch, *The Civil War Diary, 1862–1865, of Charles H. Lynch, 18th Conn. Vols.* (Hartford, 1915), p. 55.

10. *O.R.*, I, 33, pp. 1215, 1272, 1291; ? to Imboden, April 13, 1864, Charles S. Venable Papers, Southern Historical Collection, University of North Carolina, Chapel Hill.

11. *O.R.*, I, 33, pp. 1289–90, 1301, 1312, 1323, 1324, 1333, I, 37, 1, p. 707; John C. Breckinridge to Braxton Bragg, April 27, 1864, Frederick M. Dearborn Collection, Houghton Library, Harvard University, Cambridge, Mass.; Louis H. Manarin, ed., "The Civil War Diary of Rufus J. Woolwine," *Virginia Magazine of History and Biography*, LXXI (October 1963), pp. 434–35 (hereafter cited as Woolwine, "Diary"); Special Orders No. 117, April 30, 1864, Chap. II, Vol. 63, RG 109, NA.

12. *O.R.*, I, 37, 1, p. 707.

13. *O.R.*, I, 37, 1, pp. 708–10, 712; William Couper, *One Hundred Years at V.M.I.* (Richmond, 1939), II, pp. 260–61.

14. John C. Breckinridge, draft of a report of the New Market Campaign, n.d., New Market File, Alumni Files, Virginia Military Institute, Lexington (hereafter cited as Breckinridge Report); Johnston, "Sketches of Operations," p. 258; *O.R.*, I, 37, 1, pp. 710, 712; Edward Younger, ed., *Inside the Confederate Government: The Diary of Robert Garlick Hill Kean* (New York, 1957), pp.

149–50; John McCausland to Samuel Cooper, May 9, 1864, John C. Breckinridge Papers, Chicago Historical Society, Chicago, Ill.

15. *O.R.*, I, 37, 1, pp. 713–15; Breckinridge to R. E. Lee, May 4, 1864, Venable Papers.

16. *O.R.*, I, 37, 1, pp. 713, 715–16; John D. Imboden, "The Battle of New Market," *Battles and Leaders*, IV, p. 481; Breckinridge Report.

Chapter 4

1. *O.R.*, I, 37, 1, p. 717; Special Orders No. 121, Chap. II, Vol. 63, RG 109, NA; Breckinridge, Memorandum, May 5, 1864, Arthur Emmerson Papers, Perkins Library, Duke University, Durham, N.C.; Breckinridge to Imboden, May 5, 1864, Sigel Papers, Cleveland.

2. H.M.B. to Breckinridge, n.d., Sigel Papers, Cleveland; Breckinridge Report.

3. Charles Harman to Imboden, April 30, 1864, T. Sturgis Davis to Imboden, May 2, 1864, Venable Papers; Thomas B. Gatch, "Recollections of New Market," *Confederate Veteran*, XXXIV (June 1926), p. 211; Imboden, "New Market," p. 480.

4. Breckinridge Report; J. Stoddard Johnston, The Battle of New Market, New Market File, V.M.I.; Johnston, "Sketches of Operations," pp. 258–59; Charles Semple, Compiled Service Record, RG 109, NA; Albert Sidney Johnston, *Captain Beirne Chapman and Chapman's Battery: An Historical Sketch* (Union, W.Va., 1903), p. 19; *O.R.*, I, 37, 1, pp. 721–23.

5. *O.R.*, I, 37, 1, p. 722; Eli Bruce to Breckinridge, June 7, 1864, Breckinridge Family Papers, Library of Congress, Washington, D.C.; New York *Turf, Field & Farm*, May 21, 1875.

6. Robert S. Rodgers, "History of the 2nd Eastern Shore Regiment," Robert S. Rodgers Papers, Perkins Library, Duke University; Walker, *Eighteenth Regiment Conn.*, p. 213; Lincoln, *Thirty-fourth Mass.*, pp. 258–59; Cushman Diary, April 30, 1864; N. Wilkinson to Sigel, April 30, Sigel to W. P. Smith, April 30, 1864, Sigel Papers, Cleveland; *O.R.*, I, 33, p. 1027, I, 37, 1, p. 364.

7. Circular, April 30, 1864, Sigel to Stahel, April 30, 1864, Sigel Papers, Cleveland; Walker, *Eighteenth Regiment Conn.*, p. 214.

8. Sigel to Stahel, May 1, 1864, Sigel Papers, Cleveland; Cushman to Caroline Cushman, May 1, 1864, Cushman Diary, May 1, 1864, Cushman Papers; Hewitt, *Twelfth West Virginia*, p. 104.

9. Henry A. du Pont to Henry du Pont, May 2, 1864, Winterthur Collection; Cushman Diary, May 1–4, 1864; Walker, *Eighteenth Regiment Conn.*, p. 214; Wildes, *One Hundred and Sixteenth Regiment*, p. 83; Strother, *Diaries*, p. 223; Campbell Diary, May 1–4, 1864.

10. Corbin, "Diary," p. 213; Robert White, *West Virginia* (Atlanta, 1899), Vol. II of Clement A. Evans, ed., *Confederate Military History*, p. 97; Imboden, "New Market," p. 480.

11. John S. Mosby, *The Memoirs of Colonel John S. Mosby*, 2d edition, (Bloomington, Ind., 1959), pp. 272–73; Samuel C. Farrar, *The Twenty-second Pennsylvania Cavalry* (Pittsburgh, 1911), p. 195; J. Marshall Crawford, *Mosby and His Men: A Record of the Adventures of that Renowned Partisan Ranger, John S. Mosby* (New York, 1867), pp. 186–87; *O.R.*, I, 37, 1, pp. 2–3.

12. Simeon M. Bright, "The McNeill Rangers, A Study in Confederate Guerrilla Warfare," *West Virginia History*, XII (July 1951), pp. 353–56; Hu Maxwell and H. L. Swisher, *History of Hampshire County, West Virginia* (Morgantown, 1897), p. 666; Lynchburg *Daily Virginian*, May 14, 1864; *O.R.*, I, 37, 1, pp. 69, 382, 390–91; John T. Peerce, "Capture of A Railroad Train," *Southern Bivouac*, Old Series, II (April 1884), pp. 352–55.

13. Strother Journal, II, May 5, 1864, Sigel Papers, Cleveland; *O.R.*, I, 37, 1, pp. 401–2; Farrar, *Twenty-second Pennsylvania*, p. 199.

14. John A. Mastin Diary, May 6–8, 1864, Roy Bird Cook Collection, West Virginia Collection.

15. John Echols to Breckinridge, June 1, 1864, Breckinridge Family Papers; *O.R.*, I, 51, 2, pp. 981–82.

16. Mastin Diary, May 8–9, 1864; *O.R.*, I, 37, 1, pp. 725, 727; Woolwine, "Diary," p. 435; Johnston, *Chapman's Battery*, p. 19.

17. Johnston, New Market, New Market File, V.M.I.; *O.R.*, I, 37, 1, pp. 722, 724, 725, 726.

18. *O.R.*, I, 37, 1, pp. 724–28; McCausland to Cooper, May 9, 1864, Breckinridge Papers, Chicago.

19. Farrar, *Twenty-second Pennsylvania*, pp. 195–96; Chauncey S. Norton, *The Red Neck Ties: or History of the Fifteenth New York Volunteer Cavalry* (Ithaca, 1891), pp. 30–31; David Powell, Memoirs, in possession of Dr. R. Pascall, Valdes, N.C.; Lincoln, *Thirty-fourth Mass.*, pp. 260–61, 263–65; Wildes, *One Hundred and Sixteenth Regiment*, pp. 84–85; John Scott, *Partisan Life with*

Col. John S. Mosby (New York, 1867), p. 216; William H. Beach, *The First New York (Lincoln) Cavalry* (New York, 1902), pp. 318–19; Cushman to Caroline Cushman, May 6, 1864, Cushman Papers; Sigel, Campaign in May, Kelley to Sigel, May 8, 1864, Sigel Papers, Cleveland.

20. Sigel, "Campaign in May," Sigel Papers, Cleveland; *O.R.*, I, 37, 1, p. 370.

21. *O.R.*, I, 37, 1, pp. 402, 407; Walker, *Eighteenth Regiment Conn.*, pp. 215–17; Sigel, "Sigel in the Shenandoah," p. 488; Lincoln, *Thirty-fourth Mass.*, p. 271; Strother Journal, II, May 10, 1864, Sigel Papers, Cleveland; Sigel to Elise Sigel, May 8, 1864, Sigel Papers, New York.

Chapter 5

1. Couper, *Shenandoah*, II, p. 925.

2. John G. Barrett and Robert K. Turner, eds., *Letters of a New Market Cadet, Beverly Stanard* (Chapel Hill, 1961), p. 58; Couper, *One Hundred Years*, II, p. 261; General Orders No. 17, May 9, 1864, V.M.I. Order Book, 1864, Preston Library, V.M.I.

3. Lexington *Gazette*, May 18, 1864; Jennings C. Wise, *The Military History of the Virginia Military Institute from 1839 to 1865* (Lynchburg, 1915), p. 288; John S. Wise, *The End of an Era* (New York, 1965), pp. 286–87.

4. Wise, *The End of an Era*, pp. 287–88; Couper, *Shenandoah*, II, p. 926; *Report of the Board of Visitors of the Virginia Military Institute, July 1864* (Lexington, 1864), p. 40.

5. Wise, *Military History*, p. 321; Henry A. Wise, "The Cadets at New Market, Va.," *Confederate Veteran*, XX (August 1912), pp. 361–62; F. N. Boney, *John Letcher of Virginia: The Story of Virginia's Civil War Governor* (University, Ala., 1966), p. 205.

6. Wise, *Military History*, p. 285; Nelson B. Noland to St. George Noland, May 3, 1864, Noland Family Papers, Alderman Library, University of Virginia, Charlottesville.

7. William Couper, *The V.M.I. New Market Cadets* (Charlottesville, 1933), pp. 34, 61, 118, 120, 143, 254; Noland to Mary Noland, March 16, 1864, Noland Papers; Wise, *Military History*, p. 332.

8. *O.R.*, I, 37, 1, p. 730.

9. John S. Wise, "The West Point of the Confederacy: Boys in Battle at New Market, Virginia, May 15, 1864," *Century Magazine*,

XXXVII (January 1889), p. 465; Raymond Weeks to Couper, June 6, 1946, New Market File, V.M.I.; Noland to Mary Noland, May 11, 1864, Noland Papers.

10. Elizabeth Preston Allen, *The Life and Letters of Margaret Junkin Preston* (Boston, 1903), p. 179; Wise, "West Point of the Confederacy," p. 465; Couper, *Shenandoah*, II, pp. 928–29; Couper, *New Market Cadets*, pp. 106, 253. The figures given here are at odds with those of Couper, who misread Ship's report of July 4 in Alumni Files, V.M.I.

11. *O.R.*, I, 37, 1, pp. 89, 730; General Orders No. 18, May 11, 1864, V.M.I. Order Book; Wise, "West Point of the Confederacy," p. 46.

12. Breckinridge Report; John Avis to T. Sturgis Davis, May 10, 1864, Breckinridge to Davis, May 10, 1864, Sigel Papers, Cleveland; *O.R.*, I, 37, 1, p. 727.

13. Imboden, "New Market," p. 480; Imboden to "Dear Major," April 25, 1864, Imboden Papers; Staunton *Vindicator*, April 29, 1864.

14. Eva Lee to Gilmor, April 9, 13, 1864, Kane to Gilmor, April 1, 1864, J. Louis Smith to Gilmor, May 1864, Special Orders No. 1, May 10, 1864, Gilmor Papers; Harry W. Gilmor, *Four Years in the Saddle* (New York, 1866), pp. 146–47; *O.R.*, I, 33, pp. 152–54, I, 37, 1, p. 729.

15. Record Book of Company D, 51st Virginia, May 10, 1864, Rufus J. Woolwine Papers, Virginia Historical Society, Richmond; Daniel H. Bruce, "The Battle of New Market," *Southern Historical Society Papers*, XXV (1907), p. 156; Mastin Diary, May 10–11, 1864; Breckinridge Report; Johnston, "Sketches of Operations," p. 259.

16. Woolwine, "Diary," p. 436; Record Book of Company D, May 11, 1864, Woolwine Papers; Mastin Diary, May 12, 1864; *O.R.*, I, 37, 1, p. 89; Jennings C. Wise, *Personal Memoir of the Life and Service of Scott Shipp* (n.p., 1915), pp. 5–10, 17, 20–21. Ship added the second "p" to his name after 1883.

17. Barrett and Turner, *New Market Cadet*, p. 61; Preston Cocke, *The Battle of New Market* (n.p., 1914), p. 5; Richmond *Times-Dispatch*, June 23, 1912; Wise, "West Point of the Confederacy," p. 465; Couper, *Shenandoah*, II, p. 927; Wise, *The End of an Era*, p. 289; Louis C. Wise, Reminiscences of the Battle of New Market, Louis C. Wise File, V.M.I.

18. Breckinridge Report; Wise, "West Point of the Confederacy," p. 465; Couper, *New Market Cadets,* pp. 255–56; Wise, *Military History,* p. 306; Thomas E. Jackson, Compiled Service Record, RG 109, NA; Randolph Blain to John B. Castleman, January 15, 1917, John B. Castleman Papers, Filson Club, Louisville, Ky.

19. *O.R.,* I, 37, 1, pp. 71, 73, 728–29, 732.

20. Johnston, New Market; Breckinridge Report; J. Stoddard Johnston, *Kentucky* (Atlanta, 1899; Vol. IX of Evans, *Confederate Military History*), p. 186; Johnston, "Sketches of Operations," p. 259; *O.R.,* I, 37, 1, pp. 728, 732; Seddon to Bragg, May 12, 1864, Breckinridge Papers, Chicago; Imboden, "New Market," p. 481; General Orders No. 1, May 12, 1864, J. Stoddard Johnston Papers, Museum of the Confederacy, Richmond, Va.; Richmond *Whig,* May 13, 1864.

21. New York *Tribune,* May 16, 1864; Wheeling *Daily Register,* May 7, 17, 1864; Horace Porter, *Campaigning With Grant,* 2d edition, (Bloomington, Ind., 1961), p. 91; Strother Journal, II, May 9, 1864; Sigel Papers, Cleveland; Farrar, *Twenty-second Pennsylvania,* p. 220; Lynch, *Diary,* p. 57; Lincoln, *Thirty-fourth Mass.,* pp. 272–74; Campbell Diary, May 10, 1864; Cushman Diary, May 10, 1864.

22. Walker, *Eighteenth Regiment Conn.,* p. 216; James H. Stevenson, *"Boots and Saddles": A History of the First Volunteer Cavalry of the War, Known as the First New York (Lincoln) Cavalry* (Harrisburg, Pa., 1879), pp. 260–61, 274; Josiah Staley to Maria Staley, May 10, 1864, Josiah Staley Letters, Ohio Historical Society, Columbus; Sigel to Stahel, May 8, 10, 1864, Strother Journal, II, May 10, 1864, Sigel to Frederick D. Grant, June 17, 1885, Sigel Papers, Cleveland; Strother, *Diaries,* p. 224.

23. Lincoln, *Thirty-fourth Mass.,* p. 274; Lang, *Loyal West Virginia,* p. 112; *O.R.,* I, 37, 1, pp. 446–47; Sigel, Campaign in May, Sigel, General Report, May 17, 1864, Sigel Papers, Cleveland; Sigel, "Sigel in the Shenandoah," p. 488.

24. *O.R.,* I, 37, 1, p. 421.

25. Imboden, "New Market," p. 481; Richmond *Sentinel,* May 25, 1864; Imboden to ?, [May 8, 1864], Sigel Papers, Cleveland; Farrar, *Twenty-second Pennsylvania,* pp. 199–202, 218; John W. Elwood, *Elwood's Stories of the Old Ringgold Cavalry, 1847–1865* (Coal Center, Pa., 1914), pp. 187, 188–91; Corbin,

"Diary," p. 213; Norton, *Red Neck Ties*, p. 32; *O.R.*, I, 37, 1, pp. 27–28, 70, 71, 427–28, 438; Staunton *Vindicator*, May 13, 1864; Maxwell and Swisher, *Hampshire County*, p. 557; Bright, "McNeill Rangers," pp. 356–57.

26. Walker, *Eighteenth Regiment Conn.*, p. 217; Cushman Diary, May 12–13, 1864; Hewitt, *Twelfth West Virginia*, p. 105; George Templeton Strong, *Diary of the Civil War 1860–1865*, ed. by Allan Nevins (New York, 1962), p. 446; Farrar, *Twenty-second Pennsylvania*, p. 221; Lincoln, *Thirty-fourth Mass.*, pp. 275–76; *O.R.*, I, 37, 1, p. 109.

Chaper 6

1. Arthur L. Hildreth, *A Brief History of New Market and Vicinity* (New Market, 1964), pp. 2, 4; Couper, *Shenandoah*, II, p. 1126; Francis A. Walker, comp., *The Statistics of the Population of the United States . . . Ninth Census* (Washington, D.C., 1872), p. 282.

2. Richmond *Sentinel*, May 16, 1864; Harrisonburg *Rockingham Register*, May 20, 1864; Corbin, "Diary," p. 213; *O.R.*, I, 37, 1, p. 734; Imboden, "New Market," p. 481.

3. J. N. Potts, "Who Fired the First Gun at New Market?" *Confederate Veteran*, XVII (September 1909), p. 453; Frank Imboden, Compiled Service Record, RG 109, NA; Carter Berkeley, "Imboden's Dash into Charlestown," *Confederate Veteran*, XXV (April 1917), pp. 149, 152.

4. J. J. Lafferty, "Col. George Imboden," John D. Imboden Papers, Alderman Library; Gilmor, *Four Years*, pp. 147–49, 151–56; *O.R.*, I, 37, 1, p. 734; Imboden, "New Market," p. 481; Stevenson, *Boots and Saddles*, p. 269.

5. *O.R.*, I, 37, 1, p. 733.

6. Stevenson, *Boots and Saddles*, pp. 263–65; Beach, *First New York*, pp. 322–24.

7. New Market *Shenandoah Valley*, May 22, 1930; Charles T. O'Ferrall, *Forty Years of Active Service* (New York, 1904), pp. 94–95; Richmond *Sentinel*, May 25, 1864.

8. Stevenson, *Boots and Saddles*, pp. 265–69; Beach, *First New York*, pp. 324–27, 331; *O.R.*, I, 37, 1, p. 73; Cushman Diary, May 14, 1864.

9. Strother Journal, II, May 14, 1864, Sigel to Grant, June 17, 1885, Sigel Papers, Cleveland; August Moor Memoir, John E.

Wynkoop Report, May 19, 1864, August Moor Collection, Illinois Historical Survey, Urbana; Ephram Frost to his mother, May 13–14, 1864, H. Matheny Collection, West Virginia Collection; Farrar, *Twenty-second Pennsylvania*, p. 221; Lynch, *Diary*, p. 59; *O.R.*, I, 37, 1, pp. 79, 85; Beach, *First New York*, p. 349; Charles J. Rawling, *History of the First Regiment Virginia Infantry* (Philadelphia, 1887), p. 168; Strother, *Diaries*, p. 224.

10. Strother Journal, II, May 14, 1864, Sigel Papers, Cleveland; Lynch, *Diary*, p. 59; Campbell Diary, May 14, 1864; Walker, *Eighteenth Regiment Conn.*, pp. 217–18; William A. Croffutt and John Morris, *The Military and Civil History of Connecticut During the War of 1861–1865* (New York, 1868), p. 639.

11. Strother Journal, II, May 14, 1864, Michael Graham to Cole, May 16, 1864, Sigel Papers, Cleveland; Lang, *Loyal West Virginia*, p. 113; Imboden, "New Market," p. 482; Henry A. du Pont to Henry du Pont, May 14, 1864, Winterthur Collection.

12. Graham to Cole, May 16, 17, 1864, Sigel Papers, Cleveland; *O.R.*, I, 37, 1, pp. 454, 458; Lynch, *Diary*, p. 59; Sigel, "Sigel in the Shenandoah," p. 488; Stahel, Report, RG 94, NA.

13. *O.R.*, I, 33, pp. 74–75, 844; Henry A. du Pont, *The Battle of Newmarket, Virginia, May 15, 1864* (Winterthur, Del., 1923), pp. 8–9; Lincoln, *Thirty-fourth Mass.*, pp. 276–78; Ellis to Mary Phillips, May 19, 1864, Ellis Papers.

14. Imboden, "New Market," p. 482; Richmond *Sentinel*, May 20, 1864; Johnston, New Market, Breckinridge Report, New Market File, V.M.I.; Johnston, "Sketches of Operations," p. 259.

15. Breckinridge Report; Richmond *Sentinel*, May 20, 1864.

16. General Orders No. 1, May 12, 1864, Johnston Papers; Johnston, New Market, Breckinridge Report, New Market File, V.M.I.; Mastin Diary, May 13, 1864, Cook Collection; Woolwine, "Diary," p. 436; Hildreth, *New Market*, p. 9; Richmond *Sentinel*, May 20, 1864; Beach, *First New York*, p. 331; Lexington *Gazette*, May 25, 1864; *O.R.*, I, 51, 2, p. 932.

17. Potts, "Who Fired the First Gun?" p. 453; George H. Smith, *The Positions and Movements of the Troops in the Battle of Newmarket Fought May 15th, 1864* (Los Angeles, 1913), p. 13n; Imboden, "New Market," p. 482; *O.R.*, I, 37, 1, pp. 74–75, 79; Wynkoop Report, Moor Collection; Ellis to Phillips, May 19, 1864, Ellis Papers; Pittsburgh *Dispatch*, November 10, 1895; Francis S. Reader, *History of the Fifth West Virginia Cavalry . . . and of*

Battery G, First West Virginia Light Artillery (New Brighton, Pa., 1890), p. 229; Richmond *Sentinel,* May 25, 1864; John H. Mc-Clanahan, Compiled Service Record, RG 109, NA; S. T. Shank, "A Gunner at New Market, Va.," *Confederate Veteran,* XXVI (May 1918), p. 191; Harrisonburg *Rockingham Register,* May 20, 1864; Lincoln, *Thirty-fourth Mass.,* p. 278; William H. Clark, *The Soldier's Offering* (Boston, 1875), pp. 29–30; Thomas H. Neilson, "The Sixty-second Virginia–New Market," *Confederate Veteran,* XVI (February 1908), p. 60; Wheeling *Daily Intelligencer,* May 23, 1864.

18. Jessie H. Rupert, The Battle of New Market, Winterthur Collection.

19. Imboden, "New Market," p. 482; *O.R.,* I, 37, 1, pp. 79–80, 83; Potts, "Who Fired the First Gun?" p. 453; Shank, "Gunner at New Market," p. 191; Imboden to Henry A. Wise, June 6, 1895, John D. Imboden File, V.M.I.; Jasper W. Harris, "Sixty-second Virginia at New Market," *Confederate Veteran,* XVI (September 1906), p. 461; Wheeling *Daily Intelligencer,* May 23, 1864; Corbin, "Diary," p. 213.

20. Ellis to Phillips, May 19, 1864, Ellis Papers; Lincoln, *Thirty-fourth Mass.,* p. 278; Reader, *Battery G,* p. 239; Edwin Snyder, *Adventures and Misadventures, Civil and Military of a Union Veteran of the Civil War* (Topeka, 1909), p. 24; E. C. Crim, "Tender Memories of the V.M.I. Cadets," *Confederate Veteran,* XXXIV (June 1926), p. 212; Rupert, Battle of New Market, Winterthur Collection.

21. Ward to Julia Ward, June 5, 1864, Ward Letters; "Col. Francis Lee Smith," *Confederate Veteran,* XXVI (February 1918), pp. 83–84; John C. Howard, "Recollections of New Market," *Confederate Veteran,* XXXIV (February 1926), p. 57; Wise, "West Point of the Confederacy," pp. 465–66, 470; Wise, *Military History,* p. 300; Wise, *End of an Era,* p. 293; Noland to Charles Read, October 18, 1895, Noland File, V.M.I.; *O.R.,* I, 37, 1, p. 89; *New Market Day at V.M.I.* (Lexington, 1903), p. 12.

Chapter 7

1. Imboden, "New Market," p. 482; Benjamin A. Colonna to George H. Smith, November 1, 1910, George S. Patton, Jr., Papers, Library of Congress.

2. Wise, "West Point of the Confederacy," p. 466; Peter J. Otey,

Response . . . at the Alumni Banquet, June, 1896, to the Toast, "The War Cadets" (n.p., 1896), p. 6; *O.R.,* I, 37, 1, p. 89; Couper, *Shenandoah,* II, p. 928; Richard B. Tunstall to Wise, December 27, 1894, Tunstall File, V.M.I.; "Col. Francis Lee Smith," p. 84.

3. Wise, "West Point of the Confederacy," p. 466; Harrisonburg *Rockingham Register,* May 20, 1864; Woolwine, "Diary," p. 436; Mastin Diary, May 15, 1864; Neilson, "Sixty-second Virginia," p. 60; William M. Patton to Wise, June 10, 1895, Patton File, George H. Smith to Wise, March 7, 1896, Smith File, George M. Edgar to Wise, February 18, 1896, Edgar File, G. T. Lee to Wise, n.d., Lee File, V.M.I.; Gatch, "Recollections," pp. 211–12; Johnston, "Sketches of Operations," p. 259; George M. Edgar, Report, August 8, 1864, George M. Edgar Papers, Southern Historical Collection, University of North Carolina.

4. Imboden to Wise, June 6, 1895, Imboden File, Breckinridge Report, V.M.I.; Corbin, "Diary," p. 213.

5. Harrisonburg *Rockingham Register,* May 20, 1864; Baltimore *Sun,* July 23, 1903; Potts, "Who Fired the First Gun?" p. 453; John Echols, *Address . . . on the Life and Character of Gen. John C. Breckinridge* (New Market, 1877), p. 6.

6. Imboden, "New Market," pp. 481–83; Johnston, New Market, New Market File, Edgar to Wise, February 18, 1896, Edgar File, V.M.I.; Johnston, "Sketches of Operations," pp. 259–60; Johnston, *Kentucky,* pp. 186–87; *O.R.,* I, 37, 1, p. 736; Wise, "West Point of the Confederacy," p. 466; J. W. Parsons, "Capture of Battery at New Market," *Confederate Veteran,* XVII (March 1909), p. 119.

7. *O.R.,* I, 37, 1, pp. 80, 83, 461; Norton, *Red Neck Ties,* p. 36; Clark, *Soldier's Offering,* p. 30; Lincoln, *Thirty-fourth Mass.,* p. 280; Wheeling *Daily Intelligencer,* May 23, 1864; New York *Tribune,* May 25, 1864; Rawling, *First Regiment Virginia,* p. 165; F. Wyneken to Breckinridge, August 2, 1865, Breckinridge Family Papers; Theodore F. Lang, Recollections of the Battle of New Market, Va. May 15th, 1864, New Market File, V.M.I.; Document No. 52, Julius Stahel-Szamwald Papers, Hungarian National Archives, Budapest.

8. Rupert, Battle of New Market, Winterthur Collection.

9. *O.R.,* I, 37, 1, p. 90; Imboden, "New Market," p. 483; Noland to Read, October 18, 1895, Noland File, Breckinridge Report, V.M.I.; Staunton *Spectator and Vindicator,* May 20, 1904; Pulaski, Va., *Southwest Times,* December 12, 1911; Richmond *Whig,* May 23, 1864.

10. *O.R.*, I, 37, pp. 89–90; Wise, *Shipp*, p. 29; T. Morton to Edgar, February 20, 1906, Morton to Wise, February 12, 1896, New Market File, V.M.I.; Wise, "West Point of the Confederacy," pp. 467–68; Cocke, *Battle of New Market*, p. 10.

11. Imboden, "New Market," p. 483; George H. Smith, *Battle of New Market Fought May 15th, 1864, Revised Copy* (n.p., n.d.), p. 32; Edgar to Smith, November 2, 1908, George S. Patton, Jr., Papers; Johnston, New Market, New Market File, V.M.I.; Smith to Edgar, April 22, 1908, F. C. Burdette to Edgar, March 12, 1906, Edgar Papers; George S. Patton, Jr., notes, Patton Papers.

12. Staunton *Spectator and Vindicator*, May 20, 1904; Edgar to Smith, May 5, 1908, George S. Patton, Jr., Papers; James H. Dwyer to R. Turner, March 18, 1912, New Market File, Edgar to Wise, February 18, 1896, George M. Edgar, Notes on E. Raymond Turner's *New Market Campaign*, Edgar File, V.M.I.; George M. Edgar, The Battle of New Market, p. 3, Edgar Papers; Richmond *Times-Dispatch*, October 8, 1905; Harrisonburg *Rockingham Register*, May 20, 1864; Johnston, *Chapman's Battery*, pp. 19–20.

13. Richmond *Sentinel*, May 20, 1864; Shank, "Gunner at New Market," p. 191; Frank M. Imboden, New Market memoranda, n.d., Imboden Papers, Alderman Library; Johnston, "Sketches of Operations," p. 260; Johnston, New Market, Breckinridge Report, V.M.I.; New Market *Shenandoah Valley*, May 12, 1898; Gilmor, *Four Years*, p. 156.

14. Staunton *Spectator and Vindicator*, May 20, 1904; New Market *Shenandoah Valley*, May 12, 1898, May 20, 1930; J. H. V. Wharton, "Gen. G. C. Wharton," *Confederate Veteran*, XIV (July 1906), p. 318; James A. Davis, "The 51st Regiment, Virginia Volunteers, 1861–1865," *West Virginia History*, XXIX (April 1968), p. 179; Wise, "West Point of the Confederacy," p. 446; Smith, *Positions and Movements*, p. 33; G. W. Hines to Edgar, February 24, 1906, Wharton to Edgar, n.d., Edgar, Battle of New Market, p. 3, Edgar Papers; Smith, *Battle of New Market*, p. 32; Otey to Ship, April 14, 1875, Otey File, J. Lyle Clark to Wise, March 25, 1895, New Market File, V.M.I.; Otey, *"The War Cadets,"* p. 6; George H. Smith, "More on the Battle of New Market," *Confederate Veteran*, XVI (November 1908), pp. 570–71; Pulaski, Virginia, *Southwest Times*, December 12, 1911.

15. Lang, Personal Recollections, New Market File, V.M.I.; Pittsburgh *Dispatch*, November 10, 1895; Cushman to Caroline Cushman, May 22, 1864, Cushman Papers; E. Raymond Turner,

The New Market Campaign, May, 1864 (Richmond, 1912), pp. 6–7n, 28; John W. Wayland, *Battle of New Market. Memorial Address . . . May 15, 1926* (New Market, 1926), pp. 17–18; Lang, *Loyal West Virginia*, pp. 113–14; *O.R.*, I, 37, 1, pp. 81–82; Walker, *Eighteenth Regiment Conn.*, pp. 222–23; Croffutt and Morris, *Connecticut During the War*, p. 639.

16. Otey to Ship, April 14, 1875, Otey File, Smith to Wise, March 7, 1896, George H. Smith File, V.M.I.; Staunton *Spectator and Vindicator*, May 20, 1904; New Market *Shenandoah Valley*, May 12, 1898; Edgar to Smith, March 24, 1908, George S. Patton, Jr., Papers.

17. Wise, *Military History*, p. 306; Wise, "West Point of the Confederacy," p. 470; M. B. Corse to S. B. Adams, April 8, 1931, Adams File, V.M.I.; Howard, "Recollections," p. 57; Baltimore *Sun*, June 21, 1903; Wise to Smith, April 23, 1910, George S. Patton, Jr., Papers.

18. "Col. Francis Lee Smith," p. 84; Wise, "West Point of the Confederacy," p. 468; Wise, *End of an Era*, p. 298; Couper, *New Market Cadets*, pp. 96, 170, 166; Ruth Ellen Patton Totten to the author, February 8, 1972; Morton to Wise, February 12, 1896, New Market File, Tunstall to Wise, December 27, 1894, Tunstall File, J. H. Clarkson to Wise, June 29, 1909, Clarkson File, V.M.I.; Benjamin A. Colonna, "The Battle of New Market," *Journal of the Military Service Institution of the United States*, LI (November 1912), p. 345; Staunton *Spectator and Vindicator*, May 20, 1904; Smith, "More on the Battle," p. 570; Otey, "The War Cadets," p. 7; Crim, "Tender Memories," p. 212; Howard, "Recollections," p. 57; New Market *Shenandoah Valley*, May 12, 1898; James L. Merritt to W. H. C. Merritt, May 16, 1864, New Market Battlefield Park, New Market, Va.; Wise, *End of an Era*, p. 299; *O.R.*, I, 37, 1, p. 90; Baltimore *Sun*, July 23, 1903; Lexington *Gazette*, May 25, 1864.

19. Smith, *Positions and Movements*, p. 264; Smith to Edgar, March 16, 1906, Thrasher to Edgar, July 21, 1908, E. Read to Edgar, June 12, 1908, Edgar Papers; Smith to Edgar, April 22, 1908, George S. Patton, Jr., Papers; Dwyer to Turner, March 18, 1912, New Market File, Noland to Read, October 18, 1895, Noland to Wise, May 31, 1909, Noland File, John McGavock to Wise, May 20, 1909, McGavock File, Tunstall to Wise, December 27, 1894, Tunstall File, Wyndham Kemp to James Goggin, March 25, 1888, Kemp File, V.M.I.; New Market *Shenandoah Valley*, May

22, 1930; Lexington *Gazette*, May 25, 1864; Cocke, *Battle of New Market*, p. 6; Smith, "More on the Battle," p. 570; General Orders No. 5, May 4, 1864, Cadet Order Book, Preston Library; Charles J. Anderson to Margaret Anderson, May 17, 1864, Virginia Historical Society.

20. George D. Wells, Report of the Battle of New Market, May 21, 1864 (misquoted in *O.R.*), Graham to Cole, May 17, 1864, Strother Journal, II, May 15, 1864, Sigel, "Campaign in May," Sigel Papers, Cleveland; Stahel Report, RG 94, NA.

21. Strother, *Diaries*, pp. 224–25; Sigel, "Campaign in May," Additional Remarks to General Report of Operations, Strother Journal, II, May 15, 1864, Sigel Papers, Cleveland; *O.R.*, I, 37, 1, p. 109; Lang, *Loyal West Virginia*, pp. 113–14; New York *Tribune*, May 25, 1864; Ellis to Mary Phillips, May 19, 1864, Ellis Papers; Sigel, "Sigel in the Shenandoah," p. 488; *New Market Day at V.M.I.*, p. 81; Hewitt, *Twelfth West Virginia*, p. 111.

22. Strother, *Diaries*, pp. 225–26; Strother Journal, II, May 15, 1864, Sigel to Grant, June 17, 1885, Graham to Cole, May 17, 1864, Sigel Report, Sigel, "Campaign in May," Sigel Papers, Cleveland; Lang, *Loyal West Virginia*, p. 114; Hewitt, *Twelfth West Virginia*, pp. 111–13, 116–17; Lynch, *Diary*, p. 60; Sigel, "Sigel in the Shenandoah," pp. 488–89; Document No. 52, Stahel-Szamwald Papers; Lincoln, *Thirty-fourth Mass.*, p. 289; Lang, Personal Recollection, New Market File, V.M.I.

Chapter 8

1. Colonna to Wise, April 14, 1909, Colonna File, Breckinridge Report, New Market File, V.M.I.; Harrisonburg *Rockingham Register*, May 20, 1864; Smith statement, n.d., Edgar to Smith, March 24, 1908, George S. Patton, Jr., Papers; Richmond *Sentinel*, May 20, 1864; Crim, "Tender Memories," p. 212.

2. Colonna to Smith, October 21, 1910, George S. Patton, Jr., Papers; Rupert, Battle of New Market, Winterthur Collection; Crim, "Tender Memories," p. 212; Martha Henkel to R. J. Marshall, May 23, 1909, assorted clippings, Breckinridge Report, New Market File, V.M.I.; Harrisonburg *Rockingham Register*, May 20, 1864; John W. Wayland, *A History of Shenandoah County Virginia* (Strasburg, 1927), p. 324; Richmond *Sentinel*, May 20, 1864; Johnston, "Sketches of Operations," p. 260.

3. Richmond *Whig*, May 20, 1864; Johnston, New Market,

Breckinridge Report, New Market File, Smith to Edgar, October 1, 1910, Smith File, William McLaughlin to Wise, January 27, 1897, McLaughlin File, V.M.I.; Charles M. Keyes, *The Military History of the 123d Regiment of Ohio Volunteer Infantry* (Sandusky, 1874), p. 54; William T. Hart, Report, May 16, 1864, Organization table of Breckinridge's command, n.d., Sigel Papers, Cleveland; C. W. Humphreys, "Rev. Dr. Humphreys Replies to Criticism," *Confederate Veteran*, XVI (November 1908), p. 573; Smith to Edgar, May 14, 1908, Edgar Papers; Lexington *Gazette*, May 25, 1864; Smith, "More on the Battle," p. 570; Johnston, "Sketches of Operations," pp. 260–61.

4. Imboden to Wise, June 6, 1895, Imboden File, V.M.I.; Imboden, "New Market," p. 483.

5. Richmond *Sentinel*, May 25, 1864; Echols, *Address*, p. 7; Ward to Julia Ward, June 5, 1864, Ward Letters; Howard, "Recollections," p. 58; Johnston, "Sketches of Operations," p. 261; Johnston, New Market, New Market File, V.M.I.; Turner, *New Market*, p. 47; Bruce, "New Market," p. 155; Imboden, "New Market," p. 483; Lexington *Gazette*, May 25, 1864; "Battle of Newmarket, Va.," Frank Moore, ed., *The Rebellion Record* (New York, 1868), XI, p. 517.

6. Strother, *Diaries*, pp. 225–26; Keyes, *123d Regiment*, p. 55; *O.R.*, I, 37, 1, pp. 80, 82, 83; New York *Tribune*, May 20, 25, 1864; Johnston, New Market, New Market File, V.M.I.; du Pont to Edgar, October 1, 1908, Edgar Papers; Table of Breckinridge's command, Julius Stahel, Map of Battle of New Market, 1877, Sigel Papers, Cleveland; Harrisonburg *Rockingham Register*, May 20, 1864; Hewitt, *Twelfth West Virginia*, p. 107; du Pont, *Battle of Newmarket*, p. 28; Order and Descriptive Book, 30th Independent Battery, New York Light Artillery, RG 94, Kleiser to du Pont, June 13, 1864, Alfred von Kleiser, Compiled Service Record, RG 94, NA; Baltimore *Sun*, July 23, 1903; Turner, *New Market*, p. 99n; Henry S. Clapp, *Sketches of Army Life in the Sixties* (Newark, N.J., 191[?]), p. 16; Bruce, "New Market," p. 157.

7. John Carlin, Compiled Service Record, RG 94, NA; Wheeling *Daily Intelligencer,* May 23, 1864; Sigel, "Sigel in the Shenandoah," p. 489; Frank Imboden, "Gen. G. C. Wharton," *Confederate Veteran*, XIV (September 1906), p. 392; Lincoln, *Thirty-fourth Mass.*, p. 281; *O.R.*, I, 37, 1, p. 86.

8. Imboden, "New Market," p. 483; Harrisonburg *Rockingham*

Register, May 20, 1864; Smith, "More on the Battle," p. 572; Imboden to Wise, June 6, 1895, Imboden File, V.M.I.; Sigel, "Sigel in the Shenandoah," p. 489n; Stahel, Map of the Battle of New Market, Sigel, Campaign in May, Map of New Market, Strother Journal, II, May 15, 1864, Sigel Papers, Cleveland; Fitz-Simons, "Sigel's Fight," p. 63; Turner, *New Market,* p. 61; Strother, *Diaries,* p. 226.

9. Campbell to Sigel, May 1, 1867, Sigel Papers, Cleveland; Wheeling *Daily Intelligencer,* May 24, 1864; Fitz-Simons, "Sigel's Fight," p. 64; Clapp, *Sketches of Army Life,* p. 16; Strother, *Diaries,* p. 226; du Pont, *Battle of Newmarket,* p. 26.

10. Sigel, Campaign in May, Theodore Meysenburg Journal, May 15, 1864, Sigel, Additional Remarks, Sigel to Grant, June 17, 1885, Sigel Papers, Cleveland; Hewitt, *Twelfth West Virginia,* pp. 112–13; du Pont, *Battle of Newmarket,* pp. 14–15; George Crook, *General George Crook, His Autobiography* (Norman, Okla., 1946), ed. by Martin F. Schmitt, p. 122; Strother, *Diaries,* p. 226; *O.R.,* I, 37, 1, p. 80; Sigel, "Sigel in the Shenandoah," p. 489; Turner, *New Market,* p. 55n.

11. Lexington *Gazette,* May 25, 1864; Otey to Ship, April 14, 1875, Otey File, Breckinridge Report, New Market File, V.M.I.; Adolphus P. Young to Wharton, January 7, 1874, Gabriel C. Wharton Papers in possession of Anne Wharton von Poederoyen, Van Nuys, Calif.; Strother Journal, II, May 15, 1864.

12. Johnston to Wise, October 25, 1910, Johnston, New Market, Breckinridge Report, New Market File, Micajah Woods to John Woods, May 16, 1864, Micajah Woods File, V.M.I.; Blain to Castleman, January 15, 1917, Castleman Papers; Johnston, *Kentucky,* p. 187; Imboden, "Wharton," p. 392; Neilson, "Sixty-second Virginia," p. 61; James B. Clay, Jr. to Susan M. Clay, July 26, 1864, Thomas J. Clay Papers, Library of Congress; Smith, *Positions and Movements,* p. 31; Johnston, *Chapman's Battery,* pp. 19–20; Johnston, "Sketches of Operations," p. 261; Richmond *Sentinel,* May 20, 1864; Fitz-Simons, "Sigel's Fight," pp. 64–65; *O.R.,* I, 37, 1, p. 84.

13. Breckinridge Report; Echols, *Address,* p. 7; New Market *Shenandoah Valley,* July 30, 1908; Smith to Edgar, April 13, 1908, Edgar to Smith, July 3, 1906, George S. Patton, Jr., Papers; Smith, *Positions and Movements,* p. 27; Staunton *Spectator and Vindicator,* May 20, 1904; Howard Morton, "The New Market Charge,"

Southern Historical Society Papers, XXIV (1896), p. 302; Edgar Report, Edgar to Wise, February 18, 1896, T. R. Maddy to Edgar, March 18, 1896, Samuel Cunningham to Edgar, April 20, 1908, Edgar Papers; Richmond *Times-Dispatch,* October 15, 1905.

14. Sigel, "Sigel in the Shenandoah," p. 489; Graham to Cole, May 17, 1864, Sigel Papers, Cleveland; Breckinridge Report, Upshur to Wise, March 21, 1909, J. N. Upshur File, V.M.I.; Pittsburgh *Dispatch,* November 10, 1895; Pulaski *Southwest Times,* December 12, 1911; Wheeling *Daily Intelligencer,* May 24, 1864; David Jones to Smith, July 17, 1913, Edgar to Smith, March 10, 1908, George S. Patton, Jr., Papers; New York *Tribune,* May 20, 1864; Bruce, "New Market," pp. 155–57; Staunton *Spectator and Vindicator,* May 20, 1904.

15. Pulaski *Southwest Times,* December 12, 1911; Otey, *The War Cadets,* pp. 7–8; Otey to Ship, April 14, 1875, Otey File, Ship to Young, April 28, 1873, Ship File, V.M.I.; Colonna to Smith, November 1, 1910, George S. Patton, Jr., Papers; Colonna, "New Market," p. 346.

16. Smith to Wise, June 26, 1911, George S. Patton, Jr., Papers; Smith, "More on the Battle," pp. 569, 570, 572; New Market *Shenandoah Valley,* July 30, 1908; Neilson, "Sixty-second Virginia," p. 60–61; Staunton *Spectator,* May 17, 1864; *O.R.,* I, 37, 1, p. 226; Staunton *Vindicator,* May 27, 1864; "Meville Davidson Lang," *Confederate Veteran,* XVIII (May 1910), p. 240; Smith, *Positions and Movements,* pp. 2–3; F. D. Kildow to Turner, March 14, 1912, New Market File, V.M.I.

17. Smith, "More on the Battle," p. 569; New Market *Shenandoah Valley,* May 19, 1910; Turner, *New Market,* p. 55n; Charles H. Woodson to R. E. Lee, October 21, 1863, Charles H. Woodson, Compiled Service Record, RG 109, Consolidated Morning Report Book, 30th Independent Battery New York Light Artillery, May 16, 1864, RG 94, NA; James F. Smith, "Inquiry," *Confederate Veteran,* VI (June 1898), p. 277; William T. Price, *Memorials of Edward Herndon Scott, M.D.* (Singer's Glen, Va., 1873), pp. 10–11, 14–15; Wayland, *Shenandoah County,* p. 319; Harrisonburg *Rockingham Register,* May 20, 1864; Richmond *Sentinel,* May 30, 1864.

18. Richmond *Times-Dispatch,* October 8, 1905; Smith to Edgar, May 14, 1908, Derrick to Edgar, n.d., Edgar, Battle of New Market, p. 9, Edgar Papers; Wise, "Cadets at New Market," p. 361.

19. Clay to ?, April 23, 1905, in possession of Mrs. John M. Prewitt, Mount Sterling, Ky.; Edwin P. Thompson, *History of*

the Orphan Brigade (Louisville, 1898), p. 453; clipping from un-identified newspaper in New Market File, V.M.I.; Bennett Young, "John Cabell Breckinridge," *Confederate Veteran*, XIII (June 1905), pp. 259–60.

20. Richmond *Whig*, May 25, 1864; Lexington *Gazette*, May 25, 1864; Staunton *Spectator*, May 31, 1864; Gideon Davenport to Preston Cocke, January 28, 1895, Davenport File, R. H. Cousins to Wise, May 12, 1909, Cousins File, Porter Johnson to Wise, June 8, 1909, Johnson File, Colonna to Wise, April 14, 1909, Colonna File, Noland to Read, October 18, 1895, Noland File, V.M.I.; Wise, "West Point of the Confederacy," p. 470; Harrisonburg *Rockingham Register*, May 20, 1864; *New Market Day*, pp. 15–16; *O.R.*, I, 37, 1, p. 90; Couper, *New Market Cadets*, p. 23; Crim, "Tender Memories," p. 213; Wise, *Military History*, p. 313; Howard, "Recollections," p. 59; Turner, *New Market*, p. 81n; Cocke, *Battle of New Market*, p. 8; Sigel, "Sigel in the Shenandoah," p. 489.

21. Johnston, "Sketches of Operations," p. 261; Johnston, New Market, New Market File, V.M.I.; Lexington *Gazette*, May 25, 1864.

Chapter 9

1. Sigel to Elise Sigel, May 27, 1864, Sigel Papers, New York.

2. Sigel, Additional Remarks, Sigel Papers, Cleveland; Wyneken to Breckinridge, August 2, 1865, Breckinridge Family Papers.

3. Casualties in battle of Newmarket, Sigel Papers, Cleveland; Stevens to Edgar, June 4, 1908, Derrick to Edgar, n.d., Edgar, Battle of New Market, p. 9, Thompson to Edgar, n.d., C. W. Humphreys to Smith, May 9, 1908, Smith to Edgar, May 5, 1906, Edgar Papers; Edgar to Smith, May 5, 1908, George S. Patton, Jr., Papers; Otey to Ship, April 14, 1875, Otey File, V.M.I.

4. Echols to J. R. Tucker, July 1, 1863, George S. Patton, Compiled Service Record, RG 109, NA; Patton to Susan Patton, December 29, 1863, March 18, 1864, Patton Papers; Couper, *New Market Cadets*, p. 150.

5. Johnston, New Market, New Market File, V.M.I.; Johnston, "Sketches of Operations," p. 261; Echols, *Address*, p. 7; C. Minge to Edgar, June 5, 1908, P. Thrasher to Edgar, July 21, 1908, Stevens to Edgar, June 4, 1908, Edgar Papers; Gatch, "Recollections," p. 212; Smith, *Positions and Movements*, p. 33; Edgar to Smith, March 10, 1908, George S. Patton, Jr., Papers.

6. Richmond *Sentinel,* May 20, 1864; McLaughlin to Wise, January 27, 1897, McLaughlin File, Woods to John Woods, May 16, 1864, Woods File, V.M.I.; Minge to Edgar, June 5, 1908, Thompson to Edgar, n.d., Edgar Papers; Strother, *Diaries,* p. 226; New Market *Shenandoah Valley,* July 30, 1908; Strother Journal, II, May 15, 1864, Sigel Papers, Cleveland; Reader, *Battery G,* p. 239; du Pont, *Battle of Newmarket,* pp. 27–28; Chatham T. Ewing, Compiled Service Record, William B. Tibbits, Report of Service, March 18, 1874, RG 94, NA; Frank Imboden, New Market Memoranda, Imboden Papers, Alderman Library; Roll of Company H, 22d Virginia Infantry, Virginia State Library, Richmond; Fitz-Simons, "Sigel's Fight," pp. 64–65; Christopher A. Newcomer, *Cole's Cavalry; or, Three Years in the Saddle in the Shenandoah Valley* (Baltimore, 1895), p. 124; New York *Tribune,* May 23, 1864; Gatch, "Recollections," p. 212; Wyneken to Breckinridge, August 2, 1865, Breckinridge Family Papers; Charles Halpine Diary, March 22, 1864, Halpine Collection.

7. Wheeling *Daily Register,* May 20, 1864; *O.R.,* I, 37, 1, p. 84; Wheeling *Daily Intelligencer,* May 24, 1864; Sigel, "Sigel in the Shenandoah," p. 489; Otey to Ship, April 14, 1875, Otey File, V.M.I.; Hewitt, *Twelfth West Virginia,* pp. 108, 117–18; Strother, *Diaries,* p. 226.

8. *O.R.,* I, 37, 1, pp. 84, 86; Sigel, Campaign in May, Sigel Papers, Cleveland; Wheeling *Daily Register,* May 20, 1864; Lincoln, *Thirty-fourth Mass.,* p. 282; Richmond *Sentinel,* May 20, 1864; New Market *Shenandoah Valley,* July 30, 1908; Rawling, *First Regiment Virginia,* p. 166; Clark, *Soldier's Offering,* p. 31; William H. Clark, *Poems and Sketches, with Reminiscences of the "Old 34th"* (South Framingham, Mass., 1890), p. 38; New York *Tribune,* May 27, 1864; Wheeling *Daily Intelligencer,* May 24, 1864.

9. Edgar Report, Morton to Edgar, February 16, 20, March, 1906, Read to Edgar, February 24, March 29, 1906, Smith to Edgar, May 5, 1906, Edgar Papers; Richmond *Times-Dispatch,* October 15, 1905; Edgar to Wise, February 18, 1896, Edgar File, V.M.I.; Staunton *Spectator and Vindicator,* May 20, 1904.

10. Richmond *Sentinel,* May 20, 1864; *O.R.,* I, 37, 1, p. 84; Lexington *Gazette,* May 25, 1864; Baltimore *Sun,* July 23, 1903; Pulaski *Southwest Times,* December 12, 1911; Wise, "Cadets at New Market," p. 361; Noland to Read, October 18, 1895, Noland to Wise, May 24, 1909, Noland File, V.M.I.; W. W. George state-

ment, March 6, 1906, Edgar Papers; Staunton *Spectator and Vindicator,* May 20, 1904; Bruce, "New Market," p. 157.

11. Lexington *Gazette,* May 25, 1864; Harrisonburg *Rockingham Register,* May 20, 1864; Cocke, *Battle of New Market,* pp. 8–9; Wayland, *Battle of New Market,* pp. 12–14; Couper, *New Market Cadets,* pp. 75–76, 164; Adams to Wise, July 26, 1909, Adams File, Woods to John Woods, May 16, 1864, Woods File, Otey to Ship, April 14, 1875, Otey File, clipping from unidentified newspaper, November 29, 1887, New Market File, V.M.I.; Ward to Julia Ward, June 5, 1864, Ward Letters; Richmond *Whig,* May 31, 1864; Thompson, *Orphan Brigade,* p. 454; Anderson to Margaret Anderson, May 17, 1864, Virginia Historical Society.

12. New Market *Shenandoah Valley,* July 30, 1908; Smith to Edgar, March 16, 1906, Edgar Papers; Corbin, "Diary," p. 213; Baltimore *Sun,* July 23, 1903; Woods to John Woods, May 16, 1864, Woods File, V.M.I.; *O.R.,* I, 37, 1, pp. 86–87; Campbell Report, correct copy in Sigel Papers, Cleveland; Wise to Smith, August 19, 1910, George S. Patton, Jr., Papers; Wise, "Cadets at New Market," p. 361; Turner, *New Market,* p. 162; Keyes, *123d Ohio,* p. 55.

13. Wise, *Shipp,* pp. 29–30; Staunton *Spectator,* May 24, 1864; Turner, *New Market,* pp. 159–60; Tunstall to Wise, March 30, 1909, Tunstall File, V.M.I.; Richmond *Times-Dispatch,* June 23, 1912; Parsons, "Capture of a Battery," p. 119; Staunton *Spectator and Vindicator,* September 2, 1904; Ward to Julia Ward, June 5, 1864, Ward Letters.

14. Dwyer to Turner, March 18, 1912, New Market File, Woods to John Woods, May 16, 1864, Woods File, V.M.I.; Richmond *Times-Dispatch,* June 23, 1912; A. F. Bronner to Sigel, December 29, 1891, Sigel Papers, New York; Kleiser to du Pont, June 13, 1864, Kleiser, Service Record, RG 94, NA; Richmond *Whig,* May 23, 1864; Lexington *Gazette,* May 18, 1864; Strother, *Diaries,* p. 230; Turner, *New Market,* pp. 152–61; Ward to Julia Ward, June 5, 1864, Ward Letters; Richmond *Sentinel,* May 20, 1864; Staunton *Spectator,* May 24, 1864. The capture of this gun from Kleiser's battery is the genesis of the greatest of several controversies which have grown about the battle. Indeed, it is the principal reason that the fight is so well known, thanks to the legend that the Cadets captured a battery and thereby won the battle. For over a century the facts behind this episode have been

so clouded with myth and hearsay that the truth was almost lost before the smoke of battle cleared away. The account here given is gleaned from the sources cited above—eyewitness, contemporary, corroborating, sources. They conclusively establish that the Cadets took one gun from Kleiser and that it was abandoned to them, not taken in hand-to-hand combat.

15. Colonna to Wise, April 14, 1909, Colonna File, Garrett to Wise, April 26, 1909, Garrett File, V.M.I.; Colonna, "New Market," p. 349; Morton, "The Newmarket Charge," p. 303; *New Market Day*, p. 181; T. C. Morton, "Gave His Life for His Flag," *Confederate Veteran*, XII (February 1904), p. 70; Lincoln, *Thirty-fourth Mass.*, p. 295; Clark, *Soldier's Offering*, p. 32; *O.R.*, I, 37, 1, pp. 84–85; Strother Journal, II, May 15, 1864, Sigel Papers, Cleveland; Turner, *New Market*, p. 145.

16. *O.R.*, I, 37, 1, pp. 85–86; New York *Tribune*, May 18, 1864; Charles G. Halpine [Miles O'Reilly], *Baked Meats of the Funeral* (New York, 1866), p. 30; Halpine to James G. Bennett, May 27, 1864, James Gordon Bennett Papers, Library of Congress; Sigel, "Sigel in the Shenandoah," pp. 489–90; Sigel, Additional Remarks, Strother Journal, II, May 15, 1864, Sigel Papers, Cleveland; Wheeling *Daily Intelligencer*, May 24, 1864; Wheeling *Daily Register*, May 20, 23, 1864.

17. Turner, *New Market*, pp. 142–43; Staunton *Spectator and Vindicator*, May 20, 1904; Pulaski *Southwest Times*, December 12, 1911; Robert Wolfe to Turner, February 6, 1912, New Market File, V.M.I.; Edgar Report, Read to Edgar, March 29, 1906, W. W. Jones to Edgar, March 1906, Morton to Edgar, March 1906, Edgar Papers; Richmond *Times-Dispatch*, October 15, 1905. This part of the battle, equally controversial with the actions of the Cadets, is difficult to sort out, and the account given here is based on a very careful study of the field, a wary weighing of the sources, and a good knowledge through long acquaintance of the characters and personalities of the chief protagonists: the modest Wharton for the 51st Virginia and the glory-seeking Edgar for the 26th.

18. Strother, *Diaries*, p. 227; *O.R.*, I, 37, 1, pp. 84, 109; New York *Tribune*, May 20, 1864; Smith, "More on the Battle," p. 570; Smith to Edgar, April 22, 1908, Edgar Papers; Couper, *New Market Cadets*, p. 161; Wheeling *Daily Intelligencer*, May 24, 1864; Blain to Castleman, January 15, 1917, Castleman Papers.

19. *O.R.*, I, 37, 1, p. 85; Hewitt, *Twelfth West Virginia*, p. 118;

John Carr to Edgar, March 25, 1906, Edgar Report, Smith to Edgar, March 16, 1906, April 22, 1908, Edgar Papers; Richmond *Times-Dispatch*, October 15, 1905; Lexington *Gazette*, May 25, 1864; Ward to Julia Ward, June 5, 1864, Ward Letters; Woods to John Woods, May 16, 1864, Woods File, Wolfe to Turner, February 6, 1912, New Market File, V.M.I.; Neilson, "Sixty-second Virginia," p. 61; Couper, *One Hundred Years*, II, p. 336; Colonna, "New Market," p. 347; New Market *Shenandoah Valley*, May 16, 1895; Anderson to Margaret Anderson, May 17, 1864, Virginia Historical Society.

20. B. A. Colonna, "Light Battery B, Fifty U.S. Artillery, May 15, 1864," *Journal of the Military Service Institution of the United States*, LI (November 1912), p. 350; Smith to Edgar, April 22, 1908, George to Edgar, March 6–7, 1906, Edgar Papers; Richmond *Times-Dispatch*, October 15, 1905; Edgar to Wise, May 9, 1895, February 18, 1896, Edgar to Smith, February 18, 1896, Edgar File, V.M.I.

21. Stahel Report, RG 94, NA; du Pont, *Battle of Newmarket*, p. 16; Turner, *New Market*, p. 162; *O.R.*, I, 37, 1, p. 86; Pittsburgh *Dispatch*, November 10, 1895.

22. Colonna, "Battery B," pp. 350–51; du Pont, *Battle of Newmarket*, pp. 9, 15–18; Henry A. du Pont to Henry du Pont, May 17, 1864, Winterthur Collection; du Pont to Edgar, October 1, 1908, Edgar Papers.

23. Breckinridge Report, Otey to Ship, April 14, 1875, Otey File, V.M.I.; Edgar Report, Stevens to Edgar, June 4, 1908, Edgar Papers; Staunton *Spectator and Vindicator*, May 20, 1904; Imboden, "New Market," pp. 484–85; Cocke, *Battle of New Market*, p. 6; New Market *Shenandoah Valley*, May 16, 1895; Smith to Turner, n.d., George S. Patton, Jr., Papers; Gilmor, *Four Years*, p. 156; Parsons, "Capture of Battery," p. 119; Baltimore *Sun*, July 23, 1903; Shank, "Gunner at New Market," p. 191.

24. Kleiser to du Pont, June 13, 1864, Thomas McKee to George D. Ramsay, May 28, 1864, Kleiser, Service Record, RG 94, NA; Sigel, "Sigel in the Shenandoah," p. 490; Strother, *Diaries*, p. 227; Sigel, Campaign in May, Strother Journal, II, May 15, 1864, Stahel, Map of the Battle of New Market, Sigel Papers, Cleveland; Sigel to Elise Sigel, May 27, 1864, Sigel Papers, New York; Moor memoir, Moor Collection; *O.R.*, I, 37, 1, p. 80; Wildes, *One Hundred and Sixteenth Regiment*, p. 87.

25. Breckinridge Report, Woods to John Woods, May 16, 1864, Woods File, V.M.I.; Baltimore *Sun,* July 23, 1903; McLaughlin to Johnston, May 19, 1864, Sigel Papers, Cleveland; Blain to Castleman, January 15, 1917, Castleman Papers.

26. Strother, *Diaries,* pp. 227–28; Sigel, "Sigel in the Shenandoah," p. 490; Sigel to Grant, June 17, 1885, Sigel Report, Sigel, Additional Remarks, Sigel Papers, Cleveland; *O.R.,* I, 37, 1, pp. 76, 80, 81, 84, 87, 109; Walker, *Eighteenth Regiment Conn.,* pp. 223–24; Breckinridge Report, Kildow to Turner, March 14, 1912, New Market File, V.M.I.; Staunton *Spectator and Vindicator,* May 20, 1904; Baltimore *Sun,* July 23, 1903; Norton, *Red Neck Ties,* p. 36; Wheeling *Daily Intelligencer,* May 23, 24, 1864; Stevenson, *"Boots and Saddles,"* p. 272; du Pont to Edgar, October 1, 1908, Edgar Papers; du Pont, *Battle of Newmarket,* pp. 10, 18–19; William A. McIlhenny Diary, May 15, 1864, in possession of Mrs. Janet Elliott, Brooklyn, N.Y.; Tibbits Report, RG 94, NA; Frost to his mother, May 17, 1864, Matheny Collection.

27. Wayland, *Battle of New Market,* pp. 14, 17–18; Woods to John Woods, May 16, 1864, Woods File, Kemp to Goggin, March 25, 1888, Kemp File, Edgar to Wise, May 9, 1895, Edgar File, V.M.I.; Johnston, "Sketches of Operations," p. 262; Wise, "West Point of the Confederacy," p. 470; Breckinridge to Lee, May 15, 1864, Venable Papers; New Market *Shenandoah Valley,* May 16, 1895; Hildreth, *New Market,* pp. 7, 24; Crim, "Tender Memories," p. 212; Hewitt, *Twelfth West Virginia,* p. 120; Colonna and H. P. Whitehead to Smith, October 21, 1910, George S. Patton, Jr., Papers; Rupert, Battle of New Market, Winterthur Collection.

Chapter 10

1. Noland to Mary Noland, May 19, 1864, Noland Family Papers; Merritt to W. H. E. Merritt, May 16, 1864, New Market Battlefield Park; Anderson to Margaret Anderson, May 17, 1864, Virginia Historical Society; Ward to Julia Ward, June 5, 1864, Ward Letters; Barrett and Turner, *New Market Cadet,* p. 64; Couper, *New Market Cadets,* pp. 6, 15–16, 34, 190, 255–56; Baltimore *Sun,* June 21, 1903; Cornelia McDonald, *A Diary with Reminiscences of the War and Refugee Life in the Shenandoah Valley, 1860–1865* (Nashville, 1935), p. 202; New Market *Shenandoah Valley,* June 23, 1921; Couper, *One Hundred Years,* II, pp. 328–29; Crim, "Tender Memories," p. 213; Wise, "West Point

of the Confederacy," p. 471; Gilmor, *Four Years*, p. 157; Louis C. Wise, Reminiscences of the Battle of New Market, 1909, Louis Wise File, Ship Report, copy in Ship File, V.M.I.; Staunton *Spectator*, May 17, 1864.

2. Wise, *Military History*, p. 340.

3. Warner, "First Gun at New Market," p. 237; Richmond *Whig*, May 23, 1864; Quartermaster's Receipt, May 17, 1864, Randolph H. Blain, Compiled Service Record, RG 109, NA; Woods to John Woods, May 16, 1864, Woods File, V.M.I.

4. Hewitt, *Twelfth West Virginia*, pp. 114, 120; Corbin, "Diary," p. 213; Rupert, Battle of New Market, Winterthur Collection; Beach, *First New York*, p. 355; Harrisonburg *Rockingham Register*, May 20, 1864; Parsons, "Capture of a Battery," p. 119; Gatch, "Recollections," p. 212; Mastin Diary, May 16, 1864, Cook Collection; Woolwine, "Diary," p. 436.

5. Lee to Breckinridge, May 16, 1864, copy in possession of William L. Breckinridge, South Haven, Mich.; Richmond *Enquirer*, May 24, 1864; Staunton *Spectator*, May 17, 1864; Harrisonburg *Rockingham Register*, May 20, 1864; Richmond *Whig*, May 23, 1864; Gilmor, *Four Years*, p. 158; Wise, *Military History*, p. 339; *O.R.*, I, 37, 1, pp. 91, 738; Johnston to Wise, October 25, 1910, New Market File, V.M.I.

6. *O.R.*, I, 37, 1, pp. 738, 740, 742, 743; Woolwine, "Diary," p. 436; Mastin Diary, May 17–19, 1864; Susan G. Patton to Andrew ——, May 30, 1864, Patton Papers; Susan M. Baldwin to Breckinridge, May 19, 1864, Breckinridge Family Papers; Richmond *Whig*, June 13, 1864; Johnston, *Kentucky*, p. 188.

7. Lincoln, *Thirty-fourth Mass.*, p. 290; Strother, *Diaries*, p. 229; Halpine, *Baked Meats*, pp. 300–1; Sigel, "Sigel in the Shenandoah," p. 490; "Battle of Newmarket, Va.," Moore, *Rebellion Record*, XI, p. 517; Hewitt, *Twelfth West Virginia*, pp. 110, 115–16; Powell, Memoirs; du Pont to Henry du Pont, May 17, 1864, Winterthur Collection; Walker, *Eighteenth Regiment Conn.*, p. 225; Graham to Cole, May 16, 17, 1864, Sigel, Campaign in May, Sigel Papers, Cleveland; New York *Tribune*, May 25, 1864; Wheeling *Daily Intelligencer*, May 23, 1864; Cushman to Caroline Cushman, May 20, 1864, Cushman Papers; Frost to his mother, May 17, 1864, Matheny Collection; Rodgers, 2nd Eastern Shore Regiment, pp. 180–81, Rodgers Papers; Moor memoir, Moor Collection.

8. New York *Tribune,* May 18, 25, 1864; Wheeling *Daily Register,* May 19, 1864; Harrisburg *Weekly Patriot and Union,* May 26, 1864; *O.R.,* I, 37, 1, pp. 475, 478, 485, 492, 507, I, 36, 1, pp. 840–41; Grant, *Memoirs,* II, pp. 147, 238; Porter, *Campaigning with Grant,* p. 124; Sigel, Campaign in May, Sigel Papers, Cleveland; Strother, *Diaries,* pp. 230–32; Strong, *Diary,* p. 455; Sigel to Elise Sigel, June 1, 1864, Sigel Papers, New York.

9. *O.R.,* I, 37, 1, p. 477, I, 37, 2, pp. 340, 366, I, 40, 3, p. 59; Sigel, "Sigel in the Shenandoah," p. 490; Sigel, Campaign in May, Halpine to Sigel, June 12, 1864, Graham to Cole, May 17, 1864, Campbell to Sigel, May 1, 1867, Lyon to Sigel, May 18, 19, 20, 1864, Franz Sigel, Autobiographical Sketch, Sigel Papers, Cleveland; Rodgers, 2nd Eastern Shore Regiment, Rodgers Papers; Halpine Diary, May 22–23, 1864, Halpine to Bennett, July 12, 1865, Halpine Collection; Sigel to Elise Sigel, June 1, 16, 1864, Isaac Arnold to Sigel, May 30, 1864, Sigel Papers, New York; Wheeling *Daily Register,* May 28, 1864; Wheeling *Daily Intelligencer,* May 23, 1864; New York *Tribune,* May 25, 1864; Strother, *Diaries,* p. 230; Stevenson, *"Boots and Saddles,"* pp. 273–74; H. C. Vogel to Bennett, May 28, 1864, Theodore Wilson to Bennett, May 27, 1864, Bennett Papers; Ambrose Thompson to Sigel, August 22, 1867, January 8, July 9, 1868, Ambrose W. Thompson Papers, Library of Congress.

10. *O.R.,* I, 37, 1, pp. 494, 516; Jacob Weddle, Compiled Service Record, Kleiser to du Pont, June 13, 1864, Kleiser, Service Record, George D. Wells, Compiled Service Record, Joseph Thoburn, Compiled Service Record, Stahel to E. D. Townsend, February 6, 1865, Julius Stahel, Personnel File, RG 94, NA; Sigel to Elise Sigel, June 16, 1864, Sigel Papers, New York; Halpine Diary, July 12, 1864, Halpine Collection.

11. Harrisonburg *Rockingham Register,* May 20, 1864; Halpine Diary, June 3, 1864, Halpine Collection; J. Cutler Andrews, *The South Reports the Civil War* (Princeton, 1970), p. 421; Staunton *Vindicator,* July 8, 1864; John D. Imboden, Autobiographical Sketch, John D. Imboden Letters, Library of Congress; Martin Blumenson, *The Patton Papers, I: 1885–1940* (Boston, 1972), p. 24; Wayland, *Shenandoah County,* pp. 329–30; Blain, Service Record, George B. Chapman, Compiled Service Record, Edgar, Service Record, Wharton to Cooper, August 30, 1864, Samuel Jones to Patton, July 6, 1864, George S. Patton, Compiled Service Record, Woodson, Service Record, RG 109, NA; Davis, "51st Regi-

ment," pp. 199–201; Echols to Breckinridge, June 1, 1864, A. Caperton to Breckinridge, May 31, 1864, Breckinridge Family Papers; Ransom, "Echols," pp. 316–17; Lee Wallace, *A Guide to Virginia Military Organizations 1861–1865* (Richmond, 1964), p. 136; F. Hines to Edgar, February 26, 1906, Edgar Papers; Totten to the author, February 8, November 24, 1972.

12. Couper, *New Market Cadets*, pp. 7, 16, 86, 130, 251; A. Thompson to Wise, April 1, 1909, Thompson File, V.M.I.; Wise, *Military History*, p. 341; Harrisonburg *Rockingham Register*, May 20, 1864; Couper, *Shenandoah*, II, pp. 933–34; Richmond *Daily Dispatch*, May 28, 1864; Frank E. Vandiver, ed., "Proceedings of the Second Confederate Congress, First Session, Second Session in Part, 2 May–14 June, 1864, 7 November–14 December 1864," *Southern Historical Society Papers*, LI (1958), p. 131; Wise, "Cadets at New Market," p. 362; Wise, *Shipp*, p. 52; Richmond *Sentinel*, June 1, 1864; Lynchburg *Daily Virginian*, June 2, 1864; Richmond *Whig*, May 31, 1864; "Col. Francis Lee Smith," pp. 84–85; Baltimore *Herald*, October 28, 1894.

13. Charles J. Faulkner to Breckinridge, October 11, 1864, Confederate Collection of Stanley E. Butcher; Couper, *New Market Cadets*, pp. 68, 106, 110, 194; Young, "Breckinridge," p. 259; Louisville *Courier-Journal*, April 3, 1869; John C. Breckinridge Diary, March 3, 1868, in possession of Mrs. John M. Prewitt; Staunton *Vindicator*, May 20, 1864; Johnston, "Sketches of Operations," p. 261; Johnston, New Market, Johnston to Wise, December 31, 1909, Lang, Personal Recollections, New Market File, Edgar to Wise, February 18, 1896, Edgar File, Woods to John Woods, May 16, 1864, Woods File, V.M.I.; Wise to Smith, April 23, 1910, George S. Patton, Jr., Papers; Echols, *Address*, p. 11; Staunton *Spectator and Vindicator*, May 20, 1904; Imboden, "New Market," p. 485; Gilmor, *Four Years*, p. 156; Wyneken to Breckinridge, August 2, 1865, Breckinridge Family Papers; Wise, *Military History*, p. 343; O.R., I, 37, 1, pp. 744–45; Pay voucher, May–September 1864, John C. Breckinridge, Compiled Service Record, RG 109, NA.

14. Douglas S. Freeman, *Lee's Lieutenants: A Study in Command* (New York, 1944), III, pp. 515–16; Fitz-Simons, "Sigel's Fight," p. 66; Richmond *Sentinel*, May 20, 1864; McChesney to Johnson, May 31, 1864, McChesney Papers; Bristol *Gazette*, May 19, 1864; Richmond *Whig*, May 17, June 13, 1864; Richmond *Daily Dispatch*, May 19, 31, 1864; Richmond *Enquirer*, May 20,

1864; Johnston, "Sketches of Operations," p. 262; Lynchburg *Daily Virginian*, June 13, 1864; Edgar to Wise, February 18, 1896, Edgar File, V.M.I.; Gilmor, *Four Years*, pp. 263–64; Faulkner to Breckinridge, October 11, 1864, Confederate Collection, Butcher. For a full account of Breckinridge's career before and after New Market see William C. Davis, *Breckinridge: Statesman, Soldier, Symbol* (Baton Rouge, 1974).

15. Richmond *Whig*, May 31, 1864; John D. Imboden, "Fire, Sword, and the Halter," *Annals of the War* (Philadelphia, 1879), p. 170; Fitz-Simons, "Sigel's Fight," pp. 66–67; Halpine Diary, June 5, 1864, Halpine Collection.

Appendix A

1. *O.R.*, I, 37, 1, pp. 81–82; E. B. Culver to William A. Buckingham, May 18, 1864, Adjutant General's Files, Connecticut State Library, Hartford; Sigel, Additional Remarks, Strother Journal, II, March 30, 1864, Sigel Papers, Cleveland; Wildes, *One Hundred and Sixteenth Regiment*, p. 82. The figure for the 123d Ohio is entirely an estimate.

2. Strother Journal, I, March 30, 1864, Sigel Papers, Cleveland; Return of the 12th West Virginia, March 1864, Campbell Papers; *O.R.*, I, 37, 1, pp. 85, 87; James L. Bowen, *Massachusetts in the War, 1861–1865* (Springfield, 1889), p. 514.

3. Beach, *First New York*, p. 349; *O.R.*, I, 37, 1, pp. 503, 565, 571; Farrar, *Twenty-second Pennsylvania*, p. 197; Morning Report, February 29, 1864, Campbell Papers; Wynkoop Report, Moor Papers; New York *Tribune*, May 27, 1864. Some of these figures require careful interpolation of the above sources. The figure of 2,000 engaged is arrived at by subtracting Higgins' 500 and Boyd's 300, and by allowing 200 more for the numerous bridge guards, etc., left by Sigel.

4. *O.R.*, I, 33, p. 479, I, 37, 1, pp. 105, 701; Consolidated Morning Report Book, 30th Independent Battery, New York Light Artillery, May 15, 1864, RG 94, NA; New York *Tribune*, May 27, 1864. The figure for total artillery engaged is an estimate based on subtracting du Pont from the other units.

5. Casualties in battle of Newmarket, n.d., Sigel Papers, Cleveland; Edgar Report, Edgar Papers; Field Report of First Brigade, May 21, 1864, New Market File, V.M.I.

6. Casualties in battle of Newmarket, n.d., Sigel Papers, Cleveland; *O.R.*, I, 37, 1, p. 226; Richmond *Sentinel*, May 30, 1864;

Field Report of Wharton's Brigade, May 21, 1864, New Market File, V.M.I. The figure shown for the 62d Virginia is reached by deducting Woodson's numbers from the figure shown in the source.

7. Report of T. Hand, May 16, 1864, J. B. Berkeley to Johnston, May 16, 1864, Sigel Papers, Cleveland; Gatch, "Recollections," pp. 211–12; *O.R.*, I, 37, 1, p. 729; Ship Report, Ship File, V.M.I. The engaged figure for the Cadets omits the three sick who stayed in Staunton.

8. Berkeley to Johnston, May 16, 1864, Sigel Papers, Cleveland; *O.R.*, I, 37, 1, pp. 3, 69, 729.

9. McLaughlin Report, May 17, 1864, Report of Casualties, Imboden's Brigade, n.d., Sigel Papers, Cleveland; Breckinridge Report, Ship Report, Ship File, V.M.I. No precise reference to the composition of Jackson's battery exists, but Breckinridge reported using his rifled guns at long range. Chapman was kept at longer range than Blain, and therefore it is presumed that this battery was made up of 12-pounder Napoleons, since Breckinridge says, "I advanced my Napoleons." Jackson is known to have had 1 Parrott rifle as well. McClanahan's makeup is also sketchy, but *O.R.*, I, 37, 1, p. 731 states that on May 12 Imboden had four rifled field guns and two howitzers. This must refer to McClanahan.

Appendix B

1. With the exception of the 54th Pennsylvania, all casualty figures for Federal units are taken from the official report published in New York *Tribune*, May 27, 1864. Figures for the 54th Pennsylvania come from Jacob Campbell's holograph report in the Sigel Papers, Cleveland. It should be noted that the *Tribune* shows a total killed of 97, a typographical error.

2. Richmond *Whig*, May 24, 1864; casualties in battle of Newmarket, n.d., Sigel Papers, Cleveland; Edgar Report, Edgar Papers.

3. Casualties in battle of Newmarket, n.d., Sigel Papers, Cleveland; Turner, *New Market*, p. 143; Staunton *Vindicator*, May 27, 1864; Richmond *Sentinel*, May 30, 1864.

4. T. Hand Report, May 16, 1864, Sigel Papers, Cleveland; Staunton *Vindicator*, May 19, 27, 1864; Couper, *New Market Cadets*, p. 254. Five Cadets were killed, five mortally wounded.

5. Berkeley to Johnston, May 16, 1864, Sigel Papers, Cleveland.

6. McLaughlin to Johnston, May 19, 1864, Berkeley to Johnston, May 16, 1864, Sigel Papers, Cleveland.

A Note on Sources

The available source materials on New Market are legion. Indeed, no other Civil War engagement of comparable size has been so extensively written about. Much is of considerable value; much is worthless. What follows is not by any means a complete bibliography of the literature on the subject, nor even a complete listing of sources consulted for this book. It is, rather, a brief evaluation of the most useful and important resources. Many others, not sufficiently significant for mention here, will be found cited in the footnotes.

The field of manuscript sources is particularly rich, and by far the most important single collection is the Franz Sigel Papers at Western Reserve Historical Society, Cleveland, Ohio. It contains not only Sigel's official papers and reports, but also diaries of his staff officers and an invaluable body of Confederate materials as well. Almost equal in importance is the collection of V.M.I. Cadet letters, memoirs, and other documents in the New Market File and various Cadet files of the Alumni Files, Virginia Military Institute, Lexington. While most of the Cadet accounts must be used judiciously, on the whole they represent an indispensable volume of information. The George M. Edgar Papers, Southern Historical Collection, University of North Carolina Library, Chapel Hill, is also worthy of special notice, containing as it does Edgar's report of the battle and an important collection of letters from men and officers of the 51st and 26th Virginia.

Among other papers of Sigel and his officers are the Franz Sigel Papers, New-York Historical Society, New York City, which contain Sigel's illuminating wartime letters to his wife. The Jacob M. Campbell Papers, West Virginia Collection, University of West Virginia, Morgantown, are an important body of materials, including the diary and reports, from a capable regimental commander.

The Winterthur Manuscript Collection, Eleutherian Mills Historical Library, Greenville, Delaware, contains the very useful Henry A. du Pont letters and Mrs. Jessie Rupert's memoir of the battle. The Charles G. Halpine Collection, Henry E. Huntington Library and Art Gallery, San Marino, California, and the James Gordon Bennett Papers, Library of Congress, Washington, D.C., are particularly useful for Halpine's frank, generally acid, comments on Sigel's administration. The August Moor Collection, Illinois Historical Survey, Urbana, contains a useful report and memoir. While Julius Stahel's wartime diary was lost after the war, the Julius Stahel-Szamwald Papers, Signature R 170, Hungarian National Archives (Magyar Országos Levéltár), Budapest, scanty though they are, provide the only available materials from the perspective of Sigel's second-in-command. The reports of service of Sigel, Stahel, and William Tibbits in the records of the Adjutant General's Office and the Compiled Service Records and pension files of these and other Federal officers, all in Record Group 94, National Archives, Washington, D.C., also provided much worthwhile information not elsewhere available.

Records are equally plentiful for the Confederates. The most rewarding sources for Breckinridge are the Breckinridge Family Papers, Library of Congress, and the John C. Breckinridge Papers, Chicago Historical Society. From his officers, the John B. Castleman Papers, Filson Club, Louisville, Kentucky; Harry W. Gilmor Papers, Maryland Historical Society, Baltimore; John D. Imboden Papers, Margaret I. King Library, University of Kentucky, Lexington, and John D. Imboden Papers, Alderman Library, University of Virginia, Charlottesville, and the Charles S. Venable Papers, Southern Historical Collection, are particularly useful. Of special interest are the George S. Patton Papers in possession of Ruth Ellen Patton Totten, South Hamilton, Massachusetts, containing Colonel Patton's wartime letters to his wife. And the George S. Patton, Jr., Papers, Library of Congress, contain a box of very important papers of George H. Smith relating to the battle. Once again, the Compiled Service Records of Breckinridge and his unit commanders, Record Group 109, National Archives, yielded additional useful data.

Papers of men in the ranks are more scanty. Useful for the Union side are the David F. Cushman Papers, American Antiquarian Society, Worcester, Massachusetts; the William M. Ellis Papers, Norman Daniels Collection, U. S. Army Military History Research Collection, Carlisle Barracks, Pennsylvania; the William McIlhenny

Diary in possession of Mrs. Janet Elliott, Brooklyn, New York; and the Ephram Frost Letters, H. E. Matheny Collection, University of West Virginia, Morgantown. An invaluable, though brief, Confederate source is the John Mastin Diary, Roy Bird Cook Collection, West Virginia University.

Official unit records have been helpful, including consolidated morning report books for the various Federal regiments in RG 94, National Archives. Vital Confederate records are Breckinridge's headquarters records, Chapter II, Volume 63, RG 109, National Archives, and the Rufus J. Woolwine Papers, Virginia Historical Society, Richmond. Several collections in addition to the alumni files are extant for the Cadets, the most useful being the Corps of Cadets Order Book, 1864, in the Preston Library, V.M.I.; the Charles Anderson Letter, Virginia Historical Society, the James L. Merritt Letter, New Market Battlefield Park; and the Noland Family Papers and George Ward Letters, Alderman Library, University of Virginia, Charlottesville. These Cadet letters are particularly significant.

Newspapers have been extremely useful, and the files of the following journals for May–July 1864 contain excellent letters on the battle by eyewitnesses and participants: Harrisonburg *Rockingham Register,* Lexington *Gazette,* New York *Tribune,* Richmond *Daily Dispatch,* Richmond *Enquirer,* Richmond *Examiner,* Richmond *Sentinel,* Richmond *Whig,* Staunton *Spectator,* Staunton *Vindicator* (later merged with the *Spectator*), Wheeling *Daily Register,* and the Wheeling *Daily Intelligencer.* Later newspapers which published important accounts of the battle include the Baltimore *Sun,* July 23, 1903, containing Carter Berkeley's very full account; the New Market *Shenandoah Valley* for several issues containing letters of participants; and the Staunton *Spectator and Vindicator* for May 20, 1904, which published Gabriel Wharton's excellent, and indispensable, memoir of the fight.

Hundreds of books and pamphlets have been published touching on the New Market affair. For basic reference, the U. S. War Department's *War of the Rebellion: Official Records of the Union and Confederate Armies* (Washington, 1880–1901), 128 vols., is absolutely vital, though many of the documents published in it are not correctly transcribed, resulting in several errors. For general background on New Market and the Shenandoah Valley, Douglas S. Freeman, *Lee's Lieutenants: A Study in Command* (New York,

1944), 3 vols.; Edward Younger, ed., *Inside the Confederate Government: The Diary of Robert Garlick Hill Kean* (New York, 1957); William Couper, *History of the Shenandoah Valley* (New York, 1952), 3 vols.; and John W. Wayland, *A History of Shenandoah County Virginia* (Strasburg, Va., 1927), have proved especially useful. John T. Peerce, "Capture of a Railroad Train," *Southern Bivouac*, Old Series, II (April 1884), pp. 352–55, is excellent for McNeill's cavalry campaign to delay Sigel's advance.

Among actual histories of the Battle of New Market, E. Raymond Turner, *The New Market Campaign, May, 1864* (Richmond, 1912), has long been the standard source. Badly dated and suffering from the fact that Turner, whose field was European history, was working out of his element, it is still useful, especially for the now-extinct sources which he quoted extensively in his footnotes. Also valuable is John W. Wayland, *Battle of New Market: Memorial Address, Sixty-second Anniversary of the Battle of New Market, Va., May 15, 1926* (New Market, 1926). Arthur L. Hildreth, *A Brief History of New Market and Vicinity* (New Market, 1964), is an excellent study on the Valley town, with a valuable map of its wartime buildings.

Published accounts by participants have been most helpful. Daniel H. Bruce, "The Battle of New Market, Virginia," *Confederate Veteran*, XV (December 1907), pp. 553–54, is perhaps the best such source for the 51st Virginia. Henry A. du Pont, *The Battle of Newmarket, Virginia, May 15, 1864* (Winterthur, Del., 1923), is a first-rate though highly opinionated account by this capable officer. John D. Imboden's "The Battle of New Market, Va., May 15th, 1864," in Robert U. Johnson and C. C. Buel, eds., *Battles and Leaders of the Civil War* (New York, 1887–88), IV, pp. 480–86, is useful only for the campaign leading up to the battle and for Imboden's actions east of Smith's Creek. By far the best over-all account by a Confederate is J. Stoddard Johnston, "Sketches of Operations of General John C. Breckinridge, No. 1," *Southern Historical Society Papers*, VII (June 1879), pp. 257–62. The only published source for the 30th Virginia Battalion is Peter J. Otey, *Response of Hon. Peter J. Otey at the Alumni Banquet, June, 1896, to the Toast, "The War Cadets"* (Lexington, 1896); it is brief but helpful. The fullest over-all Federal account is Franz Sigel's "Sigel in the Shenandoah," in Johnson and Buel, eds., *Battles and Leaders*, IV, pp. 487–91; though it suffers from his compulsion for self-justification, it is very useful. George H. Smith of the 62d Virginia produced several good accounts, including *Battle of New Market Fought May 15th, 1864, Revised Copy* (n.p., n.d.); *The Positions and Movements of the Troops in the Battle of New Market Fought May 15th, 1864* (Los Angeles, 1913); and "More on the Battle of New Market," *Confederate Veteran*, XVI (November 1908), pp. 569–72. What may be considered a history of the campaign and battle is also found in Cecil D. Eby, Jr., ed., *A Virginia Yankee in the Civil War: The Diaries of David Hunter Strother* (Chapel Hill, N.C., 1961). Presented as a diary, Strother's account was actually written up some days after the battle. He is prejudiced, but informed.

Biographical materials on the chief actors are abundant. The major source for Breckinridge is William C. Davis, *Breckinridge: Statesman, Soldier, Symbol* (Baton Rouge, La., 1974), which contains a chapter on New Market. Also helpful are John Echols, *Address of Gen. John Echols on the Life and Character of Gen. John C. Breckinridge* (New Market, 1877); Edwin Porter Thompson, *History of the Orphan Brigade* (Louisville, Ky., 1898); and Bennett H. Young, "John Cabell Breckinridge," *Confederate Veteran*, XIII (June 1905), pp. 257–61. Martin F. Schmitt, ed., *General George Crook: His Autobiography* (Norman, Okla., 1946), is very illuminating for preparations for Sigel's campaign and Crook's part in it, as are U. S. Grant, *Personal Memoirs of U. S. Grant* (New York, 1885), 2 vols., and Horace Porter, *Campaigning with Grant*, 2d edition (Bloomington, Ind., 1961).

Roy P. Basler, ed., *The Collected Works of Abraham Lincoln* (New Brunswick, N.J., 1953), 9 vols., provides full material on Sigel's background and assignment to West Virginia. John S. Mosby, *Memoirs of Colonel John S. Mosby*, 2d edition (Bloomington, 1959), gives full background on his part in the campaign. Jennings C. Wise, *Personal Memoir of the Life and Service of Scott Shipp* (n.p., 1915), offers a brief, but revealing and informative biography of the Cadets' commander. Two good sources cover Gabriel Wharton: Frank M. Imboden, "Gen. G. C. Wharton," *Confederate Veteran*, XIV (September 1906), p. 392, and J. V. H. Wharton, "Gen. G. C. Wharton," *Confederate Veteran*, XIV (July 1906), pp. 318–19.

Regimental histories and diaries of officers and enlisted men of Federal units engaged abound. William A. Croffutt and John M.

Morris, *The Military and Civil History of Connecticut During the War of 1861–1865* (New York, 1868), is a good early history of the 18th Connecticut in the battle. Theodore F. Lang, *Loyal West Virginia from 1861 to 1865* (Baltimore, 1895), gives Lang's reminiscences of the fight. Again for the 18th Connecticut, Charles H. Lynch, *The Civil War Diary, 1862–1865, of Charles H. Lynch, 18th Conn. Vols.* (Hartford, 1915), is quite valuable, while by far the best source is William C. Walker, *History of the Eighteenth Regiment Conn. Volunteers in the War for the Union* (Norwich, 1885).

Material on the Ohio units is scarce. James M. Dalzell, *Private Dalzell, His Autobiography, Poems and Comic War Papers* (Cincinnati, 1888), is good for the 116th. Better is Thomas F. Wildes, *Record of the One Hundred and Sixteenth Regiment, Ohio Infantry Volunteers, in the War of the Rebellion* (Sandusky, 1884). Charles M. Keyes, *The Military History of the 123d Regiment of Ohio Volunteer Infantry* (Sandusky, 1874) is very useful.

Charles J. Rawling, *History of the First Regiment Virginia Infantry* (Philadelphia, 1887) is very good for this unit, while William Hewitt, *History of the Twelfth West Virginia Volunteer Infantry* (Steubenville, Ohio, 1892) is an excellent account for Curtis' regiment.

The 34th Massachusetts is the best memorialized Federal unit. William H. Clark, *Reminiscences of the Thirty-fourth Regiment, Mass. Vol. Infantry* (Holliston, Mass., 1871), is a good early account, though Clark's *The Soldier's Offering* (Boston, 1875) is better. By far the best source, though, is William S. Lincoln, *Life with the Thirty-fourth Mass. Infantry in the War of the Rebellion* (Worcester, Mass., 1879).

Sources for Sigel's artillery are slim. Francis S. Reader, *History of the Fifth West Virginia Cavalry . . . and of Battery G, First West Va. Light Artillery* (New Brighton, Pa., 1890), is brief but helpful. Du Pont's *Battle of Newmarket* and Benjamin A. Colonna, "Light Battery B, Fifth U.S. Artillery, May 15, 1864," *Journal of the Military Service Institution of the United States*, LI (November-December 1912), are good for du Pont's command.

The Federal cavalry is well represented by regimentals, a few of them being distinguished. James H. Stevenson, *Boots and Saddles: A History of the First Volunteer Cavalry of the War, Known as the First New York (Lincoln) Cavalry* (Harrisburg, Pa., 1879) is first rate, particularly for Boyd's fiasco, as is William Beach, *The First New York (Lincoln) Cavalry, from April 19, 1861, to July 7, 1865* (New York, 1902). Chauncey S. Norton, *The Red Neck Ties: or History of the Fifteenth New York Volunteer Cavalry* (Ithaca, 1891), is sketchy, as is Charles Fitz-Simons, "Sigel's Fight at New Market," *Military Order of the Loyal Legion of the United States, Illinois* (Chicago, n.d.), III, pp. 61–67, for the 21st New York Cavalry. However, John W. Elwood, *Elwood's Stories of the Old Ringgold Cavalry, 1847–1865, the First Three Year Cavalry of the Civil War* (Coal Center, Pa., 1914), and Samuel C. Farrar, *The Twenty-second Pennsylvania Cavalry and the Ringgold Battalion, 1861–1865* (Pittsburgh, 1911), are extremely useful for the 22d Pennsylvania.

Confederate regimentals are almost nonexistent, but some books and articles provide material. James A. Davis, "The 51st Regiment, Virginia Volunteers, 1861–1865," *West Virginia History,* XXIX (April 1968), pp. 178–202, is a good history, supplemented by the brief but useful Louis H. Manarin, ed., "The Civil War Diary of Rufus J. Woolwine," *Virginia Magazine of History and Biography,* LXXI (October 1963), pp. 416–48. For the 62d Virginia, Jasper W. Harris, "Sixty-second Virginia at New Market," *Confederate Veteran,* XVI (September 1908), pp. 461–62, is good, while Thomas H. Neilson, "The Sixty-second Virginia—New Market," *Confederate Veteran,* XVI (February 1908), pp. 60–61, is better. An invaluable source for Woodson's command is William T. Price, *Memorials of Edward Herndon Scott, M.D.* (Singer's Glen, Va., 1873), which published the New Market diary of Woodson's second-in-command.

For the Confederate artillery, Albert S. Johnston, *Captain Beirne Chapman and Chapman's Battery: An Historical Sketch* (Union, W.Va., 1903), is extremely brief, but invaluable. Charles Warner, "Who Fired the First Gun at New Market?" *Confederate Veteran,* XVII (May 1909), p. 237, is the only source for Jackson's battery, while S. T. Shank, "A Gunner at New Market, Va.," *Confederate Veteran,* XXVI (May 1918), p. 191, is the only useful source for McClanahan. The Confederate cavalry is also scantily covered. Henry Corbin, "Diary of a Virginia Cavalry Man, 1863–4, from the Original Manuscript," *Historical Magazine,* Third Series, II (October 1873), pp. 210–15, is very good for the 18th Virginia, as is J. N. Potts, "Who Fired the First Gun at New Market?" *Con-*

federate Veteran, XVII (September 1909), p. 453. The best source for the 23d Virginia Cavalry is Charles T. O'Ferrall, *Forty Years of Active Service* (New York, 1904), and the only source for Davis' Maryland company is Thomas B. Gatch, "Recollections of New Market," *Confederate Veteran*, XXXIV (June 1926), pp. 210–12. Mosby is well represented by J. Marshall Crawford, *Mosby and His Men: A Record of the Adventures of That Renowned Partisan Ranger, John S. Mosby* (New York, 1867), and John Scott, *Partisan Life with Col. John S. Mosby* (New York, 1867), both of which are very informative. A very useful book, though sometimes suspect, is Harry Gilmor, *Four Years in the Saddle* (New York, 1866). And for McNeill, Simeon M. Bright, "The McNeill Rangers: A Study in Confederate Guerrilla Warfare," *West Virginia History*, XII (July 1951), pp. 338–94, is excellent.

The largest body of literature about any unit is that dealing with the V.M.I. Cadets, and one must be selective in its use. William Couper, *One Hundred Years at V.M.I.* (Richmond, 1959), 4 vols., is by far the best history of the Institute, though its New Market coverage merely reiterates some of Couper's early studies on the subject, the best being his *Virginia Military Institute and the Battle of New Market, May 15, 1864* (n.p., n.d.). Also useful is *Report of the Board of Visitors of the Virginia Military Institute* (Lexington, 1864).

The best battle account by a Cadet is certainly Preston Cocke, *The Battle of New Market and the Cadets of the Virginia Military Institute May 15, 1864* (n.p., 1914), and another outstanding piece is Benjamin A. Colonna, "The Battle of New Market," *Journal of the Military Service Institution of the United States*, LI (November-December, 1912), pp. 344–49. Other good accounts are John C. Howard, "Recollections of New Market," *Confederate Veteran*, XXXIV (February 1926), pp. 57–59; J. W. Parsons, "Capture of Battery at New Market," *Confederate Veteran*, XVII (March 1909), p. 119; *New Market Day at V.M.I. Celebrating the Thirty-ninth Anniversary of the Battle of New Market* (Lexington, 1903); and Henry A. Wise, "The Cadets at New Market, Va.," *Confederate Veteran*, XX (August 1912), pp. 361–62. In a class by themselves are the writings of John S. Wise, in particular "The West Point of the Confederacy: Boys in Battle at New Market, Virginia, May 15, 1864," *Century Monthly Magazine*,

XXXVII (January 1889), pp. 461–71, and his classic *End of an Era* (Boston, 1899), one of the finest of all Confederate memoirs. In addition, a few works about the Cadets are worthwhile, particularly John G. Barrett and Robert K. Turner, eds., *Letters of a New Market Cadet, Beverly Stanard* (Chapel Hill, N.C., 1961), "Col. Francis Lee Smith," *Confederate Veteran*, XXVI (February 1918), pp. 81–85, and the extremely important William Couper, *The V.M.I. New Market Cadets: Biographical Sketches of all Members of the Virginia Military Institute Corps of Cadets Who Fought in the Battle of New Market, May 15, 1864* (Charlottesville, 1933).

A few civilian accounts proved useful, particularly Elizabeth Preston Allan, *The Life and Letters of Margaret Junkin Preston* (Boston, 1903), and Cornelia McDonald, *A Diary with Reminiscences of the War and Refugee Life in the Shenandoah Valley, 1860–1865* (Nashville, 1935). George Templeton Strong, *Diary of the Civil War 1860–1865*, ed. by Allan Nevins (New York, 1962), is good for Northern public opinion on Sigel's campaign. The engaging Charles G. Halpine, while not a participant in the New Market campaign, left some good thoughts on it and its characters when he wrote as "Private Miles O'Reilly" in his *Baked Meats of the Funeral* (New York, 1866).

Index

Gilham, William, 78
Gilmor, Harry W., 90, 150, 161, 164, 177; background, 51; opinion of Breckinridge, 51, 188; harasses Sigel's advance, 63–65; on the Confederate victory, 184; ordered to ride around Sigel, 187
Gordon, John B., 188
Graham, Michael, 167, 171
Grant, Ulysses S., 184; plans W. Va. campaign, 20–22; opinion of Sigel, 21, 173; displeasure with Sigel, 55–56, 168–69

Halleck, Henry W., relations with Sigel, 9; opinion of Sigel, 23, 168–69; Sigel accuses of treason, 172
Halpine, Charles G., 1, 6, 175, 192; opinion of Sigel, 170, 173
Hardy, William C., 180
Harman, William, 82
Hart, William T., 104, 131
Hartsfield, Alva C., 180
Hausmann, Charles, 139, 140
Haynes, Luther C., 180
Henkel, Elon, 68, 96
Henkel, Martha, 103
Henkel, Socrates, 157
Henkel, Solon, 92, 157
Higgins, Jacob, 56–57, 69, 125; goes after McNeill, 39; defeated at Lost River, 58–61
Hill, Govan, 95
Howard, John C., 79, 95
Hunter, David, 178; replaces Sigel, 169–70; opinion of Stahel, 174, 175; raids the Valley, 190–91

Imboden, Frank, 63
Imboden, George, 63, 73
Imboden, Jacob, 63, 64
Imboden, James A., 63
Imboden, John D., 22, 24, 25, 64, 65, 78, 85, 161, 162; background, 18–19; fears attack, 18–19; watches Sigel advance,

26, 30, 31–32, 35–36, 41; pursues Higgins, 41, 58–61; holds New Market, 63–66; at New Market Gap, 67–70; at New Market, May 14, 72–73, 74–75, 76, 77; skirmishes at New Market, 77–78, 81, 82, 83, 86; ordered to ride around Sigel, 90, 187; crosses Smith's Creek, 104–5; forces Stahel back, 109–10; failure to trap Sigel, 150–51; opinion of Breckinridge, 165; after New Market, 175–76; harasses Sigel, 180; on the victory, 183, 190

Jackson, Thomas E., 40, 54
Jackson, Thomas J. "Stonewall," 3–5, 18, 39, 46, 47, 48, 79, 144–45, 185–87
Jackson, William, 27, 165
Jefferson, Thomas G., 123, 160, 180
Jenkins, Albert, 32, 41
Johnson, Francis S., 50, 181
Johnson, Robert W., 50
Johnson, Sallie, 181
Johnson, Walter, 180
Johnston, Albert Sidney, 90
Johnston, J. Stoddard, 103, 105, 124, 164, 185; on Breckinridge's generalship, 114, 115, 183; on the Confederate victory, 157, 183–84
Johnston, Joseph E., 189
Jones, Henry, 122, 180
Jones, J. W., 120
Jones, Samuel, 15
Jones, William E., 32

Kelley, Benjamin F., 44, 58, 61, 113; relieved by Sigel, 7, 10, 11
Kellogg, Horace, 138
Kildow, F. D., 119
Kleiser, Albert von, 117, 136; in opening of battle, 92, 99; background, 107; has gun disabled, 107–8; in Sigel's main line, 110, 112; attacked by